Men and Masks
A Study of Molière

Lucien: (. . .) Les fables de Jupiter de Neptune et de Pluton, dont je me suis tant moqué étaient des choses respectables en comparaison des sottises dont votre monde est infatué. Je ne saurais comprendre comment vous avez pu parvenir à tourner en ridicule, avec sécurité, des gens qui devaient craindre le ridicule encore plus qu'une conspiration.

Voltaire, *Conversation de Lucien, Erasme et Rabelais dans les Champs Elysées.*

MEN and MASKS

A Study of Molière

by

Lionel Gossman

THE JOHNS HOPKINS PRESS Baltimore

To Jannie and Jim.

Preface

A WORD OR TWO about the form and content of the following pages might not be out of place.

A certain amount of repetition could perhaps have been avoided if the chapters dealing with individual plays had been presented instead in the form of a study of topics and themes. It seemed to me, however, that such a schematic presentation might have several disadvantages that would offset the possible advantages of neatness and economy. It is only in their concrete embodiment in the plays themselves that the themes live and have meaning. The significance of any work of art is probably inseparable from the work itself and is never found in concepts distilled from the work. Processes of abstraction and comparison do, I imagine, have an important part to play in the reading and understanding of a piece of literature. It seems to me only that analysis and abstraction must be completed by a return to the work and to the actual flesh of the word, the gesture and the act. The reader's first meeting with a work is often a direct and intimate experience of it, and it is through processes of alienation, abstraction, judgment, and comparison that, as he reads, he succeeds in deepening this experience, but only if the universal and the particular, the abstract and the concrete, the position of alienation and the position of immersion are maintained in dialectical union with each other, illuminating each other and illuminated by each other. It is possible to consider the totality of an author's work in this way. It may even be the best way to study an author, for it sets the parts of his work in relation to the whole and enriches thereby our understanding of these parts. No individual work, perhaps, can be properly understood in isolation from the whole, any more than one movement of a sonata can stand apart from the whole sonata. Nevertheless, a total view that maintains a constant relation to the concrete parts requires far greater experience and skill than I think, at this point anyway, I possess. Rather than fall into abstraction, therefore, and drag the reader with me into arid discussions of disembodied ideas and "problems," I preferred not to stray too far from the individual plays and to allow myself and the reader to be guided and supported by them. My exposition thus follows in some measure the process of my own reading and reflection.

This explains why the selection of plays is somewhat arbitrary. It is so not because these plays best illustrate certain arguments and theories —which would hardly be arbitrary at all—but because it was from these plays that I actually set out. I could have added others, but this would have made the book rather longer than I wanted it to be. I preferred to stick to my original group of plays and to discuss or allude to others in the conclusion. Nonetheless, I am aware that the selection of plays pinpoints a shortcoming in this study. As I shall insist shortly, I tried to view Molière in the context of the experience and thought of his age. But while I think I have taken account of Molière's work in its historical situation, I do not think I have taken sufficient account of the historical development of his work itself. I have concentrated so much on the first, which it seemed to me important to do, that I have to some degree deprived Molière of his own historical evolution, by considering his work as a static bloc rather than in its dynamic growth and in its relation to possible developments of his position in the world and of his attitudes. Thus my division of the plays into two types—the *Misanthrope* type and the *Bourgeois Gentilhomme* type—may well be rather formalistic, and a fuller study of Molière would, I suspect, require that it be considerably refined. Above all it would have to be made dynamic by being set in concrete relation to the changing situation of the author, to movements in his own life and in that of his society, and to his own intellectual growth and deepening understanding of the world.

While I think it is only honest to admit this shortcoming in the present study, I do not think that I have been entirely un-historical in my approach. It might be said that I have anachronistically applied twentieth-century ideas to a seventeenth-century writer, and I could hardly deny that reading certain nineteenth-and twentieth-century philosophers or moralists (in the French sense of *moralistes*) opened my eyes to many things I had not noticed before, or at least helped me to formulate notions that had hitherto been ill-defined. Nevertheless, almost all the categories on which my reading of Molière's texts rests are brilliantly defined by Pascal, and in case anyone should think that the analysis of vanity and pride was a prerogative of Pascal or of La Rochefoucauld in the seventeenth century, I would suggest that the late Professor Lovejoy's *Reflections on Human Nature* (Baltimore, 1961) could be looked into with profit. From Lecture IV onward, Lovejoy produces countless texts of the sixteenth, seventeenth, and eighteenth centuries in which the problems of human behavior are analyzed according to the categories that I have tried to apply to the comedies of Molière. If these strike us as "modern" in some respects, it is simply because, during the heydey of positivism, which is not yet over, we forgot a great number of useful and important ideas. To people of a more positivist cast of mind, indeed, many of my categories may appear "old-fashioned."

My occasional confrontations of Molière with more recent and even with very recent writers may cause misgivings in some readers. My intention was to emphasize the present meaningfulness and relevance of Molière, not merely as an entertainer, but as an artist and in a sense as a seer, which almost every great artist has been in some degree. Molière belongs to the seventeenth century, but he also belongs to us, as every great writer of the past does. In pointing out the historical roots of a writer's work, we should aim not to imprison it in the past but to make it even more meaningful to the present.

There are many approaches to literature and many ways of opening up the immense treasures that are contained in the great texts. For my own part I am sorry that I did not look more closely into formal matters than I did. But each critic contributes as he can. If I communicate even a part of the pleasure and instruction I myself have derived from reading, seeing, and reflecting on the comedies of Molière, and if I add anything at all to the reader's understanding of them I shall be well content. For the critic's task, I believe, is not to exhaust the work, not to substitute his work for it, but to serve it. "Cependant, ce lecteur mimétique (i.e., the critic), si proche de l'auteur qu'il est plus intime à l'auteur que l'auteur lui-même, il n'est pas l'auteur," writes Jean Rousset in a recent book (*Forme et signification* [Paris, 1962]). "Il ne compose pas l'oeuvre, il la revit pour en dégager la composition, il l'explore pour la montrer. (. . .) Sans l'opération du critique, l'oeuvre court le risque de demeurer invisible. Comment serait-elle sentie si elle n'a pas été comprise et révélée? Mais il faut en convenir, cet acte indispensable à son existence ne la remplace pas. C'est le paradoxe de la critique, et peut-être son drame: l'oeuvre a besoin de la critique, c'est-à-dire d'un regard qui la pénètre, mais la critique tend à se con-stituer en oeuvre de l'oeuvre, en un au-delà de l'oeuvre, où l'oeuvre est tout entière, sauf sa présence. Cette présence concrète, la critique ne pourra jamais en fournir l'équivalent; elle nous donne toute l'oeuvre, mais quelque chose nous échappe, ce contact charnel qu'est l'oeuvre même."

Baltimore, Maryland
June, 1962

Lionel Gossman

ACKNOWLEDGMENTS

I would like to express thanks to Nathan Edelman for his patient encouragement and advice, to René Girard for the many things that I have learned from him in the four years of our professional associa-tion and personal friendship, and last, but by no means least, to my wife.

Contents

Men and Masks
A Study of Molière

1

AMPHITRYON

Lui: (. . .) Il n'y a dans tout un royaume
qu'un homme qui marche, c'est le
souverain; tout le reste prend des positions.

Moi: Le souverain? Encore y a-t-il quelque
chose à dire. Et croyez-vous qu'il ne
se trouve pas, de temps en temps, à
côté de lui, un petit pied, un petit
chignon, un petit nez qui lui fasse
faire un peu de la pantomime? Qui-
conque a besoin d'un autre est in-
digent et prend une position.

Diderot, *Le Neveu de Rameau.*

As A FOREWORD to *Amphitryon* Molière might have selected the famous passage from Descartes' first *Meditation:* "Je
supposerai donc qu'il y a non point un vrai Dieu, qui est la sou-
veraine source de vérité, mais un certain mauvais génie, non moins
rusé et trompeur que puissant, qui a employé toute son industrie
à me tromper" (*Oeuvres et Lettres*, Pléiade, p. 272). The play is
in large measure a working out of this hypothesis. Examination
of the dramatic and symbolic functions of Jupiter reveals, however, that the wicked genius of *Amphitryon* is no spirit, but
Cartesian man himself. Jupiter is not a hidden puppet-master,
but an active participant in human affairs, seeking human ends
and not just the pleasure of deluding people. His descent into the
world of ordinary mortals provides the occasion for the dramatic
action of the comedy: a world which has been well and securely
ordered until then suddenly cracks open. Everything in it becomes
potential illusion; nothing can be relied on any more; a man is no
longer even sure if he is himself or what he is. Jupiter is a liberating
force, dramatically and symbolically. His presence dissolves the
world of conventional realities and reveals a new world of possibilities, but these possibilities never achieve substance or consistency, and in the end there is no brave new world, only the old
one with all its patterns destroyed. The colorful kingdom of
fantasy is suddenly abandoned at the end of the play, and we find
ourselves back in the world of everyday empirical reality. Jupiter,
the brilliant magician, turns out to be an ordinary *grand seigneur*.

1

All that has happened after all is that an insubstantial order has been exposed, vanquished, and replaced by blatant disorder. The rule of Amphitryon has yielded to the rule of Jupiter. But whereas Amphitryon ruled in the firm conviction that the order of things, which *happened* to suit him very well, was a necessary and just order, Jupiter is without illusions. There is no rational order, no just rule for him. There is only the right of the strongest. Jupiter's justification of his own violence at the end of the play is an obvious and deliberate piece of irony on the part of the author.

As a dramatic character, Jupiter, the mythological hypothesis, turns out to be disquietingly human, and we must take this into account in evaluating his symbolic significance. Descartes' *malus genius* dissolves all forms and leaves reason incapable of determining which appearances do, and which do not, correspond to reality, which beliefs or ideas are, and which are not, grounded in truth. In *Amphitryon,* however, it is reason itself in its Cartesian or critical form that is presented as containing its own contradictions. Calling for the questioning of all immediate sense-knowledge, putting all traditional belief in doubt, it is at once a liberation and a source of new difficulties, for while it dissolves, it cannot bind, while it enables man to recognize mere opinion for what it is, it cannot of itself discern or provide the foundation of true belief. In the end the entire natural and social world—even man's own self—becomes problematic. The rational consciousness is alienated from the world not by a malevolent God, but in the very act of winning its own freedom. Nor is it possible to renounce or ignore this freedom. There is no avoiding the situation created by Jupiter's arrival on earth. To deny Jupiter, as Amphitryon does, is simply to take one possible attitude to the strange disorder that has suddenly afflicted the world: the attitude of *pretending* that nothing has happened. If Jupiter cannot be disposed of by our simply denying him outright, neither can he be disposed of by our envisaging him as a hyperbolic hypothesis. The world returns to "normal" at the end of the comedy, but it cannot flatter itself that the problems raised by Jupiter's presence in it belong to some totally unreal nightmare. The son that Alcmène is to bear will continually revive in Sosie the problem of his personal identity and in Amphitryon the problem of his wife's love and fidelity. The extraordinarily rich thematic material of *Amphitryon* is handled freely and imaginatively by Molière, but he was aware that thè situation of the play was not of purely speculative interest. The nature of the self and the nature of relations with others, the two principal themes on which the comedy turns, are urgent practical problems. The struggle of Amphitryon and of his serving man Sosie to meet the onslaught of reason, to deal each in his own way with an attack on the very basis of their existence, provides the fundamental situation of the comedy. It is represented dramatically and concretely in the efforts of Amphitryon and Sosie to establish their identity against divine impersonation, and in Amphitryon's attempt to deal with the "infidelity" of Alcmène.

Amphitryon and Sosie have the problem of self thrust upon them. They have to prove that they are who they are.

> L'un de nous est Amphitryon
> Et tous deux à vos yeux nous le pouvons paroître

Jupiter tells the characters assembled on the stage (III, 5, 1679–80). On what grounds is it to be determined who is truly Amphitryon and who merely appears to be Amphitryon, who is truly Sosie and who merely appears to be Sosie? In the master and his servant, Molière represents dramatically two possible attitudes to the problem of appearance and reality and points out with marvelous humor that if the refusal to distinguish between subject and object, which is characteristic of Amphitryon, necessarily precludes any genuine solution of the problem, the acceptance of a radical distinction between subject and object, which would seem to be the necessary prerequisite of any critical view of the world-as-object, makes all immediate knowledge of existences impossible, including knowledge of one's own self, considered as an object of consciousness. The alienated consciousness becomes locked in the spiral of its own reflection, like Monsieur Teste "me voyant; me voyant me voir, et ainsi de suite . . .". The choice in *Amphitryon* is not between alienation and no alienation, but between awareness of alienation and hypocritical refusal to recognize it.

Amphitryon cannot find a satisfactory answer to the problem of who the real Amphitryon is because he refuses to recognize that there is any problem. Entirely dedicated to the world of opinion, he never doubts anything he believes or has been taught to believe, and truth for him is simply what he believes it to be. He feels no need to convince anyone else rationally that he is right, being content to impose his opinion on others. Truth for him is not a matter of reason. It is the opinion that the right people have and that they impose on whoever does not follow it meekly. It is convention. Of course, Amphitryon never accepts complete understanding of his position; for if he did, he could no longer claim to be sure that his opinions were true, he could claim only that they were useful, whether for himself alone or for everyone. Amphitryon's attitude to truth is best understood, as we might expect, by his victims. In Act II, scene 1, Sosie properly wonders:

> Faut-il dire la vérité
> Ou bien user de complaisance?
> (II, 1, 711–12)

In Act III, Sosie again emphasizes that, in the world as it is, truth is always the opinion of the strong. He makes the point as brutally clear as Sganarelle does in *Dom Juan*:

> Non: je suis le valet, et vous êtes le maître;
> Il n'en sera, Monsieur, que ce que vous voudrez.
> (III, 1, 698–99)

Sosie might have pointed out, however, as he did later, that though the strong man can impose his own "truth" on people, he cannot make it any the more objectively true for that. No matter how powerful a man may be, he cannot make the moon a piece of cheese even if he can force everyone to say it is, and perhaps even believe it is. Things remain what they are and reality goes its own way independently of the constructions men put upon it to delude themselves and others. In the end it catches up with them, as Molière wittily suggests by subjecting Amphitryon himself to a force before which he is impotent.

Amphitryon's answer to the problem posed by his alter ego is not a rational one. Truth for him is not problematic as Naucratès maintains it is, and there is therefore no room for discussion and demonstration. Amphitryon knows only one demonstration of his own rightness—violence:

> Allons, courons, avant que d'avec eux il sorte,
> Assembler des amis qui suivent mon courroux,
> Et chez moi venons à main forte,
> Pour le percer de mille coups.
>
> (III, 5, 1732–35)

Characteristically, he finds his best support in Argatiphontidas, a grotesque and silly blusterer, who, like Dom Alonse in *Dom Juan*, is a complete slave to appearances. Argatiphontidas never has the faintest glimmering of the problematic nature of reality; he lives on a level below awareness where images are unquestioningly accepted as realities. It never occurs to him that the existence of the two identical Amphitryons poses a problem. He does not think for a moment that the Amphitryon he is so intent on defending might not be the real one and that the impostor he cannot wait to run through with his sword might be the real Amphitryon. He remains blissfully unconscious of any difficulties and, significantly, is never brought face to face with Jupiter-Amphitryon. Amphitryon

knows that doubt is possible—this much he has had to recognize
—but he considers it subversive. In Amphitryon's world there are
no questions to be answered, only betrayals to be punished. Cor-
respondingly, Argatiphontidas sees doubt not as the mark of a
rational problem, but as a disloyalty, a disavowal of the community, which it is indeed, in the sense that it implies a withdrawal
from comfortable communal certainties:

> Ecouter d'un ami raisonner l'adversaire
> Pour des hommes d'honneur n'est point un coup à faire
>
> .   .   .   .
>
> Et l'on doit commencer toujours, dans ses transports,
> Par bailler sans autre mystère,
> De l'épée au travers du corps.
>
> (III, 7, 1834–40)

Of course Amphitryon is right: he is Amphitryon and Jupiter,
or Amphitryon II, is an impostor. But since truth for Amphitryon
is a convention of the strong, since it is decided on by force rather
than by reason, his truth must inevitably yield to the truth that
is imposed by a force infinitely superior to any he can command.
He is well and truly hoist by his own petard. Of course the situation is such an obvious fancy that the Amphitryons in the audience can laugh it off if they want to. The implication is clear,
however. It is only in the hypothetical realm of fantasy that there
is any doubt as to whether Amphitryon is really Amphitryon. At
the same time this hypothetical doubt reveals the weakness of
Amphitryon's position. His rightness about himself—or about anything—can never be more than an *accident*, for what he holds to
be true is simply willful and undemonstrated belief. He cannot
and will not answer the challenge of reason, he cannot demonstrate
the validity of his beliefs, and there is consequently *no reason* to
believe that his opinions are true. Jupiter points this out neatly
in his wonderfully ironical warning to Amphitryon:

Tout beau! l'emportement est fort peu nécessaire;
Et lorsque de la sorte on se met en colère
On fait croire qu'on a de mauvaises raisons.

(III, 5, 1633–35)

Totally immersed in opinion and belief, Amphitryon is as contemptuous of empirical evidence as he is of rational demonstration.
Just as he will not demonstrate the validity of his beliefs by argument, so he will not admit that they might be put in question by
the evidence of sense. It is not as a rational man that he rejects
Sosie's story of his alter ego, it is simply as a man who refuses to
question any of the opinions he holds in any circumstances. All
Amphitryon's certainties are prejudices (*praejudicia*). It is not
surprising therefore that it should be not he, but his serving man,
who gets caught up in rational contradiction. Amphitryon himself
remains a total stranger to reason, a creature of habit and blind
belief.

Unlike his master, Sosie has a commendable respect for reason.
It is by exposing the contradictions in the attitudes and opinions
of his "betters" that Sosie "gets even" with them. He has to accept
the world of his master as an empirical fact; reason, however, gives
him a means of destroying it in theory and exposing its fundamental falseness. There is some contempt as well as disgruntlement in Sosie's comment on his conversation with Amphitryon
in Act II, scene 1:

Tous les discours sont des sottises
Partant d'un homme sans éclat;
Ce seroit paroles exquises
Si c'étoit un grand qui parlât.

(II, 1, 839–42)

Sosie is accustomed to questioning, because his most fundamental
experience is the equality of men in reason and their inequality
in fact. Almost every one of his appearances on the stage shows

him waging his eternal sniping war against prejudice, asserting now
the demands of reason, now retreating before the power of fact.
In the wonderfully burlesque second scene of Act I, he tells
Mercury plainly that no force can either alter reality or make him
believe what he is not convinced of:

> Tes coups n'ont point en moi fait de métamorphose:
> Et tout le changement que je trouve à la chose,
>   C'est d'être Sosie battu.
>
>   (I, 2, 380–82)

For his own self-preservation Sosie will indeed *profess* to believe
what his reason denies. Theoretically it is good to tell the truth.
In practice, however, for Sosie and his like, telling the truth may
be no good at all. Often it is "better" to tell lies:

> Il est vrai, jusqu'ici j'ai cru la chose claire
> Mais ton bâton sur cette affaire
>   M'a fait voir que je m'abusois.
>   (I, 2, 393–95)

Hypocrisy is not a final solution for Sosie, however. He cannot
lie for long. In order to be physically, he has to lie, but in order
to be as a separate identity, not just as an appendage of his master,
he has to question continually. His survival as an individual person
depends on his judging freely and according to his own reason.
It is through violence that Amphitryon asserts his identity, and
it is violence that he tries to use against the divine power that
threatens him. Sosie, on the other hand, has always—of necessity
—rejected violence as an argument and demanded rational proof.
He naturally defends himself against his divine impersonator with
reason, and he demands the same rational demonstration from
Mercury, from divine power, as he demands implicitly and never
receives from Amphitryon, from human power:

N'importe, je ne puis m'anéantir pour toi
Et souffrir un discours si loin de l'apparence.
Etre ce que je suis est-il en ta puissance
    Et puis-je cesser d'être moi?
                    (I, 2, 424–27)

It is because he insists on reasoning with Mercury that Sosie
discovers in grotesquely caricatural form the antinomies of reason.
First Sosie collects his evidence. Mercury has the same physical
traits as he, but that is not convincing. Mere surface appearance
of identity is not enough. As closer questioning reveals that
Mercury is intimately familiar with all the events of Sosie's past,
however, serious doubts begin to assail the little fellow:

> (. . .) A moins d'être Sosie
> On ne peut pas savoir tout ce qu'il dit;
> Et dans l'étonnement dont mon âme est saisie
> Je commence, à mon tour, à le croire un petit.
>   (I, 2, 468–71)

The evidence piles up and Sosie's doubt deepens. He had hoped
to find the usual contradiction between the power that enforces
an opinion and the evidence for it. No such contradiction is to
be found, however:

> (. . .) de moi je commence à douter tout de bon.
> Près de moi, par la force, il est déjà Sosie;
> Il pourroit bien encore l'être par la raison.
>   (I, 2, 485–87)

A further question reveals that Mercury—whom for convenience
we shall refer to as Sosie II—can describe accurately and in detail
all that Sosie I did on that very day in complete secrecy. Sosie is
overwhelmed. Reason seems to prove that Mercury is indeed
Sosie; for if Sosie is defined as a certain sum of actions and ex-

periences, and if Mercury is defined by these very actions and experiences, Mercury must indeed be Sosie. The logic of concepts
is applied rigorously by Sosie to existences, with the result that
he finds his own existence vanishing to nothing in his thought.
Yet a doubt remains: "Car encore faut-il que je sois quelque
chose." Sosie cannot think his consciousness away. He leaves the
stage in utter perplexity, convinced and unconvinced of what
seems to be true and not true at the same time:

> Tout cet embarras met mon esprit sur les dents
> Et la raison à ce qu'on voit s'oppose.
>   (I, 2, 517–18)

Sosie's dilemma is that in founding his self in a series of states
and actions he makes himself an object of consciousness. His *me*
—to anticipate a distinction between the ego as object of consciousness (me) and the ego as transcendental *subject* (I)—is no
more accessible to his own apprehension than to that of others.
It enjoys no special status (the *me* is as accessible to the psy-
chiatrist, for instance, as it is to the patient's own introspection)
and it thus falls into the category of objects that can be called
into question. Mercury confronts him with this very problem,
for Mercury's *me* appears to him as strictly identical with his own.
In so far as it is an object of consciousness, Sosie's ego cannot
therefore be established in reason as an absolute existence. The
moment it is questioned by reason—and the effect of Mercury's
arrival in the world is to instigate this questioning—its unique
unity dissolves and no reason can reconstruct it.

This conclusion is understandably disturbing to Sosie, and he
revolts against it: *la raison à ce qu'on voit s'oppose*. It will be
clear that this reason that is opposed to *ce qu'on voit* is not formal
reason, for it was formal reasoning on appearances that led to the
conclusion reason now rejects. The reason that is opposed to *ce
qu'on voit* is no other than Descartes' reason, which protests in

its very doubting the existence of a self that doubts, and thus preserves the self even from the *malus genius* who makes every other content of consciousness false. Descartes implicitly rejected the *me* as a congeries of observed states and qualities, since they are as subject to doubt as any other objects in the world. He therefore established the ego as a transcendental subject rather than as a transcendent object of consciousness.[1] The *I* was envisaged as the inseparable companion, indeed the very source of all states and acts of consciousness. My *I* is thus affirmed in the very act of doubting that I am. But what is this *I* that is so affirmed? *Encore faut-il*, says Sosie, *que je sois quelque chose*. But what? It seems that Descartes thought of the *cogito* as personal and of the ego as a real substance transcending all possible acts of consciousness. This was what Gassendi objected to: Quare et ex eo quod noris te esse, non potest inferri te nosse aut posse nosse naturam tuam (P. Gassendi, *Disquisitio metaphysica, seu Dubitationes et instantiae: adversus Renati Cartesii, et Responsa* [Amstelodami, 1644], in Meditationem II, dubitatio prima, instantia, p. 40). In dramatic terms, Sosie knows that he is (*quelque chose*), but he cannot deduce from this what he is, what Gassendi calls his *essentia* or *natura intima*. Between the abstract universal and the concrete particular there is still a gulf which Descartes has not really bridged. Gassendi's language is a little confusing. He makes use of a pronoun, the substantial reality of which as a concrete particular is precisely in question. He himself clarified this when he referred in other passages to the ego of the *cogito* as *res cogitans*. Does the *cogito* affirm the existence of a particular person (i.e., Descartes) or does it not rather affirm simply itself, consciousness, the universal reason. As Hobbes expressed it in his

---

[1] The *me* is a transcendent object of consciousness because it is the ideal unity and sum of all my states of consciousness. The *I* is a transcendental subject because it is the ideal unity and source of all my acts of consciousness. The transcendental subject for Kant determines the *possibility* of experience and has a proper place within the limits of the Kantian system. For Descartes, however, it was a *reality*.

objections to the same point, "he who understands and the understanding are identical" in the *cogito* (*Philosophical Works of
Descartes*, ed. Haldane and Ross, Dover Press edition [New York,
1955], Vol. 2, Objections III with Replies, p. 65). Where does
the transcendental ego spring from and what precisely is it? These
are surely the questions that lie behind both Gassendi's criticism
and Molière's comic presentation of Sosie's bewilderment. In
reality, Gassendi and Molière seem to hold, the *cogito* posits
man as pure consciousness at the centre of a universe from which
he is irrevocably estranged, just as it estranges him irrevocably from
himself, for the particular determinants that make him what he is,
that give him his historical and existential being—and that have to
be rejected with the rest of the world as subject to doubt—are precisely what binds him to the world and makes him part of it. The
ego of the *cogito* is no particular thing, but consciousness itself,
consciousness trapped in its own isolation, knowing nothing certain
but itself, having no sure content but itself. No being may be de-
duced from this pure consciousness or from pure reason. Descartes'
escape from this hall of mirrors rests precisely on his attributing,
quite unjustifiably, to the ego of the *cogito* a substantial reality
ontologically prior to consciousness itself. Whatever the validity
of Descartes' proofs for the existence of God and of the entire fabric by which he sought to restore the connection between the mind
and the world, his whole enterprise inevitably fails if there is no *I*.
For if there is no *I*, no distinction at all can be made between the
possible and the real, between appearance and reality. Appearance
becomes absolute as the ego joins all other phenomena in the
world and becomes part of a vast *Schauspiel* embracing spectators
and players alike. Whether the ego be considered a depository of
innate ideas or the architect and constructor of the world, the entire question of being and appearance vanishes into thin air the
moment the ego ceases to confront the world and becomes part of
it. This is what has happened in *Amphitryon*. Descartes' hypothesis
of a *malus genius* was intended to demonstrate that doubt cannot

reach the *I* itself. To Molière, as to Gassendi, it seemed that it did, since all that could be affirmed by the *cogito* was consciousness or thought itself. Everything thereby became doubtful, everything became mere appearance.[2]

In *Amphitryon*, Molière maliciously took Descartes at his word and developed the comic contradictions and absurdities to which the hypothesis of the *malus genius* leads. The world of *Amphitryon* is, seemingly, ruled by a capricious *mauvais génie* who has the power and the will to deceive us. Sosie's *I* is not maintained, however, 'against the onslaughts of Mercury: it is looked for but never apprehended. It is only when he thinks of particulars and does not doubt them, only when he resorts to experience and memory that Sosie feels sure of his existence as *Sosie*, as a real and apprehensible *moi*:

Pourtant, quand je me tâte et que je me rappelle
Il me semble que je suis moi.
(I, 2, 488–89)

[2] It would be understandable if someone objected that Gassendi's criticism of Descartes had been given an anachronistically modern twist here. Gassendi could not and did not formulate his objections to his great contemporary in terms of twentieth-century philosophy. What concerns us, however, is not so much the terms Gassendi used, or the philosophical position from which he criticized Descartes, or even the philosophical validity of his criticism, as the historical import of his criticism. Why did Gassendi, like Hobbes, adopt a negative attitude to certain essential aspects of Cartesianism? Surely because he perceived the insufficiency of Descartes' idealism, and, in the instance we are discussing, of his disincarnated transcendental ego. Most probably it was for the same reason that he protested vigorously and obstinately against even a provisional and methodological rejection of all sense experience and objected that the hypothesis of the *malus genius* was unnecessary and unreasonable. The materialism of Hobbes and Gassendi is the—equally inadequate—counterpart of Descartes' idealism. It is justified not in itself, but by its critical relation to this idealism, by its refusal to sacrifice matter, particular existence, or particular experience to a totally abstract and disincarnated spiritualism. A case in some ways similar to Gassendi's attack on Descartes is Goethe's attack on Newtonianism a century and a half later. Goethe's criticism of Newton is virtually unintelligible without an historical perspective capable of embracing a larger area than Goethe's own time or the actual reasoning and arguments he employed against Newton (cf. Erich Heller, *The Disinherited Mind* [Cambridge, 1952]).

When he doubts this—and according to Descartes we must doubt
all the *content* of consciousness including our body—he is reduced
to protesting helplessly: "encore faut-il que je sois quelque chose."
If he doubts every content of consciousness, Sosie must doubt not
indeed that he is, or rather that there is consciousness, but that he
is Sosie. If he will be Sosie, he must accept the evidence of sense
and memory and this forces him to recognize that Mercury appears
to be identical to him, so that once again his identity as an ego
escapes him as he becomes the victim of the wiles of the *mauvais
génie*:

> (. . .) la chose à chacun
> Hors de créance doit paroître.
> C'est un fait à n'y rien connoître,
> Un conte extravagant, ridicule, importun;
> Cela choque le sens commun;
> Mais cela ne laisse pas d'être.
>   (II, 1, 771–76)

Sosie's predicament is brought on by the arrival on the scene of
a *mauvais génie*. Whereas the *mauvais génie* of Descartes, however,
was envisaged as a hyperbolic hypothesis, the *mauvais génie* in the
play turns out to be no other than the force of reason itself. Descartes' *mauvais génie* could not reach the ego, the source of all
consciousness and ultimately, though indirectly, of all knowledge
of reality; Molière's *mauvais génie* destroys the ego too and thus
takes away all possibility of distinguishing between appearance
and reality. Everything dissolves into a masquerade in which the
possible and the real participate on equal terms.

Sosie's experience is the experience of reason's failure to reach
existence and to demonstrate the necessity, in its own terms, of any
existential reality. Looked at from another angle, however, this
failure of reason is the foundation of its success, for the power of
reason frees us theoretically at least from the existential by revealing its irrationality. Just as reason dissolves all traditional social

patterns and beliefs by showing that their *So-sein* is not rational, but only historical, so it releases us from the prison of the naturalistic present. Mercury, like Jupiter, enters the world both as a destructive and as a liberating force. He undermines Sosie's naïve faith in his own self, but in so doing he opens up a new and free world of possibility. The confrontation of Sosie and Mercury reveals the purely contingent, non-essential nature of Sosie's existential being. Sosie I, the Sosie we know, the Sosie of everyday reality, is a timorous, sly, debased little man, a typical valet, with a valet's outlook on life as a slippery contest in which the weak have to use all the means of skill and trickery at their disposal to avoid being trampled on by the strong. Sosie II or Mercury, on the contrary, is bold, frank, and confident—"le moi du logis qui frappe comme quatre" (II, 1)—and contemptuous of Sosie I who humiliates himself abjectly before him (III, 6). Where Sosie I mutters curses under his breath and allows his anger to turn to impotent resentment ("Que je te rosserois, si j'avais du courage, / Double fils de putain, de trop d'orgueil enflé"), Sosie II proclaims his rights as a person and defends them boldly. This vision of his alter ego, of the Sosie he might be, gives Sosie a sudden pathetic insight into his own debasement:

> Las! à quelle étrange disgrâce,
> Pauvre Sosie, es-tu réduit!
>   (III, 6, 1782–83)

On the surface the meaning of these lines is simple: to what a pass you have come, Sosie, when you cannot even be yourself. It is not extravagant, however, to discern another meaning below the surface. Mercury is the *malus genius* who destroys the foundation of Sosie's existence, his very belief in himself as a self, but he also releases Sosie from the necessity of this existence. Sosie's "disgrace" is double, for while there is a "disgrace" in not being able to define oneself at all as an existence, there is also a "disgrace" in being the slave that Mercury reveals him to be existentially. The "disgrace" of reason is that it cannot found Sosie's existence as a pure self, the "disgrace" of his existence is that it deprives him of freedom. The presence of Mercury, of a *possible* Sosie, reveals that there is no rational necessity for the existential Sosie, that in his existential being, Sosie is pure contingency. From the perspective of reason, therefore, Sosie is indeed the "ombre" that he sees himself as in relation to Mercury.

Reason in its modern critical form—Descartes notwithstanding —founds no essences, and existence cannot therefore be rationally validated as it was for many medieval philosophers by being set in some relation to essence. All existence is resolved by critical reason into infinite possibility of existence. The realm of the existential and the historical is strictly that of the contingent, which for reason is a realm without being. Thus neither Sosie I nor Sosie II has reality in the court of reason: Sosie I because he is pure contingency, Sosie II because he is pure possibility. Mercury is in no sense an allegorical representation of some real or essential Sosie, for this would suppose that there is an essence of Sosie which exists in some non-sensible way.[3] The symbolic function of Mercury corresponds exactly to his dramatic function. He is a poetic fiction, a fancy, a liberation from the world of everyday empirical reality, but not an alternative to it. Freedom, the infinite freedom of possibility, is his very nature. He cannot be captured, fixed, pin-pointed, defined, or reduced to stability: he is what his name says he is. As pure possibility, however, he exposes the contingent, irrational, and problematic nature of the entire existential world of Sosie I. In the witty second scene of Act II Amphitryon is confronted with Sosie II, not the sly, submissive "ombre," but the "moi du logis, qui frappe comme quatre." Sosie II no longer recognizes Amphitryon

---

[3] The use of allegory as an artistic device seems to be closely related to general acceptance of a philosophy of essences. Without such a philosophy allegory loses all its inner meaning and acquires a purely decorative function. The history of allegory from the Middle Ages down to the Eighteenth Century seems to confirm this.

as his master, he dismisses the social order in which Sosie is a debased and inferior creature as illusory, a mere construction arbi-
trarily invented by Amphitryon and invested by him with a reality
he, Sosie II, does not admit. Molière's technique here resembles
that used by Gogol in *The Overcoat*. Rather as Gogol represents
Akakij Akakijevich's revenge on the society that dehumanized and
finally murdered him by the humorous poetic fancy of his ghost's
haunting the streets of St. Petersburg and tormenting his erstwhile
tormentors, so Molière uses the poetic fancy of Mercury to expose
the "illusory" nature of a social order that transforms some of its
members into submissive shadows of themselves. This does not
mean that the existing social order is illusory in the sense that it is
not there. It is illusory in the sense that it cannot be rationally
justified. The dangerous implications of this scene make it far more
"revolutionary" than all the tedious moral saws of Dom Louis in
Dom Juan. (How Jacques Arnavon could find anything revolutionary in the banalities of Dom Louis is hard to understand.)
Even lines that might reassure the audience are found on closer
examination to be disturbingly ambiguous. When Amphitryon
cries: "Tout le monde perd-il aujourd'hui la raison?" we are reminded on the one hand that we are in the realm of fancy, and on
the other we are faced with the uncomfortable question: where
does reason lie? With the everyday world, or with this fanciful inversion of it? The same devices that constantly prevent us from
believing in the existential reality of this inverted world also force
us to ask if our existential world "makes sense."

Appearance and reality, existence and reason, matter and spirit,
the alienated consciousness of Cartesian and post-Cartesian man
experiences these pairs as irreconcilable opposites. The collapse of
scholastic physics, the replacement of a world in which everything
had its appointed place by an undefined space whose parts are
identical and interchangeable is paralleled by the collapse, on the
plane of human relations, of the medieval community in which
each member had an appointed place and its replacement by a

featureless agglomeration of equal, free, and isolated individuals. In this fractured world the individual experiences others as mere objects and even becomes a problem to himself in that, while his reason posits him as an absolute above all contingency, he can grasp himself only in his relativity, as a contingent object. So far, in *Amphitryon*, we have examined the way Molière dramatizes this impermeability of being to consciousness. Sosie *acts out* the problem of the relation of being to consciousness. He is unable to grasp his own being as the subject and source of consciousness, while his self as object of consciousness becomes problematic to him as a result of Mercury's impersonation. At the same time we saw that Mercury acts as a symbol of Sosie's freedom, in the sense that Sosie *at once is and is not* Sosie the miserable, cowardly servant of Amphitryon, in the sense that he *both is and is not* his naturalistic present *and is and is not* his own transcendence. In the love of Jupiter and Amphitryon for Alcmène yet another aspect of the drama of alienation is acted out for us on the stage: the relation of the individual consciousness with others.

Three ways of envisaging love are represented in *Amphitryon*: the way of Amphitryon, the way of Jupiter, and the way of Alcmène. The first two represent love as it is for alienated man, for him who refuses awareness of his alienation and for him who accepts it. Both ways make sense in the empirical world and are consistent with everyday experience. For Alcmène, on the other hand, love is a denial (not a refusal) of alienation. Where there is love, there can be no alienation and where there is alienation, there can be no love. Hence she does not distinguish between lover and husband, between the internal and the external aspect of relations. Alcmène, however—and we shall return to this point—is an ideal figure. She is right in that her kind of love is the only one that can truly be understood as a relation of equality and trust, which is what love is supposed to mean; but from the standpoint of empirical reality she is a poor dupe. The everyday world is a world of alienation, and in this world Alcmène's position is strictly untenable.

In the community (*Gemeinschaft* as opposed to *Gesellschaft* in the terminology of Tönnies) the inner and outer aspects of relations are bound together in an indestructible unity. They are experienced by the members of the community as identical. The community begins to break up when its members, separating themselves as individuals from it, look on it as an object, scrutinize it, require that its arrangements be *rationally justifiable*. As the individual becomes alienated from the group, wins his freedom or has it thrust upon him, his point of view changes. Relations that were once experienced as unquestionable and eternal become, viewed from the outside, conventions. All social relations are problematical to the outsider. Amphitryon denies that he is an outsider. He does not ask questions. On the contrary, as we saw, he considers the asking of them subversive and treacherous. But though he rejects all questioning of his own identity, the very presence of his double forces him to deal with a situation where it is *in fact* questioned. He refuses to recognize his own alienation, the fact that to others, like Naucratès, for instance, he is no longer known simply and directly as what he is, that to them he has become a problematic object, but he must deal with this situation all the same. He can deny that he is a problem to himself, but he cannot deny that he is one to others. Amphitryon is not the victim of a hallucination. Knowing that the traditional and time-hallowed pattern of things is no longer beyond questioning, by others at least, the only way he can establish order again, short of demonstrating rationally the validity and necessity of the traditional patterns, which he cannot very well do since he refuses to admit the existence of the problem, is to behave *as though* the patterns were valid and necessary. A man may enter into pretense consciously, thereby accepting full awareness of his alienation—this is what the hypocrite does—or he may hide the nature of his awareness from himself. Amphitryon chooses the second course. For a brief moment, at the height of his distress, in the monologue at the beginning of Act III, he comes close to acknowledging that he is no longer a member of the community in the same sense as he was before Jupiter's arrival, but a consciousness alone and alienated from it:

Mille fâcheux cruels, qui ne pensent pas l'être,
De nos faits avec moi, sans beaucoup me connoître,
Viennent se réjouir, pour me faire enrager.
Dans l'embarras cruel du souci qui me blesse,
De leurs embrassements et de leur allégresse
Sur mon inquiétude ils viennent tous charger.
    En vain à passer je m'apprête,
    Pour fuir leurs persécutions,
Leur tuante amitié de tous côtés m'arrête;
Et tandis qu'à l'ardeur de leurs expressions
    Je réponds d'un geste de tête,
Je leur donne tout bas cent malédictions.
Ah! qu'on est peu flatté de louange, d'honneur,
Et de tout ce que donne une grande victoire,
Lorsque dans l'âme on souffre une vive douleur!
Et que l'on donneroit volontiers cette gloire,
    Pour avoir le repos du coeur!

                  (III, 1, *1445–61*)

Amphitryon refuses complete awareness of his alienation, however. He begins to think and act on the fact of his alienation, while refusing to recognize it. The *vive inquiétude* that he opposes to the applause of the world belongs in the end to the mask and not to the man; it expresses only concern for his appearance. His distress does not come from fear that he may have lost the love of Alcmène, that this is what her "infidelity" means, but from fear that he may have been dishonored (whether inadvertently or not is irrelevant). When he is told by Mercury that Jupiter

    Est auprès de la belle Alcmène
A jouir des douceurs d'un aimable entretien
        (III, 2, *1552–53*)

his primary concern is with his image in the eyes of others, not with himself and Alcmène, with the nominal relation, not with the essential one. "Où vois-je ici réduits mon honneur et ma flamme?" he exclaims (III, 3, 1562). Characteristically, the question that comes to his mind is not whether Alcmène no longer loves him, but how best to maintain a front, how to protect his image:

> A quel parti me doit résoudre ma raison?
> Ai-je l'éclat ou le secret à prendre?
> Et dois-je, en mon courroux, renfermer ou répandre
> Le déshonneur de ma maison?
>
> (*Ibid.*, 1563–66)

If he conceals his dishonor, the world will continue to think highly of him, but it may find out and then he will "lose face"; on the other hand, if he publicly proclaims his dishonor, there may be only a momentary and partial loss of face which he can repair. Suddenly Amphitryon is struck by shame as he realizes that what he is considering is not how to deal with his real situation, but how to appear, what mask to wear:

> Ah! faut-il consulter dans une affaire si rude?
>
> (*Ibid.*, 1567)

He yields to the "natural" impulse of an honorable man. He decides to avenge his dishonor.

Amphitryon has come very close to hypocrisy and consequently to full awareness of the split between reality and appearance and of his own alienation from a community, which, as wearer of masks, he himself now looks on as an object. But at the last minute he withdraws. He cannot bear this awareness, and he sloughs it off by yielding to the natural impulse of an honorable man. Nevertheless if he can hide the truth from himself, he cannot hide it from the audience. We know that in avenging his dishonor it is still an image of himself, his appearance in the eyes of others, that he is striving to maintain. The calculating Amphitryon has shocked the man of honor, the man who would be a member of the community, who refuses to be an outsider, but *having calculated* he can no longer truly *be* a man of honor.[4] The man of honor he sets himself up as is also a mask, a mask which he presents to himself as well as to others and which thereby releases him from *awareness* of his alienation and his hypocrisy. Amphitryon's final resolution is taken in bad faith. He conceals from himself the true nature of his behavior, because he will not accept it as it truly is. His love for Alcmène thus becomes a pure matter of external appearances, and because in reality he knows this, while at the same time hiding the knowledge of it from himself, his apparently naïve and straightforward identification of nominal relations with essential relations, of the external forms of fidelity and honor with love, is a *fraud.* Despite his denial of it, Amphitryon does in fact experience alienation, and the way he experiences love is characteristic of the particular form that his alienation has taken.

At the opposite pole from the real Amphitryon, Jupiter, the false Amphitryon, distinguishes radically between the bindingness and the freedom of love. The bindingness, he tells Alcmène, is external, conventional; it is no part of love, which is all freedom:

> Mais si je l'ose dire, un scrupule me gêne
> Aux tendres sentiments que vous me faites voir;

[4] Cf. a pertinent comment by Sartre is his *Transcendence of the Ego,* trans. Forrest Williams and Robert Kirkpatrick (New York, 1957), p. 59: "Reflection 'poisons' desire. On the unreflected level I bring Peter help because Peter is 'having to be helped.' But if my state is suddenly transformed into a reflected state, then I am watching myself act, in the sense in which one says of someone that he listens to himself talk. It is no longer Peter who attracts me, it is *my* helpful consciousness which appears to me as having to be perpetuated. Even if I only think that I must pursue my action because 'that is good,' the good qualifies *my* conduct, *my* pity etc. The psychology of La Rochefoucauld has its place. And yet this psychology is not *true:* it is not my fault if my reflective life poisons 'by its very essence' my spontaneous life. Before being 'poisoned' my desires were pure. It is the point of view that I have taken toward them which has poisoned them. The psychology of La Rochefoucauld is true only for particular emotions which have their origin in reflective life, which are given first as *my emotions,* instead of first transcending themselves toward an object."

Et pour les bien goûter, mon amour, chère Alcmène,
Voudroit n'y voir entrer rien de votre devoir;
Qu'à votre seule ardeur, qu'à ma seule personne,
Je dusse les faveurs que je reçois de vous.
Et que la qualité que j'ai de votre époux
    Ne fût point ce qui me les donne.

                                            (I, 3, 569–76)

In the husband-wife relation, Jupiter argues, love is not a total and free gift to the beloved; for the very notion of duty or virtue, of a bond or pledge, implies a *conscious reflective choice* in which it is the self as object, not as subject, that is committed. It is precisely because he desires to possess Alcmène as subject that Jupiter rejects the status of husband:

Que le mari ne soit que pour votre vertu,
Et que de votre coeur, de bonté revêtu
L'amant ait tout l'amour et toute la tendresse.

                                            (I, 3, 605–7)

Beneath the dramatic irony of this separation of husband and lover lies a searching analysis of one way of understanding and experiencing the love relation. It is surely not an accident that the conception of love found in many modern novels is so closely prefigured in the consciousness of Molière's Jupiter-figure, for Jupiter is above all an outsider, totally and consciously alienated from the human community. Love for him is more than anything else the urge *to be loved*, to possess the beloved completely as a free subjectivity. It is not the possession of Alcmène as an object or thing that Jupiter craves; that is easy enough to obtain, especially for him, and he has in fact already obtained it. It is not her total enslavement to him in virtue of some blinding passion; he wants her commitment to him to be made in complete freedom. Nor is it a pledge that he asks of her; by his rejection of the husband-wife relationship he has implied that, as far as he is concerned, what is pledged is not what the lover desires, for it is no more than the external husk the subject creates around itself, the illusory limitation that consciousness sets to its own freedom. What Jupiter demands is the surrender of this freedom itself—and *for no reason!* He does not want to be loved in virtue of some quality he possesses or is invested with (in virtue of being kind or good-looking, or in virtue of being her husband). He wants to be loved as the absolute that is beyond all qualities and all judgments ("Qu'à ma seule personne, / Je dusse les faveurs que je reçois de vous"), so that the absoluteness that his reason posits in him can be experienced by him through Alcmène's recognition of it, so that it can become objectivized in the world. Such a "love" as this is inwardly contradictory and self-destructive. If Alcmène were to sacrifice her freedom in this way, she herself would cease to be experienced by Jupiter as an absolute and consequently as a rival to his own absoluteness. In order to continue experiencing himself as an absolute he would have to turn his attention to another freedom and subjugate it, and so on indefinitely. Jupiter's absoluteness can be experienced only through competition with other absolutes and destruction of them. Love for him, in short, is really a form of hate, and so also hate is a form of love.

While the relation that Amphitryon envisages is seen to be a socially and legally determined convention, a pure externality with no inner and independent reality, the absolute relation to which Jupiter refers turns out to be no relation at all, in the sense that its achievement is at the same time its annihilation.

Alcmène does not understand the subtle separation of husband and lover proposed by the outsider. She feels herself at once and inseparably mistress and wife:

> Je ne sépare point ce qu'unissent les Dieux,
> Et l'époux et l'amant me sont fort précieux.[5]
> (I, 3, 620–21)

---

[5] This reference to the Gods is itself profoundly ironical and underlines the problem of Alcmène's position. She grounds the absoluteness and essen-

Alcmène's protest is doubtless never more than a protest. Reason remains antinomous, unable to find any path between the externality of conventional bonds and the impossibility of a true inner relationship between free individual persons, between the dutiful commitment of the self as object and the destructive struggle of "lovers" to absorb each other's subjectivity. Her words do not provide a solution so much as they demand one, by their rejection of the positions held by the men.

The positions of Amphitryon and Jupiter are in fact closely related. Confronted with the problem of reconciling essential and conventional relations, appearance and reality, Amphitryon deliberately pushes away the awareness, which Jupiter has forced upon him, of the difference between them and acts, in complete bad faith, as though they were identical. In fact, however, he has *chosen* to renounce reality for appearance and to accept an utterly theatrical and inauthentic existence. Jupiter accepts the alienation which accompanies self-consciousness. But having once discovered himself as a free, independent atom *geworfen* into an alien world at which he peers out through the window of his lonely consciousness, he is unable to discover any essential relations with others at all. Neither of the two men loves Alcmène in any sense in which love can be taken as the archetype of all relations between human beings. For both of them the community has ceased to exist. Amphitryon cannot understand either the freedom or the immanent bindingness, which, for Alcmène, are inseparably linked in love. Jupiter cannot understand this immanent bindingness, nor, for that reason, the nature of the freedom with which it is associated, because he is an outsider, a transient, a god who comes and goes in a night and whose destiny is ex-centric to that of the human community. From the outset he treats Alcmène as a freedom to be enslaved. Love for him is a project to make himself the ground and

---

tiality of her relation with her husband-lover in a transcendence, but this transcendence turns out to be no good and loving God; it is, on the contrary, a fraudulent *malus genius*.

limit of the threatening freedom of the other. This project involves
him in a flagrant contradiction, however, for he who wishes to exist
for himself, to escape all existence for others and all subjection to
others, is obliged, so that the other can be induced to ground her
freedom in him, to *appear* before the other, to exist in function of
the other, to become himself a slave. Jupiter recognizes this in his
address to Amphitryon in the last act:

> Alcmène est tout à toi, quelque soin qu'on emploie;
> Et ce doit à tes feux être un objet bien doux
> De voir que pour lui plaire il n'est point d'autre voie
>   Que de paroître son époux,
> Que Jupiter, orné de sa gloire immortelle,
> Par lui-même n'a pu triompher de sa foi,
>   Et que ce qu'il a reçu d'elle
> N'a par son coeur ardent été donné qu'à toi.
>
>   (III, 10, 1905–12)

Alcmène's love for Amphitryon opens up a third perspective in
the play. The subtle distinctions of Jupiter and the clay idols of
Amphitryon are equally unintelligible to her. If Jupiter represents
the individual's desire for absolute freedom, if Amphitryon represents the unfree consciousness in bond to opinion and belief,
Alcmène stands for the transcendence of this alternative. Love for
her is neither the desperate struggle of the alienated consciousness
to annihilate the menace that the other represents for it, nor is it a
mere conventional arrangement beginning and ending in appearance. Where Amphitryon is irate at what he understands only as an
indignity to him, Alcmène is offended by her husband's lack of
trust, his inability to see that, loving him, she could not be unfaithful to him. By making Alcmène ignorant of any distinction between love as commitment and love as spontaneous desire, Molière,
of course, deliberately eschewed the tragic problem which Madame
de La Fayette took up later in her novel. In *La Princesse de Clèves*
the trust between Monsieur and Madame de Clèves is so deep that

it is itself one aspect of love; the conflict within a human soul of love experienced as trust and pledge and love experienced as arbitrary passion is the very marrow of the novel. The tragic implications of this conflict are quite properly avoided by Molière. His play is not written from the perspective of the heroine. Its problems are invested in the dramatic contrast of the two male figures and, unlike Madame de Clèves, Alcmène remains a stranger to these problems. Her position is both anterior and posterior to that of the men. If she is untainted by the destructive egocentrism of Jupiter and ignorant of the phantoms that her husband pursues, this is because, like many of Molière's "natural" characters, she belongs to a world which is historically prior to that of the male heroes, a world in which there is no awareness of the separation of names and things, appearances and realities. At the same time, however, Alcmène also evokes the transcendence of the problems incarnated in her lovers. She is both a shadow from the past and a projection into the future. The empirical position she represents is one that the men have outgrown, but she also represents symbolically an ideal and a norm—the very concept of love. Through her we evaluate the positions of the two men, rather as we measure empirical circles in the light of the concept of a circle. That is why she is absent from the denouement of the comedy. It is not because she is a secondary character, mere object of desire or honor for men, as Walter Küchler held (*Molière* [Leipzig and Berlin, 1929], p. 147), but because her dramatic and symbolic function in the comedy precludes her being robbed of her innocence and acquainted with the ambiguities and contradictions of the world as it is for the men. Her presence at the revelation of the fiction would necessarily make her appear a fool and a dupe, which *from the standpoint of empirical reality she in fact is,* as is anyone who believes naïvely in true love in a world of Jupiters and Amphitryons.

To the male characters, on the other hand, the empirical denouement is entirely appropriate. Amphitryon's honorable dishonor is a brilliant stroke of wit. Amphitryon has consistently refused to concern himself with what lies behind appearance and he must therefore be satisfied with the appearance of honor that Jupiter gives to his dishonor. It is left to Sosie to point out the reality behind this appearance:

Le seigneur Jupiter sait dorer la pilule.
(III, 10, 1913)

Sosie knows that the whole mythological fabric of the conclusion is a pure mystification, that it is a convention like other conventions and that its function is to make what suits the powerful appear right and good. The simple reality, however, is that Amphitryon has been made cuckold by a cleverer and more powerful *seigneur* than he is himself. In this sense the solution of the comedy is, as Küchler maintained, a piquantly ironical mystification which the powerful and successful *grand seigneur* uses with conscious humor to "console" the hapless and less powerful husband. Jupiter himself, however, is exposed and degraded by the denouement. His "divinity" is seen to be a hoax, a mere disguise for the inner weakness that he shares with the other characters of the play. Molière's *malus genius* turns out to be the very image of the would-be giants who invented him out of their own fears and ambitions. It was, after all, Descartes himself, with his craving for knowledge as immediate and certain as that of God, who raised the specter of the *Dieu trompeur* and this specter reflects the desire for absoluteness and the inescapable dependence of the mind that is haunted by it. In the figure of Jupiter, as on another occasion in the figure of Dom Juan, Molière created a comic hero whose imposture reveals the imposture of the human claim to quasidivine absoluteness, for by a supreme irony the supposed *malus genius* of the play is itself the most vivid illustration of the impotence and dependence that lie at the heart of the rationalist aspiration toward absoluteness. Molière's "divine" trickster is faced with the same problems as those which he imposed on mere mor-

tals like Sosie and Amphitryon. Confronted with the imposture
of Mercury and Jupiter, Sosie and Amphitryon cannot experience
with certainty their own identity. No longer finding themselves in
others, no longer receiving confirmation of their own awareness of
themselves in the recognition of them by others, they find themselves obliged to argue and battle with others in order to recover
the recognition on which their awareness of themselves depends.
But Jupiter himself is in the same boat, despite his apparent supremacy. This "God" can likewise experience his identity only in
the recognition of it by others. He too is obliged to argue and battle
with others in order to wrest from them the recognition on which
he founds his being. Indeed Jupiter is so utterly dependent on his
supposed inferiors that he is even incapable of desiring spontaneously. His desire for Alcmène is awakened only by the spectacle of
Amphitryon's enjoyment of her. We learn from Mercury in the
Prologue that his master's interest in Alcmène was first aroused by
the happiness he observed in the newly wed couple:

> L'état des mariés à ses feux est propice:
> L'hymen ne les a joints que depuis quelques jours;
> Et la jeune chaleur de leurs tendres amours
> A fait que Jupiter à ce bel artifice
>   S'est avisé d'avoir recours.
>   (Prologue, 66–70)

Jupiter could well say with Dom Juan that his love "commença
par la jalousie." And jealousy of whom? Of the supposed inferior
whom he will subsequently trick and bamboozle. One may well
wonder what kind of god this is who is jealous and fearful of his
subjects and who is so fascinated by them that he is dependent on
them both for his desires and for the satisfaction of his desires.
Jupiter's presentation of himself as Amphitryon is deeply revealing.
In his ambition to annihilate and bring into himself all that is not
himself, it is in the end himself that Jupiter loses. Alcmène's love
is not given to him, but to Amphitryon. Jupiter does not exist for

her. In the very act that is intended to confirm his absoluteness Jupiter thus discovers his utter contingency.

The theme of the *malus genius* was a common one in the literature of the early seventeenth century (cf. Jean Rousset, *La Littérature de l'âge baroque en France: Circé et le Paon* [Paris, 1954], Chaps. 1–3) and Molière did not have to borrow it from Descartes. It occurs in Rotrou's comedy *Les Sosies*, which was so successful that it was still being played when Molière wrote his *Amphitryon*. As Molière borrowed a great deal from this play, not least the very idea of his own (cf. Jarry, *Essai sur les oeuvres dramatiques de Jean Rotrou* [Lille and Paris, 1868], and the notice preceding the text of *Amphitryon* in the Grands Ecrivains de France edition of Molière, Vol. 6, pp. 311–51), it might seem as though the *malus genius* of Cartesian rationalism has nothing at all to do with *Amphitryon*. I do not think this is so, however. The new and deeper significance that the theme of the *malus genius* received from Descartes' work and from the intense discussions it provoked is reflected, it seems to me, in several important differences between Molière's treatment of the theme and Rotrou's.

Rotrou's working over of the old Amphitryon legend is a kind of noble entertainment on the fashionable and paradoxical theme of illusion and reality. The action remains deliberately circumscribed within the mythological context of the material. Thus the Prologue, spoken by Juno, announces the birth of Hercules at the very beginning of the play, and we are reminded of this mythological event half-way through in Mercury's monologue in Act III, scene 5. Indeed, the birth of the divine hero and the episode of the serpents at his cradle actually take place within the course of the play. By punctuating his play with mythological events and allusions, by maintaining a conventional style of noble diction appropriate to his gods and heroes, Rotrou sought to contain the action and the problems it raises within the limits of theatrical convention. The play of illusion and reality was to be an amusing paradox and no more.

Molière, on the other hand, as Jarry himself noted (*op. cit.*, pp. 146–47), humanizes the action as much as possible. The birth of Hercules is announced only at the end of *Amphitryon*. It comes as a supreme piece of irony and has no mythological significance whatsoever, the divinity of Jupiter having by then been completely debunked. Rotrou's Jupiter, likewise, is simply a god having his sport with poor mortals. The analysis of love which is so important a part of Molière's comedy and which makes its human meaning so real and immediate is almost entirely absent from *Les Sosies*. Thus whereas Rotrou's play opens with a pompously conventional speech by Juno, Molière's Prologue is a witty scene in which Mercury and Night discuss, as the servants of a very *grand seigneur*, the vagaries and whims of their master. From the outset Molière's Jupiter is seen to behave not as a god, but as a human outsider, and the action of *Amphitryon* is initiated not by the legend itself, but by the most human of motives in the "divine" hero—jealousy. If this hero is prima facie a god who acts as if he were a man, he is also, on a deeper level of meaning, a man who acts as if he were a god, a man with the metaphysical ambition to be God, but without the recognition of his divinity that he must have in order to experience himself fully as that which he claims he is. The love of Rotrou's Jupiter for Alcmène is that of a divine pleasure-seeker; the love of Molière's Jupiter is that of a human being whose claim to absoluteness is negated by the non-recognition of him implicit in Alcmène's love for Amphitryon.

Molière's profound humanization of the problems in the Amphitryon material gives to his treatment even of those themes that were exploited by Rotrou an urgency and a piquancy that they do not have in *Les Sosies*. Rotrou's Sosie, in particular, has not the later Sosie's witty irony or his passionate interest in what for him is an intensely personal problem. As a man whose very existence as a separate identity is shown to depend on his being smarter and more rational than his master, Molière's Sosie experiences the challenge to his reason not abstractly as a curious paradox, but with all the intensity of his being. There is in fact nothing arbitrary or abstract about the positions dramatized in *Amphitryon*. Sosie, Amphitryon, and Jupiter are not mere conventional figures taken over from an old legend. They have their being in the world of everyday reality, and we find them reappearing in different guises in the other plays of Molière. Sosie is a serving-man, Amphitryon is a swashbuckling, self-confident pillar of society, and Jupiter is a powerful *grand seigneur*, emancipated from all traditional moral and social conventions and laying claim to an absoluteness nothing short of divine. As Molière's characters are more real and less conventional, the situation in which they are involved acquires a far greater degree of concreteness than it has in Rotrou's play. What Rotrou presents as a single, abstract problem is viewed in Molière's comedy from several different angles, each of which reveals a different aspect of it. Thus in Rotrou's play, the reactions of Sosie and of Amphitryon to the dilemma that confronts them are virtually identical; in Molière's they are significantly different. Likewise Amphitryon's conception of love in *Les Sosies* is the same as Alcmène's (both are equally concerned with honor and both are equally appeased on learning that they have been "honored" by Jupiter himself); Molière's Alcmène, on the other hand, has a notably different idea of what love is from that of her husband.

Amphitryon, no less than the other great comedies of Molière, is about the real human world. Although the problems it deals with are acted out in a world of fantasy, there is no loss of relevance to the world we live in. Granted that there is an *apparent* resolution of the conflict presented in *Amphitryon*, whereas there is no resolution in *Le Misanthrope*, in *Tartuffe*, in *L'Avare*, is it true to say, as Gutkind does, that the artistic resolution of the problem within the play empties it of all *Lebensproblematik*, and that only when the conflict remains unresolved within the play "seine Problematik schwingt weiter hinüber in die Lebendigkeit des Alltags"? (Curt Gutkind, *Molière und das Komische Drama* [Halle, 1928], p. 144, note). It is not hard to think of a number of comedies (*Lustpiele* as opposed to *Komödien* in Gutkind) where the artistic resolution, precisely because it is an artistic one, is the stroke of irony that projects the problem into the world. Gogol's *Inspector General* is a striking example. The artistic solution can be even more disturbing and thought-provoking for the very reason that it obliges the audience to raise for itself the question of validity: is the resolution valid in being "true to life" or is it valid only in the *Scheinwelt* of the play?

Molière was particularly careful in *Amphitryon* to ensure that the audience would not slough off the denouement too easily. Sosie's ironical warning speech at the end makes this clear. The play has ended and the mystery has been resolved, but everything is only *apparently* in order. If we compare Molière's fantasy with modern fantasies like those of Giraudoux, for instance, the seriousness of the seventeenth-century work becomes obvious. Giraudoux's delightful fantasies are works of urbane and elegant agnosticism, not without a streak of sadness and resignation. The question of "reality" never arises in them: we have simply to choose between the vulgar and depressing reality of the Third Republic and the infinitely more charming and poetical world of personal fantasy. In Molière's *Amphitryon* we are permitted no such choice. The world that remains and is affirmed at the end of the play is the world of violence and deceit in which we live, and it is this world that absorbs and is elucidated by the poetic fiction, not the other way around. We are not invited to revolt privately, to transform and poeticize the world by the power of imagination. We are not allowed to choose between poetry and reality. Nor is this ever an alternative for Molière. Sometimes, delicately and cautiously, he suggests through his women characters the ideal world in which all contradiction is resolved, in which subject and object, love and duty, appearances and reality are inseparably one and all antinomies have been transcended, but the main action always presents the problems of the world we have created, the world of conventions, of questionable relations, of uneasy compromises, of lies and violence. At the end of *Amphitryon* it is this world that confronts us and the solution is a solution of fraud masquerading as divine will. The apparent harmony established by Jupiter is as false as the apparent order which Amphitryon insisted on identifying with real order. Quite properly, Alcmène, the innocent dupe, *is not there* at the end. Yet the memory of the harmony she experienced so naïvely and unreflectively haunts the fragmented world of her lovers in the same way that certain memories of innocence and trustfulness inhabit the minds of grown men, long after they have left the homes of childhood and set out on the journey that all must inevitably make.

2

DOM JUAN

"Non seulement il était sensible à la présence continuelle de ce qu'il y avait de distingué, mais il l'était aussi aux étages inférieurs. Il regardait à droite et à gauche à son lever, à son coucher, à ses repas, en passant dans les appartements, dans ses jardins de Versailles. . . ."

Saint-Simon, *Mémoires*.

LIKE JUPITER and almost all the comic heroes of Molière, Dom Juan is an impostor. His real being is in flagrant contradiction with the image he gives of himself, and has of himself. On the simplest level he is an impostor with each of the women he seduces. The imposture of Dom Juan is, however, no mere surface phenomenon. It reaches deep into his innermost being, into areas where he himself is no longer aware of it.

Dom Juan presents himself as a skeptic, scornful of the conventional values to which his respectable peers adhere in the foolish conviction that they are absolute and essential. Where they are bound by their illusory values, he is as free as a god, for he recognizes no power superior to that of his own will. That "deux et deux sont quatre, (. . .) et que quatre et quatre sont huit" (III, 1) he is prepared to admit as objectively true, but this "innocent silly truth," as the good Bishop of Cloyne was to describe such propositions a century or so later, has no bearing on his behavior. It belongs to a completely different realm from that of human will and action. Strangely enough, however, the Dom's freedom is, even in his own estimation, of a singularly negative kind. "Pour moi," he says of himself, "la beauté me ravit partout où je la trouve, et je cède facilement à cette douce violence dont elle nous entraîne" (I, 2). The very structure of the comedy bears the imprint of the Dom's passivity, of the complete dissipation of his personality. Like a leaf borne along by the wind, Dom Juan is carried from one adventure to another. He spends a long time telling Sganarelle about

his latest seduction project (I, 2), but after the shipwreck no more
is heard of it. Likewise the seduction of the peasant girls, Mathurine and Charlotte, is never actually carried out. At the beginning
of Act III he is on his way to the city with Sganarelle, but he is
distracted from his purpose, first by Francisque, and then by his
"chivalrous" intervention on behalf of Dom Carlos. At the end of
Act III he is again diverted from his "path"—if one can use this
word to describe the aimless existence of Dom Juan—by the statue
of the *Commandeur*. The episodic structure of the play thus underlines in itself Dom Juan's subjection to the accidental and the cir-
cumstantial. It is the desires and impulses of the moment that
guide Dom Juan, and his life is a constant meandering from event
to event, from encounter to encounter. "Je sais mon Dom Juan sur
le bout du doigt," says Sganarelle, "et connois votre coeur pour le
plus grand coureur du monde: il se plaît à se promener de liens en
liens, et n'aime guère à demeurer en place" (I, 2).

Behind the bravura and independence of Dom Juan there is in
fact a slavish preoccupation with the opinion others have of him.
This super-hero of the will is in thrall to everything and everyone
he meets, for he has constantly to prove his superiority by humiliating others. Like the proud Spanish hidalgos or the great French
noblemen who bear a modest resemblance to them, he is utterly
dependent on the opinion of others for his entire existence. But
he cannot admit this dependence without undermining his own
pretended absoluteness. For this reason it takes strange and disguised forms. It involves, however, as we shall discover, a far greater
enslavement to others than that of the ordinary nobleman who sub-
scribes blindly to the standards and judgments of his caste.

Dom Juan's peers seek, by adhering to the codes of the caste to
which they belong, to be recognized as members of that caste and
thereby to confirm their membership of it. A Dom Carlos or a Dom
Louis acquires the recognition of his peers by fulfilling certain obligations and observing certain standards, the function of which is
precisely to make this recognition possible. This is one of the prin-

cipal purposes of conventional standards, even if the people who observe them like to think, as Dom Carlos and Dom Louis both do, that they are essential. Dom Juan, on the other hand, is not satisfied to share his prestige and superiority with others, to be one of a group. Membership of a superior caste is not enough for him: what he wants is absolute superiority, "to be distinguished" to borrow a phrase from *Le Misanthrope* that we shall have occasion to allude to again and again. He himself must be the only value, and all other values, all other objects of men's veneration are obstacles to his absoluteness. His mockery of chivalry, religion, and common honesty, his demystification of all accepted values has as its goal the destruction of every possible rival. All "myths" have to be exposed and done away with in order to establish the one super-myth, the myth of Dom Juan.

Dom Juan's opposition to his peers involves, as one might expect, no genuine rejection of their world. Dom Juan flouts the world of the nobility, but he does not want to destroy it. He is, as Sganarelle properly remarks, a gentleman to his fingertips. He is supremely conscious of his birth and his rank, and he exploits the privileges they give him to the full. Only a gentleman could behave as he does with Sganarelle, with the peasants, with Francisque, or with M. Dimanche. Nor is he indifferent to the opinion his peers have of him. Far from it! He scoffs at their code of chivalry and their principles of honor, but only in order to affirm his own superiority to them. He would not be despised by them for the world, and if he breaks the rules of chivalry, he takes care that it is the anger of the noblemen that he incurs and never their contempt. His indifference to what they think of him is a sham. He is perpetually engaged in creating an image of himself for them. This image, however, is to be not the standard image that every other noble creates of himself, but an extraordinary image, the image of a super-noble, of a noble who is superior even to his own nobility, whose every action is a free creation of his own will.

The Dom's chivalrous behavior in Act III, when he goes to the assistance of a man who has been set upon by three others, has puzzled and confused some readers of the play. Jacques Arnavon, in particular, had great difficulty reconciling this Dom Juan—"le héros du troisième acte"—with the character as he appears elsewhere in the comedy. If one fails to see that all Dom Juan's behavior is determined for him by others and by the judgment of others, the apparent contradictions in it will indeed seem irreconcilable. If, on the other hand, one recognizes the Dom's dependence on others, the question becomes no longer, why is he sometimes decent and sometimes wicked, but why does he try to impress sometimes in one way and sometimes in another and completely contradictory way?

Why, in the present instance, does he seek to impress by following the chivalrous code, whereas in other instances he seeks to impress by flouting it? It is only *as a gentleman* that Dom Juan can scandalize and confound his peers by his ungentlemanly behavior. He must, therefore, behave in such a way as to be adjudged a gentleman, in order to show his independence by mocking his own behavior. Throughout the episode in question the Dom's conduct is absolutely and strictly honorable. He saves the life of another man, and when he discovers that the man he has saved is pursuing him to kill him, he generously spares him the embarrassment of revealing his own identity, in order that the other man's obligation should not be an unbearable burden to him. At the same time he does not conceal it in a cowardly way, but protests that, as an intimate friend of the gentleman who is being pursued, he is ready to defend him. Dom Carlos' brother appears, recognizes Dom Juan, and wants to attack and slay him there and then. Dom Juan does not flinch and proves ready to meet just the kind of unchivalrous assault from which he lately saved Dom Carlos. All through the scene the Dom behaves impeccably and his language is that of a perfect gentleman. At the same time words and actions are shot through with a deliberate streak of irony, the purpose of which is to affirm the Dom's freedom of these words and actions, to assert the pure willfulness and gratuitousness of his behavior. It is this assertion of freedom which exasperates Dom Juan's peers. That a man should reject the code of chivalry and act only for his own ends, that they can understand and condemn. But that he should act in a chivalrous manner, while at the same time scoffing at chivalry and affirming his independence of all codes, that they cannot stomach. Dom Juan's ridicule of them saps the very source of their power to judge him and fills them with a disturbing feeling of inferiority. What is to be said of such a man? Is he a nobleman or a blackguard? A blackguard who can, when he chooses, behave more nobly than the noblest nobleman must, one might be tempted to say, belong to a category of his own, to a unique category transcending ordinary nobility, but not excluding it. This is precisely the kind of judgment the Dom wants his peers to make of him. Through it he hopes to escape ordinary comparisons with others and become absolutely distinguished from them, an impenetrable enigma, a god or a devil. The two apparently contradictory and mutually exclusive goals of his desire would thus be realized, for he would be judged by others and at the same time judged to be beyond judgment. Whereas all he does is in reality directed at others and designed to elicit a judgment from them, he could pose as though he never sought to be judged, for how could he who is beyond judgment be judged or care about being judged?

Some readers of the play have fallen into the trap set by the hero. To Jacques Arnavon the Dom's behavior is utterly inexplicable and irrational, and he calls upon the actors and the producer to remedy what can only be accounted faults in the play; for to the degree that Dom Juan is an inconsistent and inexplicable character, the play must be considered defective. There is no need to consider it in this light, however, as we have tried to point out. The Dom's behavior appears irrational because he wants it to appear irrational, just as Alceste's love of Célimène appears irrational because he wants it to appear irrational. In both cases the hero is covering up his real motives by presenting himself as beyond ordinary reason and, precisely because of this, as mysteriously superior to those whose behavior can be accounted for and judged. It is because he is so absolutely free and so absolutely unique, so independent of any slavish obedience to common standards and so utterly self-sufficient—so Dom Juan would like people to think—that he cannot be captured and examined and judged as ordinary mortals are. The truth, however, is the very opposite of this. All the apparent contradictions in Dom Juan's behavior can be accounted for quite satisfactorily in the light of an obsessional preoccupation with others which he refuses to admit, since to admit it would be to deny the very image of himself that he is preoccupied to create in others.

Molière constantly emphasizes the Dom's fascination with others. In scene after scene the inward enslavement of this giant of independence and self-sufficiency is exposed, and we realize that the degree of his enslavement to others is in direct proportion to the magnitude of his claim to superiority. As he is content to be recognized as a nobleman by other noblemen, the ordinary nobleman is subject only to the judgment of his peers. Laying claim to a unique and absolute superiority over all others, Dom Juan is inevitably subject to the judgment of everybody. The infiniteness of his pretensions induces in him an infinite fear of being proved inferior. He is perpetually on the lookout for rivals and he finds them everywhere, not only among his peers, but in the lowliest peasant village and in the remotest rural solitude. From nobleman to beggar, everyone must be dazzled and seduced and humiliated. No one may escape, for the least admiration or devotion to someone else is an affront to the Dom's superiority, a denial of his absoluteness, a crime of *lèse-divinité*.

This super-man is so abjectly dependent on others that he is even incapable of desiring on his own account. All his desires are mediated by his "rivals." The ugliest woman would appear beautiful to him if she loved or was loved by someone else.

An incident that the Dom himself relates reveals at an early

stage in the comedy the illusory nature of his desires. He tells
Sganarelle of a young couple of whom he caught sight a few
days previously. "Jamais," he recounts, "je n'ai vu deux personnes
être si contents l'un de l'autre, et faire éclater plus d'amour. La
tendresse visible de leurs mutuelles ardeurs me donna de l'émotion;
j'en fus frappé au coeur et mon amour commença par la jalousie.
Oui, je ne pus souffrir d'abord de les voir si bien ensemble; le
dépit alarma mes désirs, et je me figurai un plaisir extrême à pouvoir troubler leur intelligence, et rompre cet attachement, dont la
délicatesse de mon coeur se tenoit offensée" (I, 2). It is not the
young fiancée herself who excites Dom Juan. She is desirable to
him only because she is desirable to her lover. What he really desires is not to possess the girl but to dispossess the man. The young
person's love for her betrothed contradicts the Dom's pretension to
absoluteness, reduces him in his own eyes to the nothingness that
he is in hers, since for her he does not exist. Any love between
others is in fact a challenge to the Dom's absoluteness, because it
excludes him, reduces him to contingency, thrusts him back upon
his own being, for which, despite all his grandiloquent claims, he
finds no solid foundation in himself.

It is not insignificant that Dom Juan seduces Elvire from a
cloister, and his blasphemy acquires a profound meaning in Molière's play. There has been discussion as to the precise conditions
of Elvire's presence in the cloister, but it makes little difference
how this question is resolved. The objective historical and juridi-
cal nature of Dom Juan's offense is of little interest. Without further examination we can take the seducer at his word: "J'ai fait
réflexion," he says to Done Elvire in Act I, scene 3, "que, pour vous
épouser, je vous ai dérobée à la clôture d'un couvent, que vous avez
rompu des voeux qui vous engageoient autre part, et que le Ciel est
fort jaloux de ces sortes de choses." What Dom Juan makes perfectly clear is that, as in the case of the incident reported in the
previous scene, his desire for Done Elvire was a mediated one, a
desire that was inspired in him by jealousy of and rivalry with the

object of Elvire's devotion, in this instance, God. What he sought
was neither her love nor even the plain physical possession of her
body, but her recognition of his absolute transcendence of all existing or possible bonds and obligations, whether human or divine.
The convent was to Done Elvire what her betrothed was to the
young fiancée in Act I, scene 2. In neither case did Dom Juan desire the woman for herself.

Dom Juan is so far from being a sensualist that he bungles the
only attempt at physical seduction in the play—the seduction of
the two peasant girls in Act II. He is so eager to secure the submission of both girls that he makes the actual physical possession
of either doubly difficult. In reality he does not really care, for he
would rather have two women adore him and possess neither, than
enjoy the possession of one of them. None of the important seductions in *Dom Juan* is truly physical or sexual. Indeed the desire to
seduce is so far from being an attribute of sexuality in Dom Juan
that it would be more accurate to describe his sexuality as an attribute of his desire to seduce.[1] And this desire to seduce is so purely
metaphysical that it extends indifferently to women and to men.
Sganarelle and Francisque are as much objects of the Dom's desire
as any of the women. The attempted seduction of Francisque reveals how utterly unimportant to Dom Juan the persons he tries to
seduce are in themselves. The noble and beautiful Done Elvire is
no more desirable to him than the starving hermit with his rags

---

[1] The idea that intense amorousness may be the *consequence* rather than
the *cause* of the desire to seduce is common coin these days in the writings
of sociologists and psychologists, even where one cannot accept all their
premises, aims, and arguments. I quote at random from a work by a director
of the Orthogenic School of the University of Chicago, the general tendency
of which is utterly unacceptable to me personally: "As a matter of fact, much
that passes for promiscuity has very little to do with sexual desire for the
new partner. (. . .) Most often the driving impulse is to find out if here, too,
one can keep up with others. (I'll show you I'm as good or better than the
other man—meaning: Assure me that I compare favourably with all my com-
petitors . . .)." (Bruno Bettelheim, *The Informed Heart: the Human Condition in Modern Mass Society* [Glencoe, Ill., 1960; London, 1961], pp.
94–95).

and dirt, for it is not Elvire or Francisque who determines the Dom's desire, it is his rival, the object of their love and veneration.

The temptation of Francisque in Act III, scene 2 confirms the pattern already defined by the seduction of Elvire and the planned seduction outlined in Act I, scene 2. In the scene with Francisque Dom Juan confronts, as Valmont was to do a century and a half later, his ultimate rival for supremacy, God Himself. Dom Juan taunts the poor hermit with his poverty and tempts him, as Job was tempted, with the insinuation that God has abandoned him. "Tu es bien mal reconnu de tes soins," he says. He offers him a gold coin, on condition he will blaspheme, that is to say, deny God and recognize Dom Juan, the possessor of gold coins, as his God. Küchler was surely wrong when he saw in this scene a witty affirmation of materialism (Küchler, *Molière*, pp. 107-9). Dom Juan is no more anxious to score a victory for materialism than he was anxious, with the women, to score a victory for sensuality. What he wants to affirm is himself; everything else has to be denied and destroyed—including materialism and sensuality—in so far as it transcends him. Sex and money are only the means that the Dom employs—because he is rich and good-looking—to seduce others. He would not be content to be adored for his money or his looks, to become a "pleasure machine" as the men who think they have seduced Madame de Merteuil are, in fact, for her. (Paradoxically enough, however, this is what happens. The very means he uses to achieve his ends constitute his own greatest rivals in so far as they become ends for others. This, as we shall see, is the point of Sganarelle's final cry "Mes gages! mes gages! mes gages!") At the end of this scene, Dom Juan, having failed to dislodge his rival in the mind of the hermit, tosses him the coin "pour l'amour de l'humanité" and some critics, among them, once again, Jacques Arnavon, have been taken in by this gesture of defiance. Walter Küchler, on the other hand, perceived the hollowness of the hero's allusion to his "love of humanity," but by treating it only as a *Witz* he missed a good deal of its meaning.

There is an undeniable frivolity about Dom Juan's gesture. Throwing Francisque the money is at once an act of petulant irritation at the power of religious belief and a theatrical affirmation of a purely humanistic faith which he does not really have. If, as was probably the case, Molière himself believed that a secular morality was possible and desirable, and that the *honnête homme* had no need of religious faith to sustain him in virtuous conduct, this purely human ideal is expressed not by a Dom Juan, but by a Cléante or a Philinte, by those characters in the comedies who represent the *honnêtes gens* of Molière's own time rather than by a spoiled nobleman who, from the depths of his own nihilism, senses the attraction and power of a morality he is unable truly to understand or to accept. Dom Juan believes in nothing. He sees through the hollowness of the traditional moral codes of his own caste, but he can only ape the dawning morality of the *honnêtes gens*. His "humanitarianism" is an empty parody, and as such it underlines the moral bankruptcy and decadence of the feudal chivalry to which Dom Juan belongs, despite all his gestures of revolt. One of the most intelligent members of a dying caste, he can only explode the myths by which it justifies its existence; inwardly he remains bound to it and he cannot adopt the new ideology that is replacing the one he himself has helped to undermine. Dom Juan's parody of humanitarianism reveals both the power of the new faith—for it intrigues him—and his inability to embrace it. To do that he would have had to transcend his caste, but, as we have seen, it is only *within* this caste that his revolt against it has any meaning.

The moral bankruptcy revealed by Dom Juan's inability to understand the humanitarianism he can only allude to in jest is confirmed by his utter incapacity to love. Love is the domain that lies out of reach for this man with his countless amorous adventures. From his skeptical-rationalist window, he looks out upon the entire world as an object to be manipulated by him. He recognizes no equals, no fellow-creatures, and he aspires to

no joy in communion with another subject, only to the satisfaction of reducing all that is not himself to the drab monotony
of object-ness, of proving over and over again his own absoluteness. "On goûte une douceur extrême," he says, "à réduire, par cent
hommages, le coeur d'une jeune beauté, à voir de jour en jour les
petits progrès qu'on y fait, à combattre par des transports, par des
larmes et des soupirs, l'innocente pudeur d'une âme qui a peine à
rendre les armes, à forcer pied à pied toutes les petites résistances
qu'elle nous oppose, à vaincre les scrupules dont elle se fait un
honneur et la mener doucement où nous avons envie de la faire
venir" (I, 2). Immediately his victory has been won, however, immediately the other recognizes his absoluteness, the "relationship"
with her is at an end. In the act of capitulation the Dom's victim
ceases to be a subject and becomes a malleable object, a thing. But
Dom Juan's absoluteness cannot be recognized by a thing. What
he desires really is to be recognized master by a free slave, what he
longs for is mastery of the other's freedom, a contradictory goal
which he naturally never realizes. The only course open to him,
short of renouncing his impossible aspirations, is therefore to substitute "extensity" for intensity, to extend over an infinite number
of others the undertaking that can never be fulfilled in any one:
"Mais lorsqu'on en est maître une fois, il n'y a plus rien à dire ni
rien à souhaiter; tout le beau de la passion est fini, et nous nous
endormons dans la tranquillité d'un tel amour, si quelque objet
nouveau ne vient réveiller nos desirs, et présenter à notre coeur les
charmes attrayants d'une conquête à faire" (ibid). It is easy to
understand why Dom Juan tired so quickly of Done Elvire and
why his desire for her is reawakened when she comes to see him at
the end of the play. When she reappears in Act IV, Done Elvire
is no longer in thrall to Dom Juan. She has regained her freedom
(significantly it is only at this point that she truly loves him) and
again represents for him a subject to be reduced, a rival to be
brought low, an affront to his absoluteness. Dom Juan can find no
peace or happiness in a real relation with another human being. As

with the sexual maniacs of our time (and not all of them are in psychiatric clinics), there is no end, because no substance to his desire. His desire is not for any person or persons. It is to be the recognized master of all in an act of submission which is at once freely renewed at each instant and yet at the same time inescapable. Such a desire cannot be fulfilled. It perpetually destroys the very conditions of its fulfillment, for in order for the other to be inescapably bound, she must be transformed into an object, and as soon as this happens she is no longer able to will her own submission. Dom Juan is perpetually cutting the ground away from under his own feet, creating a world of nothingness of which he will be the supreme—but, alas, unacknowledged!—lord and master. His imagination loses itself in visions of a hyperbolic orgy of submissions and annihilations, a never-ending succession of Pyrrhic victories: "Je me sens un coeur à aimer toute la terre (*aimer* in his sense!); et comme Alexandre, je souhaiterois qu'il y eût d'autres mondes, pour y pouvoir étendre mes conquêtes amoureuses" (I, 21). There is no satisfaction, no resting-point of fulfillment for Dom Juan, even in his successful seductions. As soon as it is realized, every success is transformed into failure. He must constantly move on so as not to contemplate the nothingness which he is perpetually fleeing and which he discovers at the heart of his "victories" as well as in his defeats.

The utter debasement of this super-hero of the will is brought out most consistently in his relation to his serving-man. Sganarelle is the constant companion of all the Dom's wanderings, the ever-present spectator and judge of his performance. All Dom Juan's actions are directed in part toward his servant, for Dom Juan does not distinguish between noblemen and lackeys. Since he would be superior to all, above all ranks and accidental privileges, his public includes every one from the stalls to the gallery, and he seeks the acclamations of the entire theater. He constantly tries to dazzle his servant with the spectacle of his absolute freedom from every convention, his superior intelligence, his independence of will. The applause, the admiration, and the reverence of Sganarelle is as important to him as the applause, admiration, and reverence of the greatest in the land. "Et ne trouves-tu pas, dis-moi, que j'ai raison d'en user de la sorte?" he asks; or "Qu'as-tu à dire là-dessus?" (I, 2). He explains his future projects to Sganarelle and the reasons why he wants to undertake them (*ibid.*). He points humorously to the unpleasant reward Sganarelle receives for attempting to defend Pierrot (II, 3)—a light-hearted foretaste of the "tu es bien mal reconnu de tes soins" in Act III. He enjoys exhibiting to Sganarelle his skeptical incredulity (III, 1). He gives Francisque the money "pour l'amour de l'humanité," in part, at least, to impress Sganarelle (III, 2). He exploits his intervention on behalf of Carlos to show Sganarelle that with all his impiety he is at the service of others, whereas Sganarelle with his piety is selfish and cowardly (III, 5), and he does not omit to tell Sganarelle that it was his enemy whom he saved: "Sais-tu bien qui est celui à qui j'ai sauvé la vie?" He mocks Sganarelle's compassion for Elvire in Act IV, scene 6 and deliberately sets out to impress him with his own cynicism in Act IV, scene 7. Even in his dealings with the statue of the Commander he is acting a part for Sganarelle. Dom Juan must brave the statue in order to maintain the image of absolute superiority he wants his servant to have of him. Just as he sought to take the place of God for Francisque, so he must ensure that Sganarelle's awe of him is greater than his awe of the statue. The seduction of the two peasant girls is likewise undertaken to arouse Sganarelle's admiration. For this reason Dom Juan takes care to draw the servant's attention to Charlotte and excite his interest in her before he moves in for the "kill": "Ah! ah! d'où sort cette autre paysanne, Sganarelle? As-tu rien vu de plus joli? Et ne trouves-tu pas, dis-mois, que celle-ci vaut bien l'autre?" (II, 2). The seduction of the peasant girls is intended to humiliate Sganarelle, to force him to recognize the gulf between his own impotent mediocrity and the irresistible charm, the sparkling gaiety, the generous sensuality, and the effortless power and prowess of a master whose every whim is immediately and, as it were, miraculously, translated into fact. It is easy to imagine that Dom Juan was always careful to whet the appetite of his servant before moving in to satisfy it in his own person. The farcical episode of the vanishing supper at the end of the play is characteristic of the Dom's relation to his serving-man. Dom Juan finds the confirmation of his super-human power and grandeur in the bewildered frustration of Sganarelle. He never tires of taunting his servant and reminding him of his inferiority and his practical enslavement. Deliberately he embroils him in the very misdeeds that Sganarelle takes pleasure in criticizing him for. In the first two scenes with Done Elvire (I, 2), he attempts to make Sganarelle his mouthpiece; in Act III, scene 5, he obliges Sganarelle to invite the statue to supper; in Act IV, scene 8, he forces Sganarelle to sit down to a meal with the statue, even though the servant protests, despite his natural gluttony and the fiasco of the vanishing supper, that he is no longer hungry. Furthermore, when the statue ultimately declines to eat and instead invites Dom Juan to sup with him on the following day, the Dom proposes to go "accompagné du seul Sganarelle," ignoring the little man's remonstrances that "il est demain jeûne pour moi" (IV, 8).

Nonetheless, although Dom Juan can humiliate Sganarelle by always reminding him of his inferiority, he never succeeds in extracting from his servant the total recognition of his absolute superiority that he desires. Sganarelle recognizes—perforce—his practical subordination to his master, but this is not enough for Dom Juan. The entertaining episode at the end of Act II where Dom Juan, pursued by his enemies, forces Sganarelle to exchange clothes with him sums up the relation of master and servant throughout the play. "Je veux que Sganarelle se revête de mes habits," says the Dom with malicious humor, "(. . .) bien heureux est le valet qui peut avoir la gloire de mourir pour son maître" (II, 5). Dom Juan thus mockingly rejects the chivalrous order in which it does a man honor to die in the service of his lord, and at the same time requires his own servant to be totally dedicated to him. But

Sganarelle refuses to submit. However pleasant and attractive he
would find it to play the part of his master in other circumstances,
he is never so infatuated as to put the Dom above his own self.
"M'exposer à être tué sous vos habits," he remonstrates. "O Ciel,
puisqu'il s'agit de mort, fais-moi la grâce de n'être point pris pour
un autre!" (II, 5). As in the rest of the play, Dom Juan has to rely
on his material authority to secure Sganarelle's submission, and this
is the touchstone of his failure to seduce his servant. By disguising
himself as a doctor, Sganarelle, as usual, succeeds in preserving his
own independence, while not disobeying his master too flagrantly.
This elusiveness of the servant is the source of his fascination for
his master. Because Sganarelle constantly asserts his independence,
Dom Juan seeks to enslave him.

Sganarelle's cry of "Mes gages! mes gages! mes gages!" at the end
of the play marks his final revenge on the master by whom he was
constantly humiliated. The absoluteness Dom Juan claimed with
respect to others was supposed to reside in his own being, in that
ineffable subject which in its very nature was absolutely superior to
all others. When he screams for his wages at the end of the comedy,
however, Sganarelle affirms the true character of his relation to his
master. The source of Dom Juan's superiority is seen to have been
nothing essential to his being, but only the accidental attributes of
rank, prestige, and power. The very power Dom Juan used in his
attempts to extract from his servant the recognition of his innate
superiority turns out to have had a boomerang effect and to have
transformed Dom Juan himself into a mere object in the eyes of
his servant. Sganarelle is discovered to have been "using" Dom
Juan, to have admired him and envied him not for himself, not for
what he *was*, but for what he *had*. In the Dom's mind he himself
was to be the end, and his money, his looks, his rank, his charm
were to be means; to his servant, however, his money, his looks, his
rank, his charm were the ends and the Dom himself was the means.

Despite the Dom's brilliance and self-confidence, despite his pretensions to absolute and divine superiority to all others, he was in

reality bound to the little man whose inward freedom was a constant affront and challenge to him. Far from elevating him upward, the Dom's exorbitant megalomania degraded him downward, reducing him to the clown and courtier of his servant. This despot was in fact the slave of the meanest of his subjects.

In many ways Molière's Dom Juan is a caricature of the heroic Baroque personality. Wandering from one end of the earth to the other, conquering empires and abandoning them, scorning every enslavement of the will, whether to others or to his own achievements, the Baroque hero restlessly seeks new obstacles to overcome and new occasions to affirm himself as will and freedom. The comic figure of Dom Juan is at once an imitation and a revelation of this hero. The meanness of his activities—seducing peasant girls, challenging statues, insulting old men, battling for authority with beggars, outwitting clumsy bourgeois—contrasts with his airs of grandeur and superiority. Likewise the martial language of his speeches, the noble tone he gives to his activity contrasts sharply with the content of his speeches and his actual exploits. This formidable and heroic individualist who compares himself with Alexander the Great engages battle with women, peasants, and beggars. To snatch a Charlotte from a Pierrot, to seduce a wretched beggar from his faith in God, to dazzle a young girl and make her elope with him, to wriggle out of paying his bills, these are the triumphs to which the Dom aspires. His life is a sorry imitation of grander lives, and it is significant that Sganarelle says to him at one point: "Vous parlez tout comme un livre." Dom Juan models himself on those fabulous conquistadores who were the undisputed masters of two worlds; like them he wanders from place to place, encountering shipwreck here, escaping his pursuers there, making a conquest at one moment and abandoning it the next. But what a debased and deformed version of these heroic and adventurous existences is the miserable existence of the Dom! He claims to be beyond good and evil, beyond the judgment of his inferiors—a kind of super-personality in the style of Corneille's Rodogune or Webster's

Duchess of Malfi. Such were, in the real life of France in the sixteenth and early seventeenth centuries, those great feudal lords whose ambition undermined the very feudal order their powers and privileges rested on and who found themselves at the same time locked in battle with the King and the bourgeoisie in defense of these powers and privileges. The true heroes of the seventeenth century, for Molière and for a large part of his public, were men like Richelieu and Louis XIV, who had imposed order on chaos and assured the unity of the French state, not the feudal rebels who had been capable only of negative and destructive action. Like the figure of Sotenville in *George Dandin,* the figure of Dom Juan, who, let us recall, is as insolvent as his less picturesque counterpart, caricatures the ambitions and pretentions of the feudal rebels by revealing the inner impotence of their revolt and their objective moral, political, and social degradation. The grandeur and the nobility of the great feudal nobles are seen to have been utterly theatrical, to have lost all objective foundation, and to have had only a subjective reality in the admiration of a public of Charlottes and Mathurines, of Sganarelles and Dandins. Compared to his larger than life models, Dom Juan is a village tyrant, a grotesque and ridiculous pygmy, but at the same time the imposture of Dom Juan reveals the imposture of his models. Through Dom Juan they too are seen for what they were, slaves to the public before which they paraded their lawlessness, actors whose successes are measured by the intensity of the illusion they create in the minds of their audience.

But it is not only the feudal rebel who is unmasked in Molière's comedy, it is the whole structure of the feudal state, which is seen as inwardly corrupt and unable to sustain its own order. The provocation of Dom Juan brings to light the violence hidden at the heart of the ordered world of Dom Carlos and Dom Louis, just as the provocation of Jupiter in *Amphitryon* brings out the willfulness in Amphitryon himself. The quarrel between Dom Carlos and Dom Alonse in Act III over the proper way to treat an enemy who has saved your life reveals the emptiness beneath the strict formalism of the chivalrous code by which the brothers live. Alonse, impetuous, blustering and willful, is the Argatiphontidas of *Dom Juan*. Above all he wants to avenge the dishonor to his family caused by the Dom's seduction and abandonment of Done Elvire. But it is also part of his code that a man of honor has an obligation to someone who has saved his life. In his anger Dom Alonse denies this obligation: "O l'étrange foiblesse, et l'aveuglement effroyable d'hasarder ainsi les intérêts de son honneur pour la ridicule pensée d'une obligation chimérique" (III, 4). In fact Alonse would be hard put to it to explain which was more *chimérique*, the "obligation" or the "intérêts de son honneur." If one is chimerical, so inevitably is the other. In Dom Alonse's hands, the code founders in contradictoriness and absurdity, and is seen to be no more than an instrument of individual willfulness. Dom Carlos is more punctilious than his brother. He restrains Alonse but warns Dom Juan: "Je ne serai pas moins exact à vous payer l'injure que le bienfait" (*ibid.*).

Carlos is humane. Unlike his brother, he is a decent person, moderate and well-meaning, and this is what makes his own failure to found his behavior in something more essential than mere opinion even more disturbing. Carlos wants to avoid violence. He would prefer "des moyens doux pour nous satisfaire" (III, 4). But there is no alternative, as far as he is concerned, to a *public* reconciliation of Dom Juan and Elvire, to a public reparation of the damage done to the family honor. Whatever the real situation may be, as long as people *believe* that Elvire has been dishonored, then in effect she has been dishonored, and her dishonor must be avenged. The ultimate ground of Carlos' behavior is not the right or the just itself, but the opinion of others. He too grounds his entire being in the eye of the other. "Sa retraite ne peut nous satisfaire," he declares in the last act, referring to Elvire's renunciation of the world, "*pouvant etre imputée au mépris que vous feriez d'elle et de notre famille; et notre honneur demande*

qu'elle vive avec vous" (V, 3—italics added). In the end Dom
Carlos is seen to be not so very different from Dom Alonse after
all. He is just as deeply concerned with what others will think
of him, and he will not tolerate being degraded by Dom Juan in
the eyes of his peers. It is not any objective justice that he is
defending, but his own image in the minds of others, and in the
last resort he is prepared to defend it by violent means. The apparent struggle between right and wrong, between justice and
wickedness resolves itself into a struggle between two individual
wills, each of them pursuing goals of vanity.

Like her brothers, Elvire is motivated at first by considerations
of honor, which in her case, as in theirs, is no more than vanity
systematized. She cries revenge on the man who has spurned and
humiliated her, not on the man who has shown that he does not
love her. An abandoned woman may long to recover the love of
the man she loves, but she knows that it cannot be got back by
violent means and if she truly loves him, she will be beyond all
thought of humiliation and revenge. It is only when Elvire turns
away from the world and the world's judgments that she discovers
the real love she has for Dom Juan and at this point she no longer
desires revenge, or even the return of his love, but only the salvation of his soul.

Dom Juan's father, Dom Louis, kind and worthy as he is, is
as bound to images as the other members of his caste. Jacques
Arnavon made much of this character. Dom Louis's peroration
on virtue, according to Arnavon, expresses a daring, almost a
revolutionary morality. That "la vertu est le premier titre de la
noblesse" (IV, 4) is, however, a time-hallowed cliché invented by
the later medieval apologists of chivalry in an attempt to justify
ideologically an institution which was already in decay. Dom
Louis does not himself see that what he puts forward as a moral
code based in "nature" ("Apprenez enfin qu'un gentilhomme qui
vit mal est un monstre dans la nature"—IV, 4) is in fact nothing
but a conventional social code designed to maintain the superiority

of some members of society to other members of society. There
is nothing in nature itself that upholds the ideology of chivalry.
It is rather the nobility itself that has laid down certain distinguishing marks, as every privileged social class does, in order
to preserve its identity.[2] Dom Louis insists frankly on these *signs*
of rank: "(. . .) nous n'avons part à la gloire de nos ancêtres
qu'autant que nous nous efforçons de leur *ressembler*; et cet *éclat*
de leurs actions qu'ils répandent sur nous, nous impose un en-
gagement de leur faire le même honneur, de suivre les pas qu'ils
nous tracent, et de ne point dégénérer de leurs vertus, *si nous
voulons être estimés leurs véritables descendants*" (IV, 3; italics
added). The *imitatio* of the perfect nobleman, as Dom Louis
conceives it, has as its final goal the judgment and approval of
others. Dom Louis does not see this, of course. He does not
realize that the foundation of his morality is nothing essential,
but only the conventional signs of a noble caste and the desire
of most noblemen to wear these signs and be recognized by them.

Dom Juan, on the other hand, does see this. In his alienation
from the world of his peers he is aware that it is possible to
counterfeit all the signs on which his father lays stress and to
reap the same reward of recognition that would be reaped by
someone who was completely unaware of any difference between
what he is and what he appears to be. His final conversion to
hypocrisy is nothing but the act by which he puts this awareness
into practice. To Dom Juan, consequently, his father's sermon
is nothing but wordy rhetoric and he expresses his impatience with
it in the rude comment: "Monsieur, si vous étiez assis, vous en
seriez mieux pour parler." Nevertheless, at this point in the play
Dom Juan refuses to placate his father with counterfeit signs. He
is unwilling at this stage to resemble or to imitate anybody, how-

[2] Cf. Marc Bloch, *La Société féodale: les classes et le gouvernement des
hommes* (Paris, 1948), pp. 59, 72 *et passim* for a good analysis of the meaning
of many chivalrous *signs*, of which Romantic historians, following the apologists of the fourteenth and fifteenth centuries, gave quite idealized interpretations.

ever fraudulently, since his aim is to be *distinguished*, to be recognized as innately superior to all communal superiorities, to be judged beyond judgment.

After repeated attempts to win his son round, Dom Louis finally threatens to cut him off. It is Dom Juan himself who provokes the old man to this violence, but in the violence, when it comes, impatient and frustrated willfulness is inseparable from love. Dom Louis does not distinguish between family honor—the opinion that others have of him and his name—and the real goodness or badness of his son. In the end he and his world react to the violence of Dom Juan in the same way that Amphitryon reacts to the violence of Jupiter and the "infidelity" of Alcmène.

The "lower orders" in *Dom Juan* are not shown in a more favorable light than the higher ones. Charlotte and Mathurine are easily dazzled by the handsome aristocrat who woos them, and Charlotte has no qualms about giving up her peasant lover for this far better catch. She already sees herself as the lady of the manor and naïvely imagines how she will impress her superiority on others. "Si je sis Madame," she tells Pierrot, "je te ferai gagner queuque chose, et tu apporteras du beurre et du fromage cheux nous" (II, 3).

As for Sganarelle, whom some critics have presented as a reassuring model of good and simple humanity, he is devoured by the resentment which almost always marks the attitude of the slave to his master. In resentment there is admiration and envy of a superiority and at the same time refusal to recognize it. The sullen slave at once accepts and rejects the absolute superiority of his master. Sganarelle constantly resists Dom Juan and it is because he resists, as we remarked earlier, that Dom Juan persists. The relationship of these two is built on perpetual struggle. Like Sosie in *Amphitryon*, Sganarelle pays lip-service to his master, but in the very heart of his being he escapes him. He puts on a show for Dom Juan, just as Dom Juan puts on a show for him. He too conceals his real person behind a mask. "Il faut que je lui sois

fidèle," he says in the first scene of the play, "en dépit que j'en
aie: la crainte en moi fait l'office du zèle, bride mes sentiments
et me réduit d'applaudir bien souvent à ce que mon âme déteste."

Sganarelle, however, is no paragon of virtue. He is cowardly,
credulous, a charlatan, and in some situations—as in Act IV, scene
3 when M. Dimanche reminds him of the money he owes him—
only too ready to ape his artistocratic master and to find himself
superior to the simple bourgeois in virtue of his relation to Dom
Juan. Sganarelle is a typical nobleman's lackey and, as Rousseau
rightly observed, "tous les laquais sont des fripons." Despite all his
reproaches he is almost always too complaisant toward Dom Juan.
This complaisance should not be attributed in any simple way to
his material dependence on his master. His social and economic
dependence may well be the specific occasion for Sganarelle's
resentment of Dom Juan, but it is in this resentment that his
complaisance and his indignation have their immediate source.
Sganarelle is at once fascinated by the Dom's cynical disregard
of everyone and everything, finding a vicarious pleasure in observing the exercise by his master of the power, money, rank, and
courage that he would like to have himself, and glad of the opportunity to assert his own freedom and even, as he imagines, his
own superiority, by expressing pious horror at the wicked goings-on
of this master. In the very first scene of the play we find him both
vaunting his master to Gusman and running him down, reveling
both in the account of Dom Juan's diabolical deeds and in the
condemnation of them, affecting both the superiority of his master
and superiority to his master, whom he describes as "un enragé,
un chien, un diable, un Turc, un hérétique, (. . .) un pourceau
d'Epicure," and protesting piously that he remains in his service
only for fear of him.

All Sganarelle's garrulous moralizing is inspired by his resentment of his worldly and successful master. For the slave mentality,
as Nietzsche pointed out, morality and divine justice are instruments of revenge. Sganarelle is secretly fascinated by his master's

careless flouting of all the laws of nature and society and if he criticizes him, it is not because he is really distressed by his behavior but because he is envious of him. He invokes divine and transcendent powers against him only in order to belittle that power which he admires and at the same time resents because it is not his. Considered abstractly, the ideas Sganarelle expresses when he arraigns his master indirectly in Act I, scene 2 are sensible; in their context, however, they express the bitter impotence of the serving-man who avenges himself on his master by condemning him morally. "C'est bien à vous," he says, "petit ver de terre, petit mirmidon que vous êtes (je parle au maître que j'ai dit), c'est bien à vous de vouloir vous mêler de tourner en raillerie ce que tous les hommes révèrent? Pensez-vous que pour être de qualité, pour avoir une perruque blonde et bien frisée, des plumes à votre chapeau, un habit bien doré, et des rubans couleur de feu (ce n'est pas à vous que je parle, c'est à l'autre), pensez-vous, dis-je, que vous en soyez plus habile homme, que tout vous soit permis, et qu'on n'ose vous dire vos vérités? Apprenez de moi, qui suis votre valet, que le Ciel punit tôt ou tard les impies, qu'une méchante vie amène une méchante mort, et que. . . ." Similarly it is hidden hostility to Dom Juan himself that inspires his horrified indignation in Act IV, scene 1 at the Dom's disrespectful treatment of his father. Many of Sganarelle's accusations are true and many of his ideas perfectly just, but he does not make his accusations because they are true or express his ideas because they are just.

In fact, Sganarelle has precious few virtues and he is not deeply moved by love of truth or justice. He is preserved from the wickedness of his master not by any moral insight or strength, certainly not by true charity, but by his very weakness. He is saved from actually doing evil himself, as many of us are, *despite himself*, saved by his social inferiority, his lack of cash, his cowardice. (How many German *Spiessbürger* are innocent of the crimes of their late masters for the same reasons!) Sganarelle's very qualities,

mediocre as they are, are inseparable from his weakness and
resentment. Like the average good citizen of our own time he is
"sensitive" and he wouldn't hurt a fly. But he does nothing to
dissociate himself in any real sense from the Dom's wickedness.
It is because he is an envious downtrodden wretch himself that
he has some sympathy with his master's victims, and his sly
siding with them is, in part at least, an expression of his profound
hostility to his master. His defense of Pierrot in Act II, scene 3,
for instance, like his attempt to warn Mathurine and Charlotte
against Dom Juan, is inspired as much by resentment of his
handsome and wealthy master as by genuine concern for the
peasants themselves. The other face of this resentment appears
in Act IV, scene 3, where the serving man delights in borrowing
the prestige and authority of his master to mock and tease M.
Dimanche, the bourgeois to whom he, as well as his master, owes
money.

The confrontation of Dom Juan and his world, like the confrontation of Jupiter and Amphitryon, reveals similarities between
the two that are damaging to both. Both turn out to be rather
different than they appear at first sight, and Dom Juan's vision
of the world is as justified as its vision of him.

In L'Amour médecin M. Tomès remarks: "Un homme mort
n'est qu'un homme mort, et ne fait point de conséquence; mais
une formalité négligée porte un notable préjudice à tout le corps
des médecins" (II, 4). The corps des médecins of M. Tomès may
be compared with the society of Dom Carlos and Dom Louis,
which has its own strict codes, standards, and formalities. Indeed
the comparison throws an interesting light on the surprising and
apparently gratuitous introduction of the doctor theme in Dom
Juan itself. In a short scene at the beginning of Act III, Sganarelle,
who has just disguised himself as a doctor, tells how he dispensed
his prescriptions "à l'aventure." "Ce seroit une chose plaisante si
les malades guérissoient, et qu'on m'en vînt remercier," he laughs
(III, 1). Dom Juan draws the full consequences of Sganarelle's

successful imposture. Since there is nothing substantial in medicine, since it is all a matter of bluff, of forms and gestures, anyone can pose as a doctor and no one will know the difference: "Tout leur art est pure grimace." Sganarelle recoils, with candid irony on this occasion, from his master's cynical disrespect for the doctors: "Comment, Monsieur, vous êtes aussi impie en médecine?" In the following act he will recoil once again when the Dom reveals the same impiety toward society as he reveals in this scene toward the doctors. For Dom Juan the one is as much a matter of forms and appearances as the other. The forms of the one can therefore be counterfeited with as much success as the forms of the other. No one will care or notice the difference provided that no formalities are neglected.

Dom Juan's conversion to hypocrisy, which some critics, notably Gutkind, Küchler, and Professor Adam, seem to hold was added to the list of the hero's crimes so that Molière could get a dig in at his enemies, is entirely appropriate to the thematic pattern of the play as a whole. Through it society and Dom Juan are equally degraded and the hollowness of both is exposed.

Dom Juan certainly suffers a defeat with the adoption of hypocrisy. He is obliged to accede to Dom Louis's demands "pour ménager un père dont j'ai besoin," as he puts it himself (V, 2), for once he ceases to be Dom Juan, the son of Dom Louis, he will be nothing but a common criminal. The legend of Dom Juan, as we pointed out earlier, depends on his being at once of the nobility and above the nobility. It is only as a gentleman that he can scandalize by his scorn of gentlemanly behavior. He cannot, therefore, afford to be renounced by his father. At the same time, however, hypocrisy, while it preserves the conditions which make his notoriety possible, prevents him from achieving notoriety. The sparkling, winning, scoffing, carefree rake must disappear behind a mask which will make him indistinguishable from all the other members of his caste. This is to say that as Dom Juan he will cease to exist, for the very nature of the legendary Dom Juan is to

appear, to be seen, to charm and fascinate with his very wickedness and disrespect. A voyeuristic Dom Juan, see-er but not seen,
is no Dom Juan at all. Such a person is *nameless*, lost among the
crowd of petty *jouisseurs* living their secret, silent, solipsistic lives.
If he is to salvage anything of his old self, Dom Juan must find
an audience; if the secret self that transcends all his appearances
is to be seen and not just to see, Dom Juan must seek an accomplice. Just as Madame de Merteuil needs Valmont in Laclos's
novel, Dom Juan needs Sganarelle at the end of Molière's play.
It is not for nothing that he expounds his theory of hypocrisy to
his serving-man at great length. By his adoption of hypocrisy, Dom
Juan increases his dependence on Sganarelle. Henceforth he is
absolutely bound to his servant, for his whole being now depends
entirely on Sganarelle's recognition of it. Dom Juan is thus degraded to the level of an actor who pays the lowest persons in
society to watch his performance.

Society, on the other hand, also suffers a signal defeat, for it
proves utterly unable to concern itself with essentials. Dom Carlos
rejects Dom Juan's sudden conversion not because he does not
believe it is genuine, but because genuine or not, it does not satisfy
his family honor. Significantly enough, he is as indifferent to the
real conversion of his sister as he is to the counterfeit conversion
of her seducer. Dom Louis, for his part, accepts his son's conversion
with alacrity. His motives, however, remain as mixed as they were
when he threatened to renounce him. It is natural that, as a
father, Dom Louis should be overjoyed at his son's change of
heart and that his love should express itself as simple trust and
eagerness to forgive. On the other hand, Dom Louis has still not
distinguished between real goodness of heart and the external
signs which bring honor to their bearer. He is duped by his son
rather as Alcmène was duped by Jupiter. But whereas Alcmène
was never made aware of the dual nature of her lover, Dom Louis
has seen the other face of his son. More than Alcmène, he resembles an Amphitryon who would believe in the fidelity of his

wife both because he loves her and because he does not want
to be dishonored, an Amphitryon who has not faced the problem
of distinguishing between his love for his wife and his concern
with his honor. Dom Louis' trust is of an inferior sort: it is not
trust that is given in full knowledge that deception is possible, but
trust that affirms itself as deliberate forgetfulness of deception. It
is his eagerness to achieve his own happiness that makes Dom
Louis overlook the possibility of deception. In the end he is
content with a shadow in place of a substance. Through his son's
"reform" Dom Louis finds all his desires satisfied: he can take
him to his bosom again, and he can at the same time be "proud"
of him before others.

Were it not for the intervention of the statue of the Commander a compromise would probably have been effected between
Dom Juan and his world, a compromise which would have preserved the formal structure of society by driving the willfulness,
egoism, and vanity of individuals underground. The kind of social
arrangement suggested by Dom Juan's "conversion" precludes the
possibility of any Baroque heroics and imposes a uniform respect
for outward forms on all, but leaves the vanity and egoism of
individuals intact at the heart of the formal order.

The comedy begins with the abandonment of Done Elvire by
Dom Juan and with Done Elvire's call for revenge on the man who
has dishonored her. By the end there have been two conversions,
the authentic conversion of the woman and the hypocritical conversion of the hero. Done Elvire's conversion effectively removes
her from social life, Dom Juan's—were it not for the intervention
of the Commander—would have restored him to it. The only
fully authentic characters in *Dom Juan* are in fact those who are
not concerned with society and its vanities and those who have
renounced them, the simple peasant boy Pierrot on the one hand,
and Elvire and Francisque on the other. Yet these authentic
characters have something of the ambiguity that hovered over
the character of Alcmène. If there is no God, then Elvire and

Francisque are victims of illusion, dupes whose lives are as empty and senseless as those of the worldly characters, for it is as futile to ground one's being in a non-existent God as it is to ground it in the recognition of other men. In the same way the existence of a simple fellow like Pierrot is equally senseless, if he can be tricked by his beloved into believing in a love which she does not have for him, and it seems likely enough that this will happen, given Pierrot's naïve confidence in the signs of love and the far greater sophistication and vanity of his mistress.

Dom Juan is damned at the end of the play. Jacques Arnavon's suggestion that modern producers should provide the play with a naturalistic ending and that Dom Juan should be shot by one of Elvire's brothers is singularly crude and insensitive. Molière could not have his hero finally judged by his own society, for Dom Juan is simply an extraordinarily egocentric and conscious actor in the same comedy as that in which all the others—the Dom Alonses and the Dom Carloses, the Dom Louis's and the Sganarelles—participate. If Dom Juan was to be condemned, he could be condemned only from beyond his own society. Within the framework of the play itself—and let us not forget that the world of the comedy is anterior to the age of Louis XIV and of the *honnêtes gens* of *la Cour et la Ville*—such a condemnation could come only from an otherworldly source. To Molière's own audiences, however, the very pettiness and absurdity, the utterly comic nature of the Dom's existence were in themselves the condemnation of that existence. By and large Molière's audiences—bourgeois and aristocrats alike—considered themselves, above all, *honnêtes gens*. In so far as they professed, in theory at least, the rather vaguely formulated ideology of *honnêteté*, they must have discerned in the action of Molière's comedy and in the antics of its hero a grotesque mimicry of a way of life that they had already rejected and left behind. From their vantage point, the world of *Dom Juan* belonged to a dying and doomed past, and they doubtless saw the play as a satire of those ultra-conservative forces which, in

their own time, continued to resist the new order of the absolute
monarchy, the order of good sense, of reason and of *honnêteté*.
In Dom Juan's petty and ridiculous acts of bravura as well as in
the ineffectual and contradictory moral saws of his right-minded
peers, they must have recognized the total incapacity of the opponents of the new order to do more than parody the former
greatness of their caste. The very violence of some of the attacks
directed at Molière's comedy reveals that the conservative opponents of absolutism themselves discerned the profound meaning of the satire. *Dom Juan* does not glorify the libertine nobleman,
who is, after all, the hero of the comedy, nor does it undertake to
defend the feudal nobility with its Christian and chivalrous ideology against the monsters to which it gives birth. It mocks all the
political and moral pretensions of an outmoded social order which
is shown to be in full dissolution and thus utterly incapable of
founding either morality or social harmony. The humanitarianism
to which the Dom alludes in Act III may well have been close
enough to Molière's own ethics and to that of his audiences, in
theory anyway; what Act III makes perfectly clear is not that this
ethics is foolish, but that the old feudal nobility is incapable of
understanding it or acting on it.[3]

[3] On different adaptations and interpretations of the Don Juan legend, cf.
a succinct treatment by Jacques Arnavon, *L'Interprétation de la comédie class-
ique; le Dom Juan de Molière* (Copenhagen, 1947); A. de Salgot, *Don Juan
Tenorio y Donjuanismo* (Barcelona, 1953); Shaw's entertaining preface to
Man and Superman; and an article by Jean Rousset, "Don Juan and the
Baroque," *Diogenes*, 14, Summer 1956, pp. 1–16. On the Mozart-Da Ponte
Don Giovanni, cf. Denis de Rougemont, *Passion and Society* (*Originally
L'Amour et l'occident*) (London, 1950), and Geoffrey Clive, *The Romantic
Enlightenment* (New York, 1960). Clive refers to useful studies and comments
by Kierkegaard and Karl Barth. The literature on the opera is more extensive
than that on the more austere and intellectualized seventeenth-century comedy.
Clearly Rougemont's opinion that of the two works, Mozart's and Molière's,
the latter is "by far the less significant" is widely held. In a recent and first-
rate contribution to the literature on the Don Juan legend (*L'Eternel Don
Juan* [Paris, 1962]), however, Michel Berveiller goes a long way toward
pointing out the profound interest and astonishingly modern relevance of
Molière's text. I hope the present study of this mysterious and difficult play
contributes something to the invaluable achievement of M. Berveiller.

3

LE MISANTHROPE

"Quoiqu'il fuie le tumulte des villes, et qu'il se communique peu, il n'est occupé depuis le matin jusqu'au soir qu'à faire parler de lui."

Montesquieu, *Lettres Persanes.*

"J'étais transporté d'amour dans un cercle; tête à tête j'aurais été contraint, froid, peut-etre ennuyé."

Rousseau, *Confessions.*

"It is only as one who is seen, marked and attended to that he has any sense of his own reality, and his own personality, wishes and feelings are completely hidden from him by the 'personage' he enacts."

Max Scheler, *The Nature of Sympathy* (*Wesen und Formen der Sympathie*).

To ALL APPEARANCES, Alceste is a seeker after authenticity in a world profoundly marked by inauthenticity. Looking around him, he sees every one of his fellow men, including his best friend Philinte, bound over to others. Their behavior, their judgments, their whole lives are inauthentic in Alceste's view, entirely determined by the public of others before whom they parade a mask that constantly changes and adapts itself according to circumstances. Life is a vast comedy in which each man plays as many parts as he has friends and enemies. At no point is a man truly himself. Appearances, Alceste complains, do not reveal reality; they hide it. Alceste would transform this world of falsehood and illusion into a world in which appearance mirrors reality:

> Je veux qu'on soit sincère, et qu'en homme d'honneur,
> On ne lâche aucun mot qui ne parte du coeur.
>
> (I, 1, 35–36)

The inauthenticity of these noble aspirations is revealed, however, at the very beginning of the play. Alceste is not concerned with his own honesty and sincerity, which he would have us accept unquestioningly. He is concerned only with the honesty and sincerity of others, and it is for them that he is constantly laying down the law. "Je veux" is never far from his lips. Alceste is deeply disturbed by the insincerity of others because he cares a great deal what people think of him and feel toward him. Although he affects to despise their judgments and to reject their advances, there is nothing he longs for more than to be esteemed and loved by others, and not by one or two others, but by all others. Furthermore he is not content to be esteemed and loved, he longs to be esteemed more highly than anyone else and loved more wholeheartedly. He suffers from the polite formality of the compliments addressed to him, not because they are meaningless to him, but because they mean so much to him, not because they are insincere, but because he so desperately wants them to be sincere:

> Quel avantage a-t-on qu'un homme vous caresse,
> Vous jure amitié, foi, zèle, estime, tendresse,
> Et vous fasse de vous un éloge éclatant,
> Lorsqu'au premier faquin il court en faire autant?
>
> (I, 1, 49–52)

Because he cares so deeply what others think of him, Alceste wants to be sure that they really think what they say. He cannot have this certainty, however, for not only is no one prepared to give it, no one can give it. Just as he wants the love of Célimène, which he cannot be sure of, and turns down Eliante, Alceste craves the admiration and esteem of the very people whom he accuses of insincerity. He desires whatever escapes him and only what escapes him. What is given to him is never what he wants, only what is withheld. He cannot, consequently, be given what he wants. He can only try to seize it by trickery or violence. Alceste and those he complains of on account of their "insincerity" are thus seen to belong to the same world. While they refuse to reveal themselves, he desires only what is concealed, while they resist, he attacks. The changing appearances of others confound, as they are intended to do, all attempts to "see through" them. Only those can be balked, however, who make the attempt.

Desiring as he does the complete approbation of others, Alceste

longs to see into every heart, so that he can be sure of his place
in the esteem of others. Inevitably, whatever he cannot see is
experienced by him as a menace. He senses that what lies beyond
the limit of his vision is the freedom of others, and it is precisely
by this freedom that he feels constantly threatened. Anxious to
have himself recognized by others as superior and absolute, he
affects indifference to their opinions, but in his heart he is
constantly interrogating them and constantly being frustrated
by the answers. He loudly protests his uprightness, sincerity, and
independence, but when this evokes the compliments and respect
that it was intended to, he finds that the gold has turned to ashes
before his eyes, for he cannot believe the compliments that are
paid to him. He who sets himself up to be an absolute in the eyes
of others finds another absolute when he looks into theirs, he who
would look on others as objects finds himself reflected as an object
in theirs. Not surprisingly, he experiences the whole world as an
infernal web of lies and deceit:

> Je ne trouve partout que lâche flatterie,
> Qu'injustice, intérêt, trahison, fourberie.
> (I, 1, 93–94)

Alceste's world is made up of innumerable atoms which are
absolute and relative at the same time. Absolutes for themselves,
they find that they are relatives for others; the relativeness of
others for them, on the other hand is transformed into an absoluteness the moment an attempt is made to grasp and hold it.
Alceste cannot tolerate this situation. He refuses to find himself
in the same boat with everybody else; he wants to be above all
others; unfortunately, however, only they can set him above them,
and this they will not do. "Je veux qu'on me distingue," Alceste
cries in petulant rage (I, 1, 63), but his words resound in a
terrifying void. In this cry of need the supposed misanthrope who
experiences "des mouvements soudains / De fuir dans un désert
l'approche des humains" (I, 1, 143–44) acknowledges his utter

dependence on the humanity he despises, his total infatuation
with that which he professes indifference to. What he craves is
the love and recognition of those whom he scorns, what he longs
for is to be adored by those very "gens à la mode" from whom he
ostensibly turns away in disgust. But he wants this adoration to
be real, not conventional. The world which refuses to adore
Alceste, to doff the mask and reveal itself to him in its defenseless
nakedness, is at once the object of his desire and the enemy to be
humiliated.

The quarrel between Alceste and Philinte, on which the play
opens, illustrates this situation perfectly and foreshadows the
much deeper analysis of it that follows in Alceste's love affair
with Célimène. Alceste is upbraiding Philinte for his insincerity:

> Je vous vois accabler un homme de caresses,
> Et témoigner pour lui les dernières tendresses;
> De protestations, d'offres et de serments,
> Vous chargez la fureur de vos embrassements;
> Et quand je vous demande après quel est cet homme,
> A peine pouvez-vous dire comme il se nomme.
> Votre chaleur pour lui tombe en vous séparant,
> Et vous me le traitez, à moi, d'indifférent.
>
> (I, 1, 17–24)

Alceste is shocked by Philinte's falseness, but not because it is
"immoral." He is deeply disturbed personally by it. ("What does
he say to others about *me*, behind my back?") He sees that
Philinte has the power to annihilate him in the same way as he
annihilates others, by looking on him as an object. Petulantly
Alceste—the sincere Alceste—reminds Philinte that he can play
the same game. He is not to be captured so easily:

> Moi, votre ami? Rayez cela de vos papiers.
> J'ai fait jusques ici profession de l'être.
>
> (I, 1, 8–9)

Even Alceste's relations with his closest friend are poisoned by
his unbridled desire to be superior, and by the terror of inferiority
that accompanies it. He finds no confidence and no repose in
friendship; *all* others are rivals and enemies for him. He must,
therefore, affirm his superiority, regain, as he imagines, the upper
hand, by affecting to be indifferent to Philinte, to the extent
that—what delight!—he finds the impeccably masked Philinte
running after him, pleading to be allowed to defend himself,
begging for a gracious word or look, for this is how Alceste interprets Philinte's concern for him.

Alceste desperately needs Philinte. His rejection of him is as
much a pose as his frequently repeated threats to abandon the
world. At the same time as he turns away, he is constantly looking
over his shoulder, as it were, to make sure that Philinte is still
there. But precisely because he wants Philinte's recognition of him
as a being different from and above every other being, he cannot
bear Philinte's freedom to accord or to refuse this recognition.
Alceste can never have been on terms of real friendship and trust
with Philinte, and his own remark about having only affected
friendship is truer than he himself imagines when he makes it.
He wants Philinte to believe that he has only pretended to be
his friend. He himself, however, really believes that he was
Philinte's friend. His remark about having only pretended to be
his friend is, in his own mind, a deliberate lie, which he tells to
"protect himself." In fact Alceste's very lack of trust, his very
need to "protect himself" reveals that he is incapable of friendship, just as he will later be shown to be incapable of love. As
soon as he becomes aware of Philinte as a person independent of
him, an otherness and a freedom, he sees in him no longer a friend,
but an enemy and a rival. To this would-be absolutist every otherness is a menace.

Alceste is in an intolerable position. He craves genuine and
sincere recognition from others, not the conventional respect of
the mask. This recognition can be given, however, only by a free

subject. It would no longer be worth anything to Alceste if it were not freely willed by the giver. Yet the freedom which is the condition of the recognition he desires is inevitably experienced by him as a menace, since freedom to give must mean also freedom not to give. What Alceste requires is an impossible contradiction —a freedom that is not free. The absolute freedom of others confounds his own claim to absoluteness by making him relative with respect to them. Others must therefore be brought to recognize his absoluteness and to admit their own dependence. Alceste's need of the recognition of others thus places him, the would-be absolute, in the strictest dependence on others. He is obliged to woo the world in order to wrest from it a recognition that, if he were truly the absolute he claims to be, he would not have to ask for. Alceste must conceal this dependence from others and from himself, by affecting to despise the world, by *presenting himself* as the absolute he claims to be. His sincerity, his disgust, and his indifference are thus the *poses* of an independence he does not in fact possess, while the sincerity he demands from others is the indispensable condition of the recognition he desires from them. All the contradictions in Alceste's behavior can be traced back to this fundamental and initial imposture.

Alceste's own world is far less the dupe of his posturing than more recent readers—including Rousseau and even Goethe—have been. It refuses to change its ways for him; it will not give up its freedom in order to feed his. Philinte makes this clear:

> Le monde par vos soins ne se changera pas;
> Et puisque la franchise a pour vous tant d'appas,
> Je vous dirai tout franc que cette maladie,
> Partout où vous allez, donne la comédie,
> Et qu'un si grand courroux contre les moeurs du temps
> Vous tourne en ridicule auprès de bien des gens.
>   (I, 1, 103–8)

It is not that society is put out by Alceste's non-conformism, or that it laughs at him because he is different. It laughs at him because he is the same but pretends to be different. Great comedian that it is, the world recognizes the comedian in Alceste, and it laughs because it sees in him a comedian *who acts as if he were not one, and who is completely trapped by his role.*

Alceste's frantic coming and going, his wooing of the world, and his resentment of it are manifested at the deepest level in his relation with Célimène.

As Alceste himself presents it, his love for Célimène is so great and so absolute that it can be realized only through the exclusion from it of all that is contingent, of all that has value in the eyes of others alone:

> Oui, je voudrois qu'aucun ne vous trouvât aimable,
> Que vous fussiez réduite en un sort misérable,
> Que le Ciel, en naissant, ne vous eût donné rien,
> Que vous n'eussiez ni rang, ni naissance, ni bien,
> Afin que de mon coeur l'éclatant sacrifice
> Vous pût d'un pareil sort réparer l'injustice,
> Et que j'eusse la joie et la gloire, en ce jour,
> De vous voir tenir tout des mains de mon amour.
>   (IV, 3, 1425–32)

His love for Célimène, Alceste protests, is pure giving; it is its own beginning and its own end, for it is independent of anything beyond itself, the pride of conquest, the charm of wit, the advantage of wealth.[1]

---

[1] It might be instructive to compare Alceste's speech here with Bérénice's speech in Act II of Racine's *Bérénice:*

> (. . .) Ah! plût au ciel que, sans blesser ta gloire,
> Un rival plus puissant voulût tenter ma foi,
> Et pût mettre à mes pieds plus d'empires que toi;
> Que de sceptres sans nombre il pût payer ma flamme,
> Que ton amour n'eût rien à donner que ton âme!
> C'est alors, cher Titus, qu'aimé, victorieux,
> Tu verrois de quel prix ton coeur est à mes yeux.
>   (II, 5, 656–62)

While it is not suggested that Bérénice's love for Titus is as inauthentic as Alceste's for Célimène, the theatricality of lines such as these does seem to me to require explanation.

Many critics—notably Arnavon and Bénichou—have justly observed that the love of this champion of sincerity is darkly tainted with fanatically possessive egoism. Alceste does not dream of a situation in which all contingency and public approval or disapproval would be abolished in the simple and pure equality of love. On the contrary, he needs the judgment and the values of others in order to manifest his "love" ("Afin que de mon coeur l'*éclatant sacrifice* / Vous pût d'un pareil sort réparer l'injustice"—italics added) and he needs the contingent in order to make himself the absolute for Célimène that he wants to be. It is through Célimène's destitution—a destitution in terms of the values of others: money, prestige, power—that he hopes to become the very ground of her existence ("Vous voir tenir tout des mains de mon amour"). Just as he is hardly concerned with his own sincerity but greatly concerned with the sincerity of others, Alceste does not want to love, but *to be loved*. The language he speaks is the language of power, not the language of love.

The tyrannical aspect of Alceste's "love" does not escape Célimène, who retorts drily to his strange declaration: "C'est me vouloir du bien d'une étrange manière." Her insight is justified at the end of the play. If there was ever a time for Alceste to prove the constancy and purity of his love, this was it. Célimène at the end of the play is as destitute as he could have wished. But Alceste does not want or know how to give love. He wants only to be loved, to be preferred absolutely. Rounding on Célimène harshly and cursing his love for her, he brutally lays down the conditions on which alone she can redeem herself in his eyes:

> Oui, je veux bien, perfide, oublier vos forfaits;
> J'en saurai, dans mon âme, excuser tous les traits,
> Et me les couvrirai du nom d'une foiblesse
> Où le vice du temps porte votre jeunesse,
> Pourvu que votre coeur veuille donner les mains
> Au dessein que j'ai fait de fuir tous les humains,
> Et que dans mon désert, où j'ai fait vœu de vivre,

Vous soyez, sans tarder, résolue à me suivre:
C'est par là seulement que, dans tous les esprits,
Vous pouvez réparer le mal de vos écrits,
Et qu'après cet éclat, qu'un noble coeur abhorre,
Il peut m'être permis de vous aimer encore.
                                        (V, 4, 1757–68)

Célimène replies that she cannot renounce the world. She offers Alceste her hand in marriage, however, only to find herself interrupted by an irate "lover" who rejects her offer in insulting terms:

(. . .) Non: mon coeur à présent vous détēste,
Et ce refus lui seul fait plus que tout le reste.
Puisque vous n'êtes point, en des liens si doux,
Pour trouver tout en moi, comme moi tout en vous,
Allez, je vous refuse, et ce sensible outrage
De vos indignes fers pour jamais me dégage.
                                        (V, 4, 1779–84)

The contradictoriness and inauthenticity of Alceste's position is mercilessly exposed in this scene. By stipulating that Célimène must withdraw to a desert place with him, Alceste is attempting to realize *literally* his goal of complete and utter domination. In his desert he would *in fact* be the whole world for Célimène. If Célimène had accepted, however, Alceste would no longer have wanted to go with her. This is one reason for the alacrity with which he accepts her refusal. Alceste can desire Célimène only as long as she is an "enemy," a freedom to be reduced to slavery. Had she accepted his offer, he would have ceased to "love" her, since, having renounced her freedom, she would no longer be in a position to give it up for him. Like Dom Juan, Alceste cannot find the recognition and admiration he longs for in the love of a devoted mistress. At the same time, he cannot accept her offer of marriage, for marriage, as Jupiter made amply clear in *Am-*

phitryon, does not constitute a sufficient abandonment by the beloved of her freedom. Alceste's "love" for Célimène is such that he can neither accept her as free, nor accept her as unfree. If she is free he does not possess her freedom, and if she is unfree she no longer has any freedom for him to possess. Alceste is condemned by the very nature of his desire to desire indefinitely without satisfaction. In the debased romantic parlance of recent times, he is "in love with love."

As we discover the true nature of Alceste's "love" for Célimène, we also discover the true nature of his supposed spontaneity and sincerity. Alceste's love for Célimène is not an inconsistency or "comic flaw" as has sometimes been held, not at least in the sense in which it has been described as one. The fact that reason does not determine love in no way contradicts the position Alceste *professes* to hold; it is, on the contrary, essential to it. When Philinte compares Eliante favorably with Célimène and expresses surprise that Alceste does not choose the former rather than the latter, since Eliante is in every way a more "suitable" match than Célimène ("Et ce choix plus conforme étoit mieux votre affaire"—I, 1, 246), Alceste's reply is no banal comment on the irrationality of passion, it is a rejection of the level on which Philinte is discussing love. From the point of view of prudence and advantage, Philinte is no doubt right ("Il est vrai: ma raison me le dit chaque jour"—*ibid.,* 247), but, Alceste observes, the realm of love like that of justice lies beyond reason (read: the calculating reason) and it is not governed by interest. "Mais la raison n'est pas ce qui règle l'amour," he says (*ibid.,* 248), and he might have added: "nor ought it to." Alceste cannot admit that reason ought to govern love, for reason in the sense of "sagesse," the shrewd accommodating of ends, means, and interests, is precisely what Alceste ostensibly rebels against in the world of his fellow creatures. Nothing is more opposed to the "sincerity" he advocates than careful calculation of advantages and disadvantages. Alceste's own description of his love for Célimène as passing reason is thus entirely consistent with the position he claims to hold and the free, natural, spontaneous, and sincere person he claims to be.

At the same time, however, Alceste appreciates that his infatuation with the worldly and sophisticated Célimène must appear strange to his public. People must inevitably wonder what he, the bluff and uncompromising champion of simplicity and sincerity, finds so attractive in this cultivated and self-conscious society lady. Philinte's words to Eliante express a bewilderment that many of Alceste's acquaintances must have shared:

> De l'humeur dont le Ciel a voulu le former,
> Je ne sais pas comment il s'avise d'aimer.
> Et je sais moins encor comment votre cousine,
> Peut être la personne où son penchant l'incline.[2]
>   (IV, 1, 1171–74)

To justify his behavior and conceal his real motives, from himself as well as from others, Alceste must despise Célimène at the same time as he "loves" her, he must present his love as at once *irrational*—an enslavement, unworthy of him—and *super-rational* —a manifestation of his perfect freedom and a higher emotion than anything his contemporaries, with their mean calculations, can possibly achieve. Like the Romantic lovers who were to succeed him, he swithers ambiguously between both these presentations of his relation to Célimène in an attempt to make both seem true at the same time. This explains why the words "la raison n'est pas ce qui règle l'amour" have so often been taken as an expression of his shame at the totally irreducible and uncontrollable fact of love. The ambiguity of Alceste's attitude to his love for Célimène is understandable. On the one hand, he must posit

---

[2] One recalls the questions that were asked about Rousseau's predilection for rich and aristocratic patronesses. The *Confessions* make it quite clear that Rousseau was aware of a dangerously revealing contradiction in his attachment for ladies like Madame du Luxembourg; on several occasions he tries to justify himself.

his love as transcending the cunning calculations of his fellow-
men, as absolute, coming from the heart, sincere and free. In this
sense his love acts as a mark of his superiority. At the same time,
however, he must appear to despise Célimène, in order to show
that he is not really the slave that he seems to be. He must remind
his audience that he is superior even to his own desire. His love
must be shown to be at once super-rational, the free creation of
his own sincere and spontaneous nature, and irrational, not
consented to, beneath him.

In reality, Alceste's love for Célimène is neither super-rational
(above all reason and all explanation) nor irrational (below all
reason and explanation). It is quite simply a peculiar and contradictory fascination which goes by the name of love in the
vocabulary of the Alcestes of the world. It *can* be explained, and
the explanation reveals that far from being the sincere and spontaneous being he says he is, Alceste is as calculating as anyone
else.

It is precisely because Célimène is the most sought after and
worldly of women (to all *appearances* the most unsuitable for
Alceste) that he falls in love with her. It is not Célimène that
Alceste loves or desires. She is irrelevant *as a person* to his "love."
It is the world that he seeks to reach and possess through her.
To have at his feet this woman whom all the world admires and
courts would be to win the recognition of the world for himself.
Alceste's love is entirely mediated by those very "gens à la mode"
for whom he so loudly protests his contempt. He "loves" Célimène
because she has what he wants—the admiration of the world—
and cannot admit he wants, without at the same time admitting
that he is not the free, frank, and independent person he wants
to be admired as. The object of his desire is thus also his unavowed rival, and this *for the very same reason* that she is the
object of his desire. While he protests his love for Célimène,
Alceste must therefore conceal the real reason for this love by
affecting to deplore her participation in the "false" society of the

gens à la mode and to despise her charms and her popularity. The final break with Célimène strikingly illustrates the ambiguity that characterizes Alceste's entire relationship with her from the beginning. Alceste calls on witnesses to observe how superior and disinterested his love is compared to the love of the elegant suitors who have abandoned Célimène, while at the same time he affirms before them his own contempt for it as unworthy of him:

> *Vous voyez* ce que peut une indigne tendresse,
> Et je vous fais tous deux *témoins* de ma foiblesse.
> Mais, à vous dire vrai, ce n'est pas encor tout,
> Et *vous allez me voir* la pousser jusqu'au bout,
> *Montrer* que c'est à tort que sages on nous nomme,
> Et que dans tous les coeurs il est toujours de l'homme.
>   (V, 4, 1751–56, italics added)

Having once proved how different his love is from that of Célimène's frivolous and calculating suitors, however, Alceste is only too quick to use her unwillingness to follow him to his desert as an excuse to drop her. Célimène without her suitors can have no attraction for Alceste.

Those who fall for Alceste's argument about the irrationality of passion are his dupes. Alceste cannot accept in the front rank of his own consciousness, or admit to others, that his whole life is pure posturing before others, that he who claims to be sincere and spontaneous is as preoccupied with the public as anybody and as mediated by it as those whom he charges with acting parts for others. Is he not, after all, the only person in the world who does not posture, whose emotions spring directly from the heart and who speaks nothing but what he really thinks and feels? Alceste uses the myth of the irrationality of passion to hide from others and from himself a character that is every bit as cold and ungenerous as the characters of those he criticizes for their coldness and lack of generosity. "Par son sérieux prudent, morne et toujours occupé du public," to use the words with which Stendhal was later to describe the Comte de Nerwinde in *Lamiel*, Alceste prefigures the innumerable misanthropes who were to come after him. Molière saw, as Stendhal was to see, that those who flaunt their freedom and eccentricity, their passions and their furies, are in reality careful and calculating actors with not a grain of natural spontaneity and sincerity in them.[3] Stendhal's Nerwinde, "ce caractère froid, contenu, calculant toujours," seems ruinously extravagant, insouciant, and a little mad. But he is extravagant by design, prudently insouciant, and carefully mad. "Avant 1789," Stendhal observes, "il eût paru souverainement ennuyeux; on eût trouvé dans les comédies ce caractère d'un Gascon froid et important" (Chap. 12). One does indeed, and rarely more clearly delineated than in Molière's *Misanthrope*.

Alceste's life is in an important sense a life not of participation but of demonstration. This is one way in which he differs from the tragic heroes of Racine. The scandalous contradiction between the ideal and the real, between being and appearance, between the world of absolute values and the world of contingent opportunities is at the heart of seventeenth-century tragedy. There is never any danger, however, that Alceste will share in the sombre destinies of Racine's heroes. His world is far removed from theirs. He does not stake his destiny, as Junie or Andromaque or Monime does, on living an authentic life in a world of inauthenticity. The inauthenticity of the world is not a menace to him; on the contrary, it is the very source of all his satisfactions. It provides the basis for his own superiority and he spends his time not in a real struggle to reach authenticity, but in endless efforts to have his superiority recognized by the very world of inauthenticity which he affects to detest. The absence of value in the world becomes, with Alceste, a matter for personal self-congratulation. Far from threatening his existence, the world of lies and deceit founds it. He exhausts himself in theatrical gestures, because all his wrestling

---

[3] Cf. likewise Pushkin's description in *The Queen of Spades* of "the young men calculating in their giddiness" who ignore Lizaveta Ivanovna at the gay balls to which she accompanies her tyrannical old benefactress.

with the ideal and the real, all his disgust with the world's falseness, however painfully experienced subjectively, is, objectively
viewed, nothing but vain, ineffectual, and deeply inauthentic
posturing. He does not really suffer because life is full of pretense
and selfishness, because men have made their lives so vain and
stupid. He suffers because he cannot bear to be like others and
because others refuse him the adulation which he wants from
them.

In the end he is so divorced by his monstrous vanity from any
authentic participation in human affairs that he is unable to
function normally in the world. (In the subtitle of the comedy
Molière described him as *l'atrabilaire*; in our more sophisticated
age he could doubtless be classified according to the categories of
modern psychology.) [4] He acts out his role so intensely that he

---

[4] In his *Wesen und Formen der Sympathie*, which we quote from the
English translation by P. Heath (*The Nature of Sympathy* [London, 1954]),
Max Scheler describes various forms of vicarious living, that of the abnormally
vain man, that of what he terms the "mental parasite," and that of the
"spiritual vampire, the hollowness of whose existence, coupled with a passionate
quest for experience, drives him to a limitless active penetration into the
inmost reaches of the other's self."

"It is common for certain psychoses to exhibit a variant form of the general
attitudes here outlined," Scheler continues: "I refer to that excessive deference
in attitude, thought and action, towards the 'spectator' and the impression
supposedly made on him, which is so especially noticeable in *hysteria*. The
presence of an onlooker immediately upsets the patient's natural self-possession,
his consciousness of himself being replaced by the *image* of himself as seen
by the onlooker, and as judged by the latter's standards of preference. He
speaks, acts and conducts himself by reference to this image and on the spur
of the moods it evokes—refusing to eat, for instance, or even committing
suicide in some cases. It would be a mistake to describe this, as many psychiatric textbooks do, simply as 'excessive vanity', 'play-acting' or 'coquetry'
on the part of the patient. (. . .) Such a patient will not be content, like
the still normal 'prima donna' type to put on a stricken air so as to make others
feel sorry for him, or a gay one to cheer them up; instead he will implement
the wished for calamity by *actually* staging one, will actually kill himself,
actually get into a state of wild hilarity, etc., but all still for the benefit of the
spectator and depending on his presence. The vain man, the play actor and
the coquette do not act thus, for they have not lost their capacity for self-
awareness and merely vacillate between their own true condition and the
image of themselves as others see them.

"All such sub-species of this general type consist of forms, which have nothing to do with fellow-feeling proper, seeing that the conditions for this, the

becomes the prisoner of his own theatricality. Incapable, as we
have seen, of any form of real communication with others, either
in love or in friendship, he loses all contact with the real world.
His entire being is demonstrative. He does not want to win his
lawsuit, preferring to lose it so that the world's unworthiness—
and his own superiority to it—can be proved:

> (. . .) Je voudrois, m'en coûtât-il grand'chose,
> Pour la beauté du fait avoir perdu ma cause.
> (I, 1, 201–2)

For the abstract satisfaction of proving—as he imagines—that
the world is not fit to judge him, he is willing to sacrifice the

consciousness and feeling of being oneself, of leading one's own life and thus
of being 'separate' from others, are only apprehended here in a degenerate
form. For this reason too *their ethical value is negative*, however much they
may be mistaken for refinements of fellow-feeling or even for love. (. . .)
All these people are capable of acts of what is commonly called 'sacrifice.'
But in fact that is merely what they look like. For a man who neither leads
his own life nor finds it worth living cannot sacrifice himself for another. (. . .)
Such neglect of self may have the quality of being useful and well-intentioned
towards others, or it may be damaging and malevolent—as in the case of pure
villainy, which may render the villain quite forgetful of his own advantage and
even reckless of damage to himself; but even where the process begins in
goodwill, it is an almost inevitable rule (. . .) that it *ends in hatred*, and the
more so, the more the agent persists in *throwing himself away* in this spurious
fashion, for it is the very opposite of real meritorious self-*devotion*. Without
a certain self-awareness and self-respect, acquired at first hand, and not derived from the effect produced on others, it is not possible to live morally. But
the more one's self-respect is impaired in the process referred to, the harder
do we struggle to retain it, and the sterner grows the conflict between this
endeavour and the countervailing tendency to lapse into absorption in another
person. Figuratively speaking, although the 'slave' has voluntarily delivered
himself into the bondage of living another's life rather than his own, he
comes at last to chafe against his fetters, and to rise up against his 'master.'
And so the expense of spirit which at first resembled love turns necessarily to
hatred, as a final means of self-assertion" (pp. 44–45).
  This passage has been quoted at some length because it seems so deeply
pertinent to the case of Alceste as we have described it. (In our conclusion
we shall discover many other comic heroes to whom Scheler's analysis applies
equally well.) Alceste—*l'atrabilaire*—is a profoundly sick man. It is remarkable that Molière's understanding of his malady transcends the simple char-
acterology of the humors as effectively as Scheler's analysis transcends that of
grosser and more positivist types of psychology.

justice of his cause. But just as Alceste is not really interested in Célimène herself, he is not really interested in justice. He claims to refuse the kind of justice that can be had in the world because it is not absolute justice; in reality, however, he is anxious to place himself beyond all possible justice, beyond good and beyond evil, to have himself recognized as an absolute that no relative—no other—*can* judge. In his frenzied efforts to achieve this recognition Alceste, rather like George Dandin in a later play, rushes joyfully toward self-destruction.

Alceste acts the part of an absolute, but no one accepts his absoluteness: he loses his lawsuit, he fails to make Célimène submit to him, and he is laughed at by the world at large. He is an absolute in the world of his own conceptualizing alone, and thither he withdraws to decide for himself the fate of all his battles. The desert to which Alceste has always thought of withdrawing and to which he makes as if to withdraw at the end of the comedy is the world of his own mind. In it there is nothing to contradict his absoluteness, but there is unfortunately nothing to confirm it either. Alceste's difficulty is that his absoluteness can be experienced as real only with reference to others. Withdrawal to the desert cannot therefore be a final solution. It can only be an *act*, just as his rejection of Philinte at the beginning of the play was an act. This withdrawal requires an audience to watch it; and this hermit seeks not to escape but to be pursued. Alceste's withdrawal is simply a pose. And this is the very marrow of Molière's play. Alceste literally *joue la comédie*. He is perpetually play-acting, whether we think of his passion for Célimène or of his passion for justice, and in this respect he resembles Molière's other comic heroes.

At first sight the legendary seducer and professed anarchist of *Dom Juan* seems to have little in common with the moralizing hero of *Le Misanthrope*. If we wipe off some of the grease paint, however, we find that the same actor plays both roles. As the individual alienates himself from the world and takes cognizance of the gulf between his own consciousness and the objects of his consciousness, he sets himself up as the absolute judge of all that exists. Man, theoretically, becomes the measure of all things. But what of men among themselves? What is to be the measure here? Inevitably, each man sets himself up as the measure of other men, measuring them in relation to himself and himself in relation to them. While inanimate objects have no eyes to return our gaze and no mouths to answer us back, the men we measure can also measure us. As we all measure ourselves in relation to others, we must be sure that others measure themselves in relation to us exactly as we do. We must be, in short, the supreme measure for others that we are for ourselves, no longer subject for ourselves and object for others, but subject for ourselves and for others, no longer judging ourselves and judged by others, but judging for ourselves and others. We cannot achieve this absolute supremacy, however, without first provoking others to judge us. We must make them try to judge and measure us so that they will judge us unjudgeable and measure us infinitely unmeasurable.

In a society that has not begun to question its values, the obvious way to provoke the judgment of others, while at the same time positing oneself as beyond judgment, is to flout and deny the values at the same time. This is the course followed by Dom Juan. By flouting the values of his peers, the Dom deliberately forces them to judge him, but by denying that their values have any bindingness in themselves, by affirming that his will is the only law, he recognizes that he puts himself out of reach of their judgments. In a society that is fully aware of its own freedom and of the conventionality of its behavior, Alceste adopts a directly contrary course. Instead of flouting values, he champions them and insists that his will is the universal moral will, his conscience the universal conscience, his reason the universal reason. In this way he forces himself on his fellows, demanding to be judged by them, and at the same time puts himself beyond their judgment, since by associating his own values with absolute values and his own will with a universal will, he presents himself as the fountainhead and the foundation of all judgments, itself necessarily beyond judgment. When Alceste says "Je veux qu'on soit sincère" and "Je veux que l'on soit homme, et qu'en toute rencontre / Le fond de notre coeur dans nos discours se montre," this is intended to be synonymous with "On doit être sincère" and "On doit être homme," etc. That Alceste's will is not in fact synonymous with the universal moral will is evident, however, from numerous other instances of it. "Je veux me fâcher, et ne veux point entendre" (I, 1, 5) cannot be transcribed as a universal moral obligation. The crux of the matter lies in the cry "Je veux qu'on me distingue," which Alceste would doubtless have everybody read "On doit me distinguer." Unfortunately for Alceste nobody accepts this as a moral law, and in presenting it as one Alceste gives himself away. He is discovered to be the same as everybody else in the very moment that he demands to be regarded as different. What he presents as a universal law is seen to be nothing but a generalized formulation of his own desire.

Alceste's desire to withdraw from the world is an inevitable reaction to the refusal of his fellow-men to recognize his will and his law as absolute. He dreams of constituting himself a one-man society, a world apart, in which his reason will in fact be the universal reason and his will the general will, while the prescriptions of his conscience will in fact inform the social order, *which he is*. The realization of Alceste's dream would be the literal realization, in what is ostensibly an effort to overcome them, of the full consequences of modern individualism. Alceste would become truly a world and a law unto himself. But Alceste can only dream. He would dearly love to annihilate all those others whose existence is the principal obstacle to his own absolute supremacy, but he cannot annihilate them, and he cannot ignore them, because it is only through them that he can hope to experience the superiority he desires for himself.

Beneath his mask of righteous sincerity, Alceste is as willful and anarchical as Dom Juan, and both are inescapably bound to those of whom they claim to be independent. Both are motivated by the same grotesquely inflated vanity and both become *poseurs* in the attempt to conceal their true desires. With astonishing insight Molière saw that idealism and cynicism, soaring romanticism and skeptical "realism," Alceste and Dom Juan are two masks of the same actor, two presentations of the same comedy.

The polite society against which Alceste rebels might seem at first sight to have nothing in common with its irascible critic. If Alceste turns out to resemble his opponents rather more than he thinks, however, they in their turn are shown to resemble him rather more than they think. Their formally polite gestures conceal the same extravagant vanity as the petulant intransigence and moral self-righteousness of Alceste. The whole universe which revolves around Célimène, like planets around a sun, is in fact held together and propelled by vanity. With the exception of Philinte and Eliante, *none* of the characters in *Le Misanthrope* is free to act spontaneously or capable of desiring anything for its own sake. Each is mediated by the others. Each sees, feels, desires, and exists uniquely through the others. Célimène is the center toward which all the conflicting forces of vanity in the comedy gravitate. Every one of the characters aspires to win her in order to find the superiority that his vanity demands reflected in the recognition of it by others. To become the acknowledged master of Célimène and to usurp her place at the center of the universe is the goal of Oronte as well as of Alceste, of Arsinoë as well as of the two marquesses. For the men this means that they must woo Célimène and win a public avowal of love from her; for Arsinoë it means that she must attempt to dethrone Célimène and deflect the adulation she enjoys toward herself. The difference between the technique employed by Arsinoë and that employed by the men obscures, but in no way cancels, the essential fact that all—the worshiping lovers and the resentful prude alike—are the rivals of Célimène herself as well as of each other.

Célimène's fascination for each of her admirers depends not on any innate charm or beauty which is desired in its own right and for itself, but on the fact that she is desired by other admirers. Alceste, as we saw, does not desire Célimène directly on her own account. His desire is mediated by the very people whom he professes to despise and disregard. Likewise Oronte desires her not for herself, but because Alceste, Acaste, and Clitandre desire her. Acaste and Clitandre are similarly mediated by the other suitors, Acaste by Clitandre, Oronte, and Alceste, and Clitandre by Acaste, Oronte, and Alceste. But just as Célimène does not arouse the men's desire for her, so she herself is incapable of satisfying it. It is not enough for any of them to be secretly preferred by Célimène or to possess her privately. Each conceives his desires only through others and each can satisfy them only through others. Only by looking at Célimène with the desire of his rivals can each of the suitors desire her, and only by looking at himself with the envy of his rivals can he hope to savor his triumph.

Célimène knows that her privileged position at the center of her world depends on her maintaining all the tensions around her in equilibrium. She must stimulate and sustain the desire of each member of her group by stimulating and sustaining the desire of all the other members at the same time. While she must constantly reassure and encourage each of her suitors by giving him marks of preference, she must also maintain him in a state of uncertainty, watchfulness, and jealousy with regard to all the others. If she were to commit herself publicly to any one of her ardent "lovers" to the exclusion of the others, Célimène would inevitably destroy the desire in them all, and even in the chosen one, since the desire of each is dependent on the desire of all the others. Even as she assures each suitor privately that he should not be put out by the favors with which she distinguishes his rivals in public, she also, therefore, sows the seeds of doubt in his mind by reminding him of the goodwill she shows to his rivals, so that he must constantly ask himself the question: do I really enjoy her favor to the exclusion of all others? The famous *scène des portraits* shows Célimène at

her best. As she draws her malicious and witty sketches, each of
those present enjoys the humiliation suffered by her victim, while
at the same time he is disturbed by the nagging question that tormented Alceste in the first scene with Philinte: "What does she
say to others about *me?*"

As long as she refuses to commit herself publicly, as long as she
envelopes her relation to them in mystery, Célimène's suitors cannot experience the success they want in the eye of their rivals. They
must consequently push her to make her choice public and unequivocal, so that in the humiliation and dismay of their rivals
they can enjoy the spectacle of their own triumph. The scene between Acaste and Clitandre at the beginning of Act III leaves us
in no doubt that Célimène's suitors are compelled by their vanity
and their rivalry with each other, and not by their "love" of her, to
demand a clear statement of preference from her. Acaste and
Clitandre are disputing as to who is truly favored by Célimène.
Clitandre says he has been given to understand by Célimène that
it is he who enjoys her special favor. Acaste, however, claims to
have been given to understand the same thing. "Tu te flattes, mon
cher, et t'aveugles toi-même," Clitandre tells his friend and rival
(III, 1, 826). Nevertheless, in the absence of any public pronounce-
ment on Célimène's part, Clitandre cannot be *sure.* His affirmative-
ness hides a nervous uncertainty, and he presses Acaste to tell him
what signs of special favor he has really had. Now it is Acaste's
turn to be tantalizingly mysterious. Absolutely none, he replies.
"Je me flatte . . . je m'aveugle." Clitandre no longer knows
whether Acaste is telling him the truth or not. His teasing irony
might be a deliberate blind, intended to disguise the fact that he
has received no special mark of favor; on the other hand it might
equally well mean that he has had very tangible signs of favor and
that he really is laughing up his sleeve at Clitandre, that it is Clitandre in fact who "se flatte" and "s'aveugle." The uncertainty is
intolerable to Clitandre. He must know for sure what lies behind
the masks of Célimène and of Acaste. He therefore suggests that

he and Acaste devise a scheme to force Célimène to show her hand.
The alacrity with which Acaste accepts this proposal reveals that,
despite his parade of assurance, he has been in turn put out by
Clitandre and is as dissatisfied as his friend by the assurances he
has received from Célimène.

In the second scene of Act V it is the rivalry of Oronte and
Alceste that brings Oronte to Célimène demanding to be told unequivocally who enjoys her absolute preference:

> Oui, c'est à vous de voir si par des noeuds si doux,
> Madame, vous voulez m'attacher tout à vous.
> $$(V, 2, 1586–87)$$

She must decide, he insists, and make her decision known publicly:

> Il s'agit de savoir quels sont vos sentiments.
> $$(V, 2, 1600)$$

> Il faut, il faut parler, et lâcher la balance.
> $$(V, 3, 1665)$$

Suddenly Alceste rises from his corner to repeat the same demand
for a clear, unambiguous, and public answer:

> C'est son éclat surtout qu'ici j'ose exiger.
> $$(V, 2, 1639)$$

The audience is confronted with the strange spectacle of the two
opponents and rivals, the one supposedly representing bluff frankness and the other conventional civility, joining forces to exact an
avowal of her feelings from Célimène.[5] In scene 4, they are joined

[5] The underlying similarity of Alceste and Oronte is suggested at the very
beginning of the play in Act I, scene 2, where Oronte reads his sonnet to
Alceste and asks his opinion of it. Oronte had already read his sonnet to
others and they had applauded it. If he brings his sonnet to Alceste, it is

by the two marquesses who produce the damning letters. It is thus not only Alceste who wants people to be sincere so that he can know what they really think. Orgon and the two marquesses are equally unwilling to accept conventional signs and polite reassurances. They are as eager as he is to see behind appearances into the true thoughts of others, because they are as dependent as he is on the opinion others have of them.

By forcing Célimène to choose, however, the suitors topple the entire structure by which they themselves are upheld. None of the suitors has anything to gain by Célimène's choosing. On the contrary, they must all lose. Célimène can choose only one: three must therefore lose. But the winner's victory will be a Pyrrhic one, for, by the very fact of choosing, Célimène will cease to have the value that she has as long as she does not choose. The value of possessing Célimène must itself vanish the moment she shows that she can be and is possessed. The desire of the suitors, in short, can never be satisfied. The idol and the object of their desire perfectly reflects the vanity that motivates it. Célimène has no being of her own. She is a Sphinx-like creature who acquires her reality from her suitors themselves and whose entire being, like theirs, is contained in her appearance for others. "Mais croyez-vous qu'on l'aime, aux choses qu'on peut voir," Philinte, speaking on behalf of Alceste, asks Eliante (IV, 1, 1179). "C'est un point qu'il n'est pas fort aisé de savoir," Eliante replies. "Comment pouvoir juger s'il est vrai qu'elle l'aime? / Son coeur de ce qu'il sent n'est pas bien sûr lui-

---

because he too, like Alceste, wants to know what others *really* think of him and of his work. When Alceste asks to be excused from passing judgment—"J'ai le défaut / D'être un peu plus sincère en cela qu'il ne faut" (299–300)— Oronte replies that it is precisely on account of his sincerity that Alceste's opinion is precious to him: "C'est ce que je demande, et j'aurois lieu de plainte, / Si, m'exposant à vous pour vous parler sans feinte, / Vous alliez me trahir, et me déguiser rien" (301–3). Oronte's desire for "sincerity" here is the very copy of Alceste's. It is not the truth he wants, as the quarrel that ensues confirms, but unreserved recognition by others of the value he claims for himself. It is amusing to see the roles reversed in this scene. Alceste is as anxious to avoid pronouncing what he thinks as he accuses others of being, while Oronte insists on absolute sincerity.

même; / Il aime quelquefois sans qu'il le sache bien, / Et croit aimer aussi parfois qu'il n'en est rien" (IV, 1, *1180–84*). It is true that Célimène is never sure of her own sentiments, and the reason for this is that she has none of her own. Like her suitors, she has no autonomous desire or will, only the desire to find herself reflected as desirable in the eyes of others. Only through the sentiments and reactions toward her that she finds in others can she experience her own self. The enigmatic being that all her suitors pursue behind her masks is perfectly elusive because it does not exist. Only what they themselves call into existence exists—the masks they try to "see behind." Apart from her masks Célimène is nothing, a pure seeing, transparent and opaque at the same time. She is completely given in her appearances, like those strange tropical fish that take on the colors of the objects surrounding them. When they finally do see through her, Célimène's suitors discover that she is not the ultimate and enigmatic foundation of all being, but an absence of being, the very reflection of their own seeing, an utter emptiness. Abandoned by everyone at the end of the play, Célimène vanishes like a shadow into the night, and the whole structure which pivoted around her vanishes with her, like froth on the surface of nothingness.

The court of Célimène with its urbanity, wit, and formal civility masking subterranean rivalries and resentments calls to mind a passage in Saint-Simon's *Mémoires* which describes another and more celebrated court:

Les fêtes fréquentes, les promenades particulières à Versailles, les voyages furent des moyens que le Roi saisit pour distinguer et pour mortifier en nommant les personnes qui à chaque fois en devaient être, et pour tenir chacun assidu et attentif à lui plaire. Il sentait qu'il n'avait pas à beaucoup près assez de grâces à répandre pour faire un effet continuel. Il en substitua donc aux véritables d'idéales, par la jalousie, les petites préférences qui se trouvaient tous les jours, et pour ainsi dire à tous moments, par son art. Les espérances que ces petites préférences et ces distinctions faisaient naître, et la con-

sidération qui s'en tirait, personne ne fut plus ingénieux que lui à
inventer sans cesse ces sortes de choses. . . . (ed. Boislisle, Collec-
tion des Grands Ecrivains de France, Vol. 28, p. 127).

While it would be ludicrous to suggest that Molière deliberately
dressed Louis XIV up as Célimène, it is worth noting that some
acute observers discovered in the supreme social reality of Molière's
own time the same structure of relations as that which binds
Célimène and her world together in the supreme comedy of that
same time.

In almost every respect Philinte and Eliante stand in striking
contrast to the other characters in *Le Misanthrope*. Although they
do have a part in the elaborate ballet of formal social relations, it
is a small part and it does not absorb their whole being. They play
the roles that are expected of them, on the understanding that roles
are never more than roles and that a stage is never more than a
stage. Neither tries to occupy the center of the stage or to take
control of the action. Philinte flatters politely where flattery seems
called for by the rules of the game, but he does not try to make his
hearer forget that his flattery is conventional. Similarly, although
he is as aware as Alceste of the imperfections of the world he does
not present himself to others as a champion of morality. He limits
his public appearances to a strict minimum. "J'observe, comme
vous," he tells Alceste, "cent choses tous les jours, / Qui pourroient
mieux aller, prenant un autre cours; / Mais quoi qu'à chaque pas je
puisse voir paroître, / En courroux, comme vous, on ne me voit
point être" (I, 1, 159–62). Philinte tempers his Hobbesian realism
with a philosophical resignation to the evils of human life and
human beings:

> Oui, je vois ces défauts dont votre âme murmure
> Comme vices unis à l'humaine nature;
> Et mon esprit enfin n'est pas plus offensé
> De voir un homme fourbe, injuste, intéressé,

> Que de voir des vautours affamés de carnage,
> Des singes malfaisants, et des loups pleins de rage.
> (I, 1, 173–78)

Philinte is certainly concerned with what people think of him
(". . . on ne me voit point être," etc.). He is not anxious to do
what would shock others or attract unwanted attention, what
would not be considered "à propos et de la bienséance." "Parfois
. . . / Il est bon de cacher ce qu'on a dans le coeur," he says (I, 1,
75–76). This is not, however, the advice of a hypocrite. Philinte
does not advocate that we conceal our true thoughts so that we
can deceive people as to what we are. He argues that it does not
matter very much that most people should know what we think,
and that if we are truly independent of others, we will not feel any
great need to tell others what we think of them or to learn what
they think of us. Philinte asks only conventional courtesies of
others and he expects them to require no more of him. In this way,
he would argue, the order of society can be upheld, while the freedom of the individual remains intact, and social life can go on
without each person's being completely absorbed by his being for
others:

> (. . .) quand on est du monde, il faut bien que l'on rende
> Quelques dehors civils que l'usage demande.
> (I, 1, 65–66)

Society requires only that we render unto it that which belongs to
it. If we try to give it more than that, we transform Caesar into a
god, and it is not surprising that we then find ourselves at once the
slaves and the rivals of the idol we ourselves have invested with
supreme power and authority.

Like Philinte, Eliante keeps her distance from the world. She
says little and scrupulously avoids becoming involved in the performances of those around her. When Célimène asks her to defend

her against Alceste and Oronte, both of whom demand that she decide between them, Eliante answers that she must beg to be excused:

> N'allez point là-dessus me consulter ici:
> Peut-être y pourriez-vous être mal adressée,
> Et je suis pour les gens qui disent leur pensée.
>   (V, 3, 1660-62)

Like Philinte, Eliante does not mean that everyone should at all times speak what is on his mind. This is certainly not her own policy, for no other important character in the comedy is as sparing of words as she. Even in these lines she expresses her opinion very reticently. She means no more than that between friends or lovers there should be good faith. Those who are open with their friends or lovers do not get into the difficulty Célimène finds herself in.

Eliante is dimly aware that neither Célimène nor Alceste is really in good faith. In one of her rare speeches she dissociates herself from Alceste's view of the lover's relation to the beloved as well as from Célimène's. The judgment of the beloved by others and the attempt to reach an "objective" judgment of her "as she really is" are equally excluded by Eliante from the relation of the lover to his beloved:

> L'amour, pour l'ordinaire, est peu fait à ces lois,
> Et l'on voit les amants vanter toujours leur choix;
> Jamais leur passion n'y voit rien de blâmable,
> Et dans l'objet aimé tout leur devient aimable:
>
> .   .   .   .
>
> La pâle est aux jasmins en blancheur comparable;
> La noire à faire peur, une brune adorable;
> La maigre a de la taille et de la liberté;
> La grasse est dans son port pleine de majesté . . .
>   (II, 4, 711-14, 717-20)

The lover's mistress is desirable to him, says Eliante, not because others find her desirable or because she has been examined "objectively" and found without blemish, but for no other reason than that he desires her. The opinion of others is so irrelevant, according to Eliante, that it may be quite the opposite of the lover's own, without his being affected by it in any way. At first glance Eliante's argument seems slight and banal, a restatement of the old idea that beauty is in the eye of the beholder and that all is appearance. While it is true that her argument is banal, however, the matter is not quite so simple. Eliante is trying to distinguish between different ways of beholding. She does not say that what the lover sees in his beloved is what is really there. She does not say either, however, that what is there is what others see. There is no complete objective truth about another person, Eliante is saying, and if we try to see another person "objectively," that is as an object, we are bound to fail. We can never have certain and objective knowledge of another person, because no person is an object of our seeing. It is therefore right and proper that a lover should see his beloved with the eyes of his love. The kind of knowledge by which love is nourished is the kind of knowledge that love provides.

This is illustrated by Eliante's own relation to Philinte, which contrasts strikingly with the relations among Célimène and her suitors. When Philinte asks Eliante to accept him in lieu of Alceste, should the latter not wish to marry her, she answers: "Vous vous divertissez, Philinte" (IV, 1, 1213). But she knows that Philinte is not teasing, and Philinte knows that she knows he is not teasing. She is simply asking for a little reassurance, which Philinte promptly supplies in a few words. Eliante is reassured. But she is reassured, paradoxically, only because she was already sure. Her "Vous vous divertissez, Philinte" is neither a request for absolute objective certainty nor an attempt to evade commitment on her part by treating his profession of love as a conventional gesture. Because she has and is willing to have faith, her faith is strengthened. Had she not had it, had she, like Alceste, wanted to know for sure, to read Philinte's heart as if it were a mathematical table, every reassurance would simply have intensified the torment of uncertainty. "For whosoever hath, to him shall be given, and he shall have more abundance: but whosoever hath not, from him shall be taken away even that he hath" (Matt., 13:12).

It is true that several of Molière's heroes, who appear to have absolute trust, are duped and deceived by those they trust. The case of Orgon springs immediately to mind. We shall see in the following chapter, however, that Orgon's love for Tartuffe is not love as Eliante understands it at all, but a desire for domination not unlike Alceste's "love" for Célimène. Wherever the original desire of Molière's lovers is not to love but to possess the beloved, they find in the end that they have been the victims of a deception on the part of the "beloved," similar to their own deception of the "beloved." Where neither is true to the other, where neither has real faith, each in the end unmasks the imposture of the other. At the end of *Tartuffe*, Orgon unmasks the hypocrite, but the hypocrite also unmasks Orgon. In Act II of *Le Misanthrope*, Alceste unmasks Célimène, pointing out that she is constantly performing for her public, but Célimène counters with the most devastating exposure of Alceste's own theatricality in the play:

> Et ne faut-il pas bien que Monsieur contredise?
> A la commune voix veut-on qu'il se réduise,
> Et qu'il ne fasse pas éclater en tous lieux
> L'esprit contrariant qu'il a reçu des cieux?
> Le sentiment d'autrui n'est jamais pour lui plaire;
> Il prend toujours en main l'opinion contraire,
> Et penseroit paroître un homme du commun,
> Si l'on voyoit qu'il fut de l'avis de quelqu'un.
> L'honneur de contredire a pour lui tant de charmes,
> Qu'il prend contre lui-même assez souvent les armes;
> Et ses vrais sentiments sont combattus par lui,
> Aussitôt qu'il les voit dans la bouche d'autrui.
> (II, 4, 669–80)

As Célimène utters these words she is doing just what Alceste accused her of doing, but the same is true of Alceste, for when he criticizes Célimène, he is doing what Célimène accuses him of doing. There are few innocent dupes in Molière. Nearly all his heroes get what they deserve: Orgon is not the innocent victim he appears to be, Alceste is not the persecuted saint he appears to be, and Dandin is not the harmless and simple peasant he appears to be. Had Alceste been willing to love another person genuinely, he would not, as Philinte in fact suggests at one point, have fallen in love with Célimène. Similarly, if Orgon had truly desired to be pious, he would not have chosen Tartuffe as his guide and counselor.

There is one notable case of an innocent dupe, the case of Alcmène in *Amphitryon*. Alcmène's case reveals that, in a world of diabolically clever tyrants and hypocrites, seeking not love but total possession, the trusting are indeed likely to be deceived. In the end, however, the tyrant is deceived too, for he never succeeds in winning the object of his desire. If Jupiter deceives Alcmène, he is paid back in his own coin, as we saw in a previous chapter. He has to recognize that Alcmène's love is given not to him but to the true object of her love. Alcmène's love bypasses Jupiter in the very moment that she gives herself to him; in the very moment that he seems to possess her, she slips from his grasp and he finds himself grasping an empty husk. All Molière's tyrants meet with the same fate. As they force others to look upon them, they find that Medusa-like they have turned them to stone.

At the same time it is true that the trusting lover is as isolated in the world as the distrustful tyrant. Jupiter cannot satisfy his own desire; nevertheless he breaks apart all the bonds that people previously imagined themselves bound together by. There is certainly no real communication between tyrannical egoists, nor, however, is there any real communication between a trustful lover and a calculating deceiver. The deceiver does not really win the love of the lover, but the lover's embrace likewise encloses a void. Molière suggests that real communication and real love are possible only between two trusting people. It is not an accident that the opposition to Célimène and her court is provided by a *couple* rather than by a single individual.

And yet it is undeniable that Eliante and Philinte preserve their authenticity and sincerity only at the cost of non-participation. In one sense they are the only truly social characters in the comedy, the only characters capable of living comfortably and decently in society with others. In another sense, however, they stand apart from society, protecting themselves from it, Eliante by her silence and Philinte by his formal civility. Their attitude is not very different from that which Lucien Leuwen decides to adopt to his army comrades, in whose affected gestures and ironical politeness he senses only nastiness and resentment. "M'abstenir est le *mot d'ordre*; agir le moins possible le *plan de campagne*," says Lucien (Chap. 7). This strange contradiction in Philinte and Eliante points to a certain skepticism with regard to social life which we find again and again in Molière's comedies. As we shall have occasion to point out once more in the conclusion of our study, Molière's reasonable characters are already on the way to becoming outsiders, exceptions, or even abstractions. The very banality of their arguments emphasizes their inability to found social relations on anything substantial, and both they themselves and their arguments acquire consistency solely from their opposition to the extravagant or "impossible" natures and demands of the comic characters. It was still possible for Molière's audiences to adopt their point of view, but it is a point of view *on* society rather than a point of view provided *by* society. In the end it is the comic heroes, the egoists and tyrants, who are the socially oriented characters. They are the ones whose entire being is determined by and directed toward others. *Le Misanthrope* illustrates this more clearly than any of the comedies. The characters who are involved in the comic action of this play are not grotesque eccentrics like Harpagon or Argan. They are recognizably common social figures. The fact that many modern audiences find it hard to see Alceste as *comic* is thus hardly surprising. The literature of the centuries after Molière shows that modern writers have experienced more and more difficulty in finding a credible and real opposition to the vanity and egoism that they see as characteristic of social life. The Alcmènes and Eliantes of Molière's world have to be sought more and more in provincial or rural environments, where their contacts with "society" are limited. Laclos made Madame de Tourvel, as Baudelaire rightly insisted, the only bourgeois character in a world of aristocrats, a woman who deliberately shunned society, since she felt that all liaisons were dangerous. Goethe placed his Gretchen in a medieval village. Stendhal set Madame de Rênal in an out-of-the-way province and virtually cut her off from the social life of Verrières, while he shut Clélia up in her father's high tower, far from the social activities of the court at Parma. A disturbing half-light plays around the two characters of Eliante and Philinte. We accept them without question, because we cannot examine them too closely without upsetting the balance of the play and transferring to them an emphasis which Molière clearly intended to place on the other characters.[6]

[6] The shadowy nature of Philinte and Eliante, or, for that matter, of many of Molière's other reasonable characters, the abstractness of their "wisdom," their failure to offer within the plays a concrete alternative to the comic characters, may well reflect the abstractness of the very concept of the *honnête homme* in the seventeenth century. *Honnêteté* might be held to be in large measure the ideology of that bourgeoisie that was growing in power and influence under the absolute monarchy. The quality of *honnêteté*, as it is thus understood, transcends nobility and bourgeoisie alike, and abolishes, ideologically at least, social and class distinctions, creating a kind of equality, under the monarch and in service to him, of all men of education, talent, taste and goodwill. The full story of the concept of the *honnête homme* would doubtless reveal that those who subscribed to the ideal were not exclusively bourgeois, any more than the ideology of the eighteenth-century *philosophes*, which is, in a way, a thoroughgoing extension of *honnêteté*, was elaborated exclusively by the bourgeoisie of that period. Historical research would, I suspect, disclose a complex pattern of different groups, all supporting, in greater or lesser degree and in accordance with their own more or less well understood interests and ambitions, the ideal of *honnêteté*. It is not surprising, at any rate, that Molière, who was of good bourgeois stock, subscribed to it. At the same time his actual work shows that, at a certain level, he understood that social conflicts and ambitions were not in reality resolved by the ideological compromise of *honnêteté*.

4

LE TARTUFFE

"Nous n'aimons rien tant que ce qui nous
ressemble."

Molière, *Dom Garcie de Navarre.*

IN HIS OWN PRODUCTIONS of *Tartuffe*, Molière is known to have played the part of Orgon. In the following pages we propose to take Orgon, rather than Tartuffe himself, as the pivot of the comedy. While this perspective is somewhat distorted, it is hoped that it will bring to light certain aspects of the play that have not, perhaps, received the attention they merit, the correct angle from which we should view *Tartuffe* being provided, in our opinion, neither by Tartuffe nor by Orgon alone, but by the partnership of both.

The type of situation we find in *Tartuffe* is characteristic of many of Molière's comedies, from the early *Précieuses ridicules* to the later *Femmes savantes*. In both these plays, as in *Tartuffe*, those who are duped by impostors are themselves impostors in their own way. They try to use others and they are used by those whom they thought to use. Dupe and deceiver—and which is which?—are seen to be partners in the same enterprise. The main characters in these plays bear, in addition, a strong resemblance to the comic heroes whom we have encountered in the foregoing chapters. Cathos and Magdelon imitate the manners of the *précieuses*, whom they consider a species of demi-gods, in the hope that they too will be recognized as *précieuses* and so share in the adulation they enjoy. Dom Juan goes a step further. Refusing, ostensibly, to imitate or be judged by anybody, he sets himself up as unique and tries to win recognition and admiration on account of his very uniqueness. Likewise Alceste rejects any imitation, but he does not

101

flout society in the way Dom Juan did. He does not *appear* to set
himself up as a supervalue. In the more settled world of Louis XIV
such blatant vanity would not be tolerated. He chooses instead to
be *plus royaliste que le roi*, to present himself as the guardian of
the very values that society professes but does not practice. Real
justice and righteousness are his model, and yet, as we saw in the
previous chapter, this supposed model is in reality only an instrument for Alceste, a means of proving his superiority to others. Justice and sincerity are nothing but the servants of Alceste's vanity.
Orgon follows Alceste in choosing to be *plus royaliste que le roi*.
He professes to be a humble servant and follower of the saintly
man whom he has taken into his home to guide him and give him
counsel. But for Orgon, as for Alceste, the model serves in fact as a
kind of instrument.

Orgon's real desire is, like Dom Juan's or Alceste's, to have himself recognized by all around him as divinely absolute and self-
sufficient. His relations with his family are profoundly marked by
this desire. Claiming absolute being for himself—absolute in relation to the contingency of all others—he cannot recognize the independence of others except as a threat to and a denial of his own.
He cannot therefore love his family or entertain any relations with
them other than relations of violence and tyranny. When, almost
despite himself, he feels a touch of tenderness for his daughter, he
drives it away ("Allons, ferme, mon coeur, point de faiblesse humaine"—IV, 3, 1293) and he rejects affection impatiently when it
is offered to him ("Je ne veux pas qu'on m'aime"—II, 2, 545). This
"Christian" is not able to give love or to receive it, since both the
giving and the receiving of love imply recognition of the equality
of the self and the other, acceptance of the freedom of the other
and, consequently, of a limitation to the freedom and absoluteness
of the self.

Orgon does in fact receive due and proper love and respect from
his wife and children, but he wants more than due and proper love
and respect. The freedom to give this love and respect irks and

alarms him, because it marks a limit to his absolute power. No protestations of filial love and obedience can satisfy him. The very
existence of his family's freedom is unbearable to Orgon and presents itself to his sickly imagination as flagrant revolt. As his desire
for absolute power and authority is insatiable, so his fear that everyone is plotting against him cannot be assuaged, and to justify this
fear, to give it a *visible* object, he deliberately seeks out the break-
ing-point of his family's respect. Deliberately he provokes his children to rebellion. He then rounds upon them and, accusing them
of disrespect and disobedience, demands recognition of his absolute authority:

> Ah! je vous brave tous, et vous ferai connoître
> Qu'il faut qu'on m'obéisse et que je suis le maître.
> (III, 6, 1129–30)

Orgon, in short, is unwilling to base his relations with others on
mutual respect and the proper exercise by each of the authority invested in him. Like Dom Juan or Jupiter, he deliberately breaks
down this system of proprieties and trusts, in order to extract from
his family, in an atmosphere of violence, a total submission due
not to his rank and function as head of the family, but due to himself alone.

The form of Orgon's vanity is recognizably similar to that of the
other heroes we have looked at. What Orgon wants is the possession of a freedom and, like the other heroes, he constantly misses
the goal of his desire—the other's freedom—in the attempt to seize
it. Thus he loses his temper with Mariane when she refuses to say
that she is glad to be marrying Tartuffe. The child has already
expressed her resignation to her father's will, but this is not enough
for Orgon. He wants to control Mariane not only as an object but
as a subject, he wants her to will her submission to him, not merely
to do what he wants her to do, but to want to do what he wants her
to do. Mariane says it is not true that she *wants* to marry Tartuffe.

"Mais je veux que cela soit une vérité," Orgon shrieks (II, 1, 451).
As he brings the marriage contract to her later, he observes sadis-
tically: "Je porte en ce contrat de quoi vous faire rire" (IV, 3,
1277), but in the tears of his daughter he finds a refusal as well as
a recognition of his absolute power. Orgon can force Mariane to do
his will, but he cannot force her to will his will.

Orgon's attempts to extract recognition of his absolute and innate superiority are doomed to failure. He does not, however, admit
that this recognition is what he wants. He constantly disguises his
desire as desire for something else, for to reveal it would be to admit
a lack, an incompleteness, an insufficiency that are incompatible
with absoluteness. Tartuffe provides him with a means of securing
the subjection of others, while at the same time appearing not to
seek it for himself.

Orgon does not demand that he should be the center of attention, he demands that Tartuffe should be; he does not put his own
health and well-being before that of his wife and children, but
Tartuffe's; he does not require that his own innate superiority be
recognized by his family, but that Tartuffe's should be. It is not he
who is quasi-divine, but Tartuffe. Is he not himself the most fer-
vent and devout of Tartuffe's admirers? Dorine cannot get over
an infatuation that is absolutely unintelligible to her:

> Enfin il est fou; c'est son tout, son héros;
> Il l'admire à tous coups, le cite à tout propos;
> Ses moindres actions lui semblent des miracles,
> Et tous les mots qu'il dit sont pour lui des oracles.
> (I, 2, 195–98)

Indeed Orgon presents Tartuffe as a kind of Christ-figure. The very
words he uses when speaking of him have a strangely evocative
ring. "Vous ne connoissez pas celui dont vous parlez," he ad-
monishes Cléante (I, 5, 267) and this wonderfully ironical connoître carries the meaning of "recognize." The nature of Tartuffe,

according to Orgon, is such that the respect and admiration due to him transcend all ordinary respect and admiration. Tartuffe reduces to nothing the bonds of nature and convention. He is to be loved and admired not as a father or a brother or a friend, but absolutely, not in virtue of any relation in which he stands to others, but in virtue of his being who he is. When Dorine tries to dissuade Orgon from marrying his daughter to a man who is socially far below her, Orgon rejects her arguments out of hand. "Enfin avec le Ciel (Tartuffe) est le mieux du monde," he declares, "Et c'est une richesse à nulle autre seconde" (II, 2, 529–30). Tartuffe's admirers, according to Orgon, should find themselves elevated above everyday affections and loyalties. They should not love and admire him for any *reason*, in virtue of anything which is extrinsic to his being. Their devotion should be absolute, determined by nothing other than the intrinsic being of Tartuffe. Thus to Orgon all thought of family ties, of rank, and of social convention vanishes to nought before the irresistible illumination that emanates from Tartuffe:

> Il m'enseigne à n'avoir affection pour rien,
> De toutes amitiés il détache mon âme;
> Et je verrois mourir frère, enfants, mère et femme,
> Que je m'en soucierois autant que de cela.
>
> (I, 5, 276–79)

These lines contain an obvious and deliberate allusion to Christ's words in Matthew 10:37 (cf. also Luke 14:26). So far from having been intended by Molière to poke fun at Christianity, however, they emphasize the radical difference between the true Christ-figure and this all too human impostor. There is nothing divine at all about Tartuffe. In Orgon's own words:

> C'est un homme . . . qui . . . ha! . . . un homme . . . un homme enfin.
>
> (I, 5, 272)

Orgon rejects the ordinary bonds of nature and convention not in the name of Christ, but in the name of an idol of his own creation, a god who is an extension of himself.

By doubling himself in the shape of Tartuffe, Orgon's plan is to be both he who is absolutely superior and he who recognizes this absolute superiority, both the master and the slave whose enslavement confirms the superiority of the master. Orgon cannot see this himself. Were he fully aware of what he was doing, he would find himself faced with the very contradiction which he has invented Tartuffe to escape from. By admitting to himself that he envisaged Tartuffe as his alter ego, he would make it impossible for himself to demand recognition for him, for this would be to avow the very inferiority which the adoration of Tartuffe is intended to conceal— from himself as well as from others. Orgon cannot therefore afford to see that he intends to use Tartuffe as a projection of himself. He must believe in his idol himself; he too must feel himself seduced, captivated, carried away, not indeed by any deliberate effort on the part of Tartuffe, but by the very nature of Tartuffe's superior being. At the same time, however, since he wants to have this idol for himself, to enjoy *through* him the absolute superiority that he recognizes *in* him, he must attach him to himself, win him over, make him into an inalienable part of himself. He must in short seduce Tartuffe. Orgon thus becomes the supreme victim of his own project to be at once master and slave. He invests Tartuffe with the absoluteness he desires for himself so that he can objectify it through his own recognition of it, but he must also make sure that he is in full control of this absoluteness that he has projected on to Tartuffe. In the attempt to acquire this control, he finds himself in the position of the lover-idolator whose every attempt to seduce and control the beloved-idol reinforces his own enslavement.[1]

---

[1] The problematic relation of Orgon and Tartuffe has become in its most fashionably modern form that of subject and object, of see-er and seen. Modern man likes to consider himself as object in order to get round the unbearable situation in which he is an object for others. By consciously transforming himself into an object, he imagines he can maintain a surreptitious control

It is through his rank and position—those very conventional and accidental sources of authority and power which in his desire for absolute power he rejects—that Orgon seeks to gain control of Tartuffe and attach him to himself. He takes him in "gueusant et

---

over this object-self, repossess it from those who see it as object and thus be at one and the same time see-er and seen, subject and object for his own consciousness. This is what Gide's Immoralist is trying to do when he watches the young Arab steal a pair of scissors from him or when he goes out on poaching expeditions on his own estate with Alcide. It is what Mann's Madame Houpflé does when she orders Felix Krull to steal from her as she lies in bed in her hotel-room. It is what Malraux's business tycoon Ferral wants from the Chinese woman he takes to bed with him in *La Condition humaine:* "il possèderait à travers cette Chinoise la seule chose dont il fût avide: lui-même. Il lui fallait les yeux des autres pour se voir, les sens d'un autre pour se sentir. Il regarda la peinture thibétaine: sur un monde décoloré où erraient des voyageurs, deux squelettes exactement semblables s'étreignaient en transe" (Livre de Poche ed., p. 194). It is what we all want from each other and what God wants from us, according to Jouhandeau: "Qu'est-ce que Dieu cherche à surprendre dans l'homme? quel mystere conditionne l'amour que l'homme inspire à Dieu? Qui sait si ce n'est pas 'la Même Chose,' à un autre degré, qui m'attire dans les autres qui attire Dieu en moi? La Même Chose: une 'différence'? Si ce n'est pas à des intervalles divers le meme mirage qui nous fascine, Dieu en moi, moi dans les autres? si ma curiosité et ma jalousie ne sont pas les mêmes sur un autre plan que celles de Dieu? si mon amour et l'amour de Dieu n'enveloppent pas quelque indigence, le même regret?" (*Algèbre des valeurs morales* [Paris, 1935], p. 107). It is the point of Francis Ponge's poem, *L'Objet poétique:*

> L'homme est un drôle de corps, qui n'a pas son centre de gravité en lui-même.
> Notre âme est transitive. Il lui faut un objet, qui l'affecte, comme son complément direct, aussitôt.
> Ne serions-nous qu'un corps, sans doute serions-nous en équilibre avec la nature.
> Mais notre âme est du même côté que nous dans la balance.
> Lourde ou légère, je ne sais.
> Mémoire, imagination, affects immédiats, l'alourdissent; toutefois nous avons la parole (ou quelque autre moyen d'expression): chaque mot que nous prononçons nous allège.
> Dans l'*écriture* il passe même de l'autre côté.
> Lourds et légers donc je ne sais, nous avons besoin d'un contre-poids.
> Il nous faut donc choisir des objets véritables, objectant indéfiniment à nos désirs.
> Des objets que nous rechoisissons chaque jour, et non comme notre décor, notre cadre; plutôt comme nos spectateurs et nos juges; pour n'en être, bien sûr, ni les danseurs, ni les pitres;
> —Enfin notre secret conseil.
> Et ainsi composer notre temple domestique.

n'ayant rien" (V, 1, 1603). From the beginning, he tells Cléante, "je lui faisois des dons" (I, 5, 293) and throughout the play he continually renews and intensifies this initial attempt to purchase Tartuffe by progressively alienating in his favor his property, his children, and in all but a formal sense his wife—for does not Orgon ignore his wife for Tartuffe's sake and even place her in the impostor's hands? To be sure he does not expect Tartuffe to want her; Tartuffe, for Orgon, is the man who is absolutely self-sufficient, who is without need or desire for others, the impassive recipient of the gifts that are laid at his feet. If Orgon wants to unite Mariane and Tartuffe, for instance, it is not because Tartuffe desires Mariane—how should he desire what is so inferior to him?—but simply because Orgon wishes to make him a gratuitous gift of his daughter, to love him as it were, through his daughter. Or so it would seem. For on another and unconscious level, Orgon is using his social and financial superiority to seduce Tartuffe, and this is so obvious that we are not at all surprised when at the end, after his betrayal by his "beloved," Orgon recalls these gifts, suddenly attaching great importance to them and looking on them as something less than gratuitous:

> Quoi? sous un beau semblant de ferveur si touchante
> Cacher un coeur si double, une âme si méchante!
> Et moi qui l'ai reçu gueusant et n'ayant rien. . . .
> (V, 1, 1601–3)

In his indignation at Tartuffe's "ingratitude," Orgon inadvertently confesses what he would never have admitted to consciously—that all along he has been trying to *buy* Tartuffe with gifts and protection. (The attempt to buy others is characteristic of Molière's comic heroes: one recalls Alceste's dream that Célimène might be stripped of all her worldly goods so that she would owe everything to him, Dandin's outright purchase of Angélique, Arnolphe's exploitation of his penniless ward, Jourdain's extravagant loans to his noble "friends.")

Of course Orgon could not possibly succeed in seducing Tartuffe, and yet he had inevitably to keep on trying. This is the ludicrous paradox in Orgon's relation to his idol. What made Orgon try to buy Tartuffe was precisely that which ensured that he could not buy him—his supposedly absolute superiority and self-sufficiency. Orgon desires Tartuffe and wishes to attach him firmly to himself only because he sees him as absolutely free; but in so far as Tartuffe is absolutely free he cannot be bought or bound by gifts of any kind. The more Orgon pursues him with gifts, the more elusive and mysterious Tartuffe becomes to him; the more elusive and mysterious he becomes, the more confirmed Orgon is in his adulation; and the more confirmed he is in his adulation, the more relentlessly he pursues him with gifts. The fantastic comedy of Orgon's fascination by Tartuffe lies in the fact that he has invented the entire situation himself. Tartuffe is in no way superior or self-sufficient, and he is in a sense being bought all the time by Orgon's gifts. Orgon's very success is thus the measure of his failure, for to the degree that he can buy Tartuffe and does buy Tartuffe, Tartuffe is not the superior and absolute being Orgon is trying to buy, while to the degree that he fails to win Tartuffe's subjection to himself, to the degree that Tartuffe remains independent of him, Orgon finds himself the *rival* of the man he sought to transform into his alter ego. Orgon's indignation when he discovers the "imposture" of Tartuffe is as grotesque as Uncle Vanya's outburst in Act III of Chekhov's comedy. Vanya screams that he has been cheated by his brother-in-law, but it was Vanya himself who invested the professor with transcendent superiority and it was Vanya who decided to dedicate his life to serving him.

The reality of the situation underlines the utter subjectivity of Orgon's infatuation with his idol. Far from being the absolute and indifferent being Orgon sees him as, Tartuffe is completely given over to presenting himself to others. The lofty piety Orgon finds in him on their first meeting is a carefully planned and executed comedy, designed to make an impression on Orgon. His indifference to the things of the world hides a very real desire for them and dependence on them. All the other characters in the play see this without difficulty. If Orgon does not see it, it is not because he is a fool, in any ordinary sense, but because he does not *want* to see it. The speech in which he tells Cléante of his first encounters with Tartuffe ("Ha! si vous aviez vu comme j'en fis recontre . . ." etc. —I, 5, 281) emphasizes that though many were witnesses of Tartuffe's "devotions," only one was duped by them, though many were present, only one was tempted. While, therefore, Tartuffe undoubtedly singled Orgon out for his attentions, Orgon in a sense invited them. If Tartuffe was looking for his Orgon, Orgon was looking for his Tartuffe. Even on the most elementary psychological level, Tartuffe must have spotted in Orgon a hidden desire to be seduced. The practiced rake always recognizes his prospective victims. He provokes and answers a desire that is already there. Tartuffe cannot be given credit for having bamboozled Orgon. Orgon is as much Tartuffe's creator as Tartuffe is himself, just as the true creators of Célimène are Alceste, Oronte, Acaste, and Clitandre. It is Orgon who invests Tartuffe's rudimentary comedy of piety with the reality he wants it to have. From Orgon's point of view the signs of piety he finds in Tartuffe are above all an indication that Tartuffe is a suitable partner who will play his game with him, enter his world, and act out the role assigned to him.

Orgon is not interested in the real qualities of Tartuffe, he is interested only in the authority that these qualities command in the world. In this respect he is no different from Monsieur Jourdain when the latter takes up music, dancing, fencing, and philosophy, not because he thinks they have any value in themselves, but because of the value they have in the eyes of others and the authority that he believes the possession of them will impart to him. Alceste's love for Célimène is of the same nature. What attracts Alceste in Célimène is nothing that is in Célimène herself, but the acclaim and admiration she enjoys. Likewise what attracts Orgon in Tartuffe is the public nature of his piety. "Il attirait les yeux de l'assemblée entière," he tells Cléante (I, 5, 285). Seeking to enjoy through the object of his love and admiration an absolute superiority to others that he cannot, without giving himself away, claim directly for himself, Orgon invests Tartuffe with the qualities that he thinks will secure this absolute superiority for his idol, thus encouraging and conniving in Tartuffe's own crude imposture.[2] He cannot consequently doubt the authenticity of Tartuffe, and inevitably he interprets his family's hostility to his favorite as a mark of their jealousy and as evidence of Tartuffe's authority. "Je sais bien quel motif à l'attaquer t'oblige," he says to Damis: "Vous le haïssez tous" (III, 6, 1118–19). His family's hatred of Tartuffe thus becomes for Orgon the "objective" recognition that confirms the reality of the superiority with which he has invested the hypocrite. The greater the efforts of his family to get rid of Tartuffe, the stronger is Orgon's conviction of the power of his beloved "frère" and the firmer his intention to keep him:

> Mais plus on fait d'effort afin de l'en bannir,
> Plus j'en veux employer à l'y mieux retenir.
>   (III, 6, 1124)

The complete subjectivity of Orgon's universe is apparent in these lines. In disagreement he sees only a conflict of wills, a struggle in which each seeks to impose his subjective vision on others. The rejection of Tartuffe by his family, far from making him doubt Tartuffe, thus confirms him in his estimation of the *dévot* as a being through whom he can accede to the absoluteness he desires. The value of Tartuffe is corroborated for Orgon by the fear he in-

[2] The relation of Madame Stavrogin to Stepan Verkhovenski in Dostoievski's *Possessed* is reminiscent in many ways of Orgon's relation to Tartuffe. Madame Stavrogin, we are told, protected old Verkhovenski "from every speck of dust, she fussed over him for twenty-two years, she would have spent sleepless nights if his reputation as a poet, a scholar, or a public man had been in danger. She had invented him, and she had been the first to believe in her own invention. He was, in a way, a sort of dream of hers. (. . .) But in return she really demanded a great deal of him, sometimes even the obedience of a slave" (I, 3, Penguin ed., pp. 29–30).

spires in his family; in reality, of course, the value of Tartuffe for Orgon *is* the fear he inspires in his family.

It is not an accident that all the other members of Orgon's household—with the exception of his mother, to whom we shall return —see through the impostor. The truth is that Orgon is himself largely responsible for Tartuffe's imposture. He does not see it because he connives in it. As long, indeed, as Tartuffe fulfills Orgon's requirements, he is not really an impostor with respect to Orgon. He is the *alter ego* that Orgon wants him to be. Orgon "sees through" Tartuffe only when he finally recognizes in him a will that is separate and different from his own.

The inward identity of the *dévot* and his devotee receives concrete expression at the end of the comedy. Before the King intervenes to put matters "right" again, the tables are turned on Orgon, and Tartuffe achieves real dominion over his erstwhile protector. All along Orgon has been playing a game which has allowed him to be at one and the same time the master and the slave of Tartuffe. He has not *consciously* played this game of course. The conscious mind cannot envisage itself as bowler and batsman at the same time; it is only by surreptitiously hiding our dreams from our own conscious minds that we can win every game by playing all the parts at once. Suddenly, however, Orgon has to pay the price of his secret cheating, when he discovers that Tartuffe has an objective existence of his own quite independent of the subjective dream in which he had enclosed him. It is not for love of Elmire that Orgon is outraged by Tartuffe's designs on her, but for "love" of Tartuffe. As Orgon sees it, Tartuffe's crime lies in having preferred Elmire to him, in having claimed an existence and a will of his own, independent of the role assigned to him in Orgon's scheme of things. Through Tartuffe's betrayal, Orgon realizes that he has all along been an object-in-the-world for the being whom he called his "brother," and whom he thought he possessed as securely as he possessed himself. One is reminded of Gide's Immoralist. Michel, it will be remembered, learns that at the very moment when he thought he possessed Moktir—as he watched the little Arab's theft of a pair of scissors in a mirror—he was in fact an object for Moktir. "Vous croyiez le tenir, et c'était lui qui vous tenait," Ménalque reveals later, when he tells his friend that Moktir was aware he was being watched. We cannot really feel that Orgon has been wronged because he burns his fingers in his own fire. He calls a halt to the game he has been playing with Tartuffe because he sees that Tartuffe, not he, has been directing it, and in so doing he reveals his true intention, which was to use Tartuffe for his own ends. He has no right to be indignant, therefore, when Tartuffe unmasks himself and engages in open combat. Tartuffe's deception of Orgon was undertaken in full lucidity, but Orgon's deception of Tartuffe was no less a deception for having been undertaken with less lucidity. Orgon is well and truly hoist—as Dandin will be in a later play—by his own petard. He wakes up to find that far from his being Tartuffe's master, it is Tartuffe who is really his. Tartuffe can even be as indignant at the "imposture" by which Orgon "deceived" him as Orgon is about his "imposture:"

> C'est à vous d'en sortir, vous qui parlez en maître:
> La maison m'appartient, je le ferai connaître,
> Et vous montrerai bien qu'en vain on a recours,
> Pour me chercher querelle, à ces lâches détours,
> Qu'on n'est pas où l'on pense en me faisant injure,
> Que j'ai de quoi confondre et punir l'imposture,
> Venger le Ciel qu'on blesse, et faire repentir
> Ceux qui parlent ici de me faire sortir.
>   (IV, 7, 1557–64)

The inversion of roles in this scene recalls a similar inversion in the last act of *George Dandin*, where Angélique, having succeeded in re-entering the house and locking Dandin out, upbraids her husband in the same terms as he upbraided her. And just as Angélique's indignation—hypocritical and affected as it is—is in a sense justified, so Tartuffe's comically bitter reproaches are also not without foundation. Dandin claims he has been betrayed by his wife, but he has himself betrayed Angélique from the very beginning, since he never loved her and married her only to exploit her. In the same way Tartuffe can claim with some justice that Orgon has all along been betraying him by acting as if he were a disciple, whereas in reality he sought only to use Tartuffe for his own ends.

The hypocrites in Molière's plays often mirror back the real nature of their apparently innocent victims. In *George Dandin*, Angélique not only turns the tables on her husband at the end of the play, she speaks the truth fearlessly, in perfect confidence that the Sotenvilles will understand it, not as it is, but as they want it to be. She is fully aware of the bad faith that shelters her parents from their own reality. She knows that they dare not question her sincerity for fear of having to examine their own. Likewise in *Tartuffe*, Orgon hides his egoism and vanity from himself, wraps it up in the mantle of religion and presents it to himself and to others as spiritual zeal. Tartuffe can therefore tell Orgon the truth about himself in perfect confidence that Orgon will understand it in terms of the very fantasies with which he conceals his own true nature from himself:

> (. . .) traitez-moi de perfide,
> D'infâme, de perdu, de voleur, d'homicide;
> Accablez-moi de noms encor plus détestés:
> Je n'y contredis point, je les ai mérités.
> (III, 6, *1101–4*)

Doubles entendres of this kind abound in Molière's plays and they are not mere "gimmicks," stock devices from the comic playwright's trick-box. They have a meaningful function in revealing the complicity of deception and self-deception, of hypocrisy and illusion. The hypocrite in whom Orgon can no longer recognize himself is precisely his true reflection.

Orgon's "frère" turns out to be his "semblable" even, and indeed especially, where Orgon no longer recognizes him as such. In the false priest who tries to seduce his wife Orgon no longer recognizes his idol and his brother. Yet it is precisely in this desire to gain control of Orgon's entire household that Tartuffe is the very image of his patron, his alter ego and his rival at the same time. Like his benefactor, Tartuffe does not know love, and his arrival in Orgon's home marks the inauguration of the reign of power and terror, violence and seduction that Orgon himself longs to impose. Even in attempting to seduce Elmire, Tartuffe is working his patron's secret will. For Orgon himself is indifferent to Elmire as a wife. He is not interested in possessing her as a husband possesses his partner in marriage. His ambition is to be recognized not as a father or a husband, but as a supreme, irresistible, and divine being, owing his power and authority to nothing beyond himself. With his mien of piety and otherworldliness Tartuffe is indeed the arch-impostor, but his imposture mirrors back the imposture of Orgon. "Du gleichst dem Geist den du begreifst," the spirit tells Faust. Seeking not a true mediator between himself and God, but a slave, an idol who is at the same time an instrument of his will, Orgon finds himself in a monster of hypocrisy who is likewise incapable of love and who likewise seeks an instrument of his will.

The rivalry of worshiper and idol is brought out beautifully by Molière in Acts IV and V of *Tartuffe*. The one person in Orgon's family from whom he has managed to win adoration for his idol is his mother. Madame Pernelle is herself as eager to be different and superior as her son. She is a possessive and tyrannical woman to whom even the freedom of her son is intolerable. In the very first scene of the comedy we find her usurping Orgon's place in his own home. Like Tartuffe, she sets herself between Orgon and his family, concealing her lust for power beneath a mask of righteousness and affecting to legislate for all in virtue of some moral authority which she claims to possess. She takes it upon herself to turn Orgon against his son, she proposes to determine who may and who may not be admitted to Orgon's house, and she criticizes Elmire, comparing her unfavorably with Orgon's first wife, whom one suspects she could not have liked either in so far as she was not more of an obedient daughter-in-law than a wife. It is no accident that Madame Pernelle encourages Orgon's infatuation with Tartuffe while undermining his relation with Elmire. She knows very well that Orgon's way to freedom lies through his assumption of his proper part as head of his family. Observing his mother's worship of Tartuffe, Orgon can fancy that he has succeeded in winning over the freedom of at least one member of his family. In fact, however, Madame Pernelle has her own motives for recognizing Tartuffe, *and they are the same as Orgon's.* Mother and son each seek to establish dominion over others through Tartuffe, and it is no accident that the only person Orgon succeeds in winning over for Tartuffe is this haughty and possessive woman. Madame Pernelle's reappearance in the last act of the comedy was to be expected. Hearing of Tartuffe's disgrace, she hurries to the scene to have matters out with her son and to restore the protégé, who is her protégé and idol as well as Orgon's, to favor. Orgon, on his side, must equally try to get his mother to recognize the fraudulence of the idol who has "tricked" him. Having discovered that, far from his using Tartuffe, Tartuffe has been using him, he must transform the submission which he believes he has won from his mother indirectly through Tartuffe into a direct submission to him. Tartuffe must now be looked at "objectively," not recognized as an idol and an absolute, but seen as a mere object, a contingency, a lack of essential being:

> Je l'ai vu, dis-je, vu, de mes propres yeux vu,
> Ce qu'on appelle vu. . . .
> (V, 3, 1676–77)

Madame Pernelle, however, will not look on Tartuffe as an object:

> Mon Dieu, le plus souvent l'apparence déçoit:
> Il ne faut pas toujours juger sur ce qu'on voit.
> (V, 3, 1679–80).

Madame Pernelle's refusal to acknowledge Tartuffe's betrayal of her son confirms that what Orgon took to be *her* submission through Tartuffe was, from her point of view, *his* submission through Tartuffe. The utter subjectivity, the total disregard for any objective truth in the infatuation of mother and son alike with this idol-instrument of their absolutist ambitions is emphasized by Molière in the wonderful irony of Madame Pernelle's defense of Tartuffe. Madame Pernelle and Orgon are so completely willful and egoistic that they can employ quite contradictory arguments to "prove" the truth of what they want to believe and to have others believe. The argument that was used against Tartuffe by Orgon's family and that was rejected by Tartuffe's adherents— that appearances are deceptive—is taken up blandly by Madame Pernelle in support of her idol.

Madame Pernelle's unwillingness to recognize the truth about Tartuffe springs from the same source as Orgon's did previously. Tartuffe is the instrument of her power over the world, as he was Orgon's before Orgon became aware of his "betrayal." She will not renounce the authority she derives through him. Orgon thus finds himself confronted in the obstinate idolatry of his mother with the very image and truth of his own obstinate idolatry. In Céline's *Voyage au bout de la nuit*, the "savant" Serge Parapine tells of his irritation with the old boy who has been his lab assistant for thirty years: "Vous l'avez vu mon vieux crétin de garçon? (. . .) Eh bien voici trente ans bientôt, qu'à balayer mes ordures il entend autour de lui ne parler que de science et fort copieusement et sin-cèrement ma foi . . . cependant, loin d'en être dégoûté, c'est lui et lui seul à present qui a fini par y croire ici même! A force de tripoter mes cultures il les trouve merveilleuses! Il s'en pourlèche. . . . La moindre de mes singeries l'enivre! N'en va-t-il pas d'ailleurs de même dans toutes les religions? N'y a-t-il point belle lurette que le prêtre pense à tout autre chose qu'au Bon Dieu que son bedeau y croit encore. . . . Et dur comme fer?" (Livre de poche ed., p. 283). Madame Pernelle is like Parapine's lab technician. She con-tinues to believe in Tartuffe even when Orgon no longer believes, and Orgon's irritation with her is like Parapine's irritation with his technician for having transferred to the idol that he has repudiated —that is to the means—the worship that he feels is due to him alone, to the end.

As Goldmann and others have shown, the rise of the *robins* coincided in France with that of the monarchy. At the same time, however, relations between the *robins* and the monarchy became strainęd as the *robins*, having formed themselves into a corps, jealous of its interests and privileges, found that the royal authority, the interests of which they no longer served so wholeheartedly, was ceasing to regard them as its favored agents. The resentment of the *robins* was such, indeed, that during the Fronde many of them sided, for their own reasons, with the feudal opposition to the King. *Tartuffe* itself contains an important allusion to this defection. Orgon, it is true, remained loyal (I, 2), as did many members of his caste, but some of his friends did not. In fact, Tartuffe's knowledge of the papers entrusted to Orgon by his friend Argan, when the latter had to flee, provides him with the instrument of his hoped-for revenge on his benefactor. The crushing of the Fronde only embittered the *robins* further, and the most scathing critics of the new régime of Louis XIV came equally from the ranks of the *robins* and from the feudal opposition. The *robins*, however, could not make as radical and open a criticism of the monarchy as the feudal nobles, since they still depended on it in very large measure. They therefore chose to emphasize rather that it had become corrupt as it had estranged itself from them. The most radical of them rejected the existing political and social order as *immoral*, or even *sinful*, for they could scarcely espouse the cause of the feudal nobility, which had even less place for them than the new monarchy. The *robins* could only reject the absolutist monarchy. They could suggest nothing to put in its stead, except a return to an earlier stage in the history of the monarchy, which was desired by nobody but themselves. As a purely negative opposition, they inevitably found themselves, willy-nilly, the allies of many opposition forces with which they had little in common except opposition. Meantime, the internal rivalries among all the forces of opposition to the monarchy simply confirmed the monarchy in its new power.

The hypocrite in Molière's play can thus be thought of as revealing the hypocrisy of an apparently religious ideology of opposition to the new society of Louis XIV. Molière shows that this ideology simply covers the resentment of an enfeebled social group that is unable to recover the place it has lost.

At the same time, however, there is a sense in which Tartuffe, the false idol, can be seen, from our later perspective, to resemble the King himself.[3] It would be madness to imagine that Louis XIV was deliberately travestied as Tartuffe by Molière. Indeed in the play it is the King himself who punishes Tartuffe and saves Orgon and his family. The significance of this intervention of the monarch cannot be overlooked. We are clearly intended to understand that Orgon's mistake was to have transferred to an impostor, a sordid and inferior schemer, the adoration that should properly be directed upward to the monarch, the sole truly supreme and absolute authority. This is doubtless how Louis XIV and those who defended the comedy against its critics, as well as Molière himself in large measure, understood the ending of the play. Nevertheless, although the Sun-King is presented as the proper idol for Orgon to worship, Molière does not question that the Orgons of the world must have an idol to worship, and his analysis of Orgon's worship of the false idol elucidates aspects of the relation of worshiper and idol that could not have been elucidated in a play in which the idol was the monarch himself. Molière could show the

[3] One might alternatively find in Tartuffe a distant reflection of some of the great ministers of the realm, subjects such as Richelieu, or outsiders such as Mazarin, who achieved enormous power as a result of struggles for power within the French court. Madame Pernelle, for instance, bears many resemblances to the Regent, Louis XIV's ambitious and power-hungry mother. The fact that the situation in Tartuffe can be applied so variously, however, far from invalidating our contention that it reflects the political and social temper of Molière's time, seems to us to confirm it.

rivalry that lies hidden in the worshiper's adoration because the idol was a Tartuffe and the idolator an Orgon. Given the historical conditions of Molière's work, there could obviously have been no question of revealing a rivalry of this nature had the idol been the King. The absolute order of the monarchy was, for the advanced minds of Molière's time, the answer to the absolute disorder represented by Tartuffe and Orgon. Molière's inverted trinity of the mother, the son, and the unholy ghost is, however, strikingly prophetic. It reveals a pattern of behavior that was to become characteristic of the society of the Court too, as the absolute monarchy gradually lost its grip on events and turned out to be itself unable to provide more than a formal solution to the real social and political conflicts within the state. In a way, indeed, the world of folly and illusion represented in *Tartuffe* foreshadows even more recent attempts to impose order on a fundamentally disunited and anarchical society by means of political myths.

As the Orgons of the world have become more and more numerous, the rivalry and resentment among them has become more and more intense, while the idolatry through which this rivalry is expressed has reached a pitch of frenzy and grotesqueness that would have astounded Molière himself. The fanaticism of the modern Orgons' worship of their idols is accompanied by a corresponding fanaticism in their rivalry with these idols. While they vie with each other at being *plus royaliste que le roi* with a passion and seriousness of intent unknown in any monarchy, they will not tolerate any idol that might turn out to have a real superiority. Their hidden resentment and envy of their idol is more intense than ever before and their enthusiasm for him is as fierce as their need to humiliate all their other idol-rivals is deep. They demand, as Molière's Orgon demanded, a God in their own image, and they worship him to the degree that they can identify themselves with him in his humiliation of others. The idol may well be the man next door or a fellow-executive in the office, in whom some superior quality is discovered. By participating in this superiority, as it were, by establishing a special relation to it, the modern Orgons hope to "get one over" on their other neighbors and fellow-workers. At the same time, however, they also hope to displace the idol and their subservience to him fills them with bitterness and discontent.

In these circumstances the old idols have inevitably fallen by the wayside and been replaced by new ones resembling their worshipers more closely than Louis XIV resembled his subjects. The Orgons get their Tartuffes in the end, those likenesses of themselves that they prefer to the remote grandeurs of a Louis XIV. A Louis XIV is too truly different, too truly superior to suit the Orgons. The new heroes, like Tartuffe himself, are grotesque and sinister at the same time. It is hard to see why the juxtaposition in the character of Tartuffe of a clever and sinister schemer and a crudely comical impostor has puzzled readers of the play or struck them as a contradiction. At no time in history, perhaps, have we been in a better position to appreciate the genial insight that enabled Molière to see the intimate relatedness of the sinister and the comic, the diabolic and the grotesque.[4] Napoleon I is both a more sinister and a more comical figure than Louis XIV, and Napoleon III is more sinister and comical than Napoleon I. The stodgy and neurotic William II is a more ridiculous and dangerous personage than his witty and cynical ancestor Frederick the Great (who would most certainly have been thought far too clever and frivolous by the solid bourgeoisie of late nineteenth-century Germany) and Adolf Hitler is more grotesque and more frightening still than the Emperor William. The idols of the modern world have become progressively more base, more empty, more dangerous, and more like Tartuffe as time has gone on. They even resemble Tartuffe in being so taken up by the roles they play for their worshipers that they are no longer aware of playing them. Tartuffe feels strong indignation when he accuses Orgon of imposture and calls

---

[4] In films like *Modern Times* and *The Great Dictator*, Charlie Chaplin rediscovered in our own day, as Molière did in his, this ancient vision of the devil as a sinister and at the same time crudely comic impostor.

for justice, and in the same way the fanatical dictators of our own times have really believed the monstrous fabrications of their deranged minds.

The degradation of the idols together with the spread of idolatry in the modern world confirms the astonishingly prophetic vision of *Tartuffe*. For that very reason, however, it is more difficult for us to recognize the comedy of the dangerous and sinister world we live in than it was for Molière and his contemporaries to portray and recognize the comedy of Orgon, Tartuffe, and Madame Pernelle. The Tartuffes of Molière's world were real and powerful enough to do quite a bit of damage, but there were far fewer Orgons in Molière's world than in ours. The rivalries of the Court, the worship and resentment of the monarch by the great nobles of the realm may indeed manifest the same structure of envy and vanity that marks the relations of Orgon, Tartuffe, and Madame Pernelle or the even more monstrous passion of modern times; at the same time, however, this courtly vanity and resentment acted as an effective brake on baser and more sinister forms of vanity and resentment. Louis XIV was after all a great monarch and his courtiers were urbane and civilized men with a notable sense of style and form. They could hardly have sunk to the crudity of Orgon's stubborn infatuation with a seedy character like Tartuffe. Inevitably they felt themselves closer to Cléante and even to Dorine, than to the grotesque hero of the comedy.

The reasonableness of Cléante and the naturalness of Dorine do not, however, represent an influential social force. The structure of the comedy makes this clear, for neither character proves able to exercise any influence on Orgon. It was never Molière's intention to mock the entire world, to belittle all humanity and all human life. No genuine satirist, perhaps, has ever attempted to do this. He exaggerated and caricaturized human folly so that his audiences might the better discern it and in laughing at it be in some measure freed of it. His claim that he was concerned to *corriger les moeurs*, conventional as it is, was probably made in all sincerity and seriousness and it should not, perhaps, be discounted as lightly as it sometimes is nowadays. Molière's purpose could not be, therefore, to expose all the Orgons and the Tartuffes in the world, which is what La Bruyère would doubtless have preferred him to do.[5] His purpose was rather to exorcize the Orgon and the Tartuffe which everyone in his audience was potentially or in some degree, and to do this he had to present Orgon and Tartuffe as creatures on whom ordinary people could look with amusement. But while the audience is expected to laugh at the comic characters, Cléante, Dorine, and Elmire do not necessarily represent what most people really are; they represent rather the healthy side of them, the side of them that looks on the darker side, on Orgon, Tartuffe, and Madame Pernelle, and laughs at it.

Far from being deeply involved *in* society, Cléante, Dorine, and Elmire all stand to some extent *outside* society. Indeed each owes his good sense and integrity to the maintenance of a certain distance between himself and others.

Cléante looks in at the world from the outside. Sainte-Beuve described his position rather well. "Le rôle de Cléante," he wrote, "est une indispensable contre-partie de celui de Tartuffe, un contrepoids. Cléante nous figure l'honnête homme de la pièce, le

---

[5] La Bruyère's Onuphre, it will be remembered, "ne dit point: *Ma haire et ma discipline,* au contraire; il passeroit pour ce qu'il est, pour un hypocrite et il veut passer pour ce qu'il n'est pas, pour un homme dévot" (*Caractères,* Les Grands Ecrivains de France ed. [Paris, 1865], Vol. 2, p. 154). Molière's hypocrite, La Bruyère implies, is so gross that he leaves the real hypocrites unscathed and for La Bruyère the real hypocrites were everywhere. Almost everybody at Court was a hypocrite. By La Bruyère's time, the inner weaknesses of the social order created by the absolute monarchy were already becoming so manifest that this social order itself began to replace the disgruntled *robins* and the feudal nobles as a subject of satire. Whereas Molière had viewed his *robins* and his *grands seigneurs* from the vantage point of a victorious absolutism, however, La Bruyère had no firm vantage point beyond the Court from which to mock it. This accounts, in part at least, it would seem, for the shriller tone of La Bruyère's satire and for the absence from his work of that confident generosity and heartiness that characterizes much of Molière's. Against a corrupt society La Bruyère could set only his own consciousness of its corruption. With La Bruyère the Alceste type is already looming on the horizon in its modern form.

morals.

représentant de la morale des honnêtes gens dans la perfection, de la morale du juste milieu. Pascal, dans ses premières Lettres, s'était mis, par supposition, en dehors des Molinistes et des Jansénistes, simple homme du monde et curieux, qui se veut instruire. Cléante de même, mais plus à distance, se tient en dehors des dévots: il se contente d'approuver les vrais, il les honore; il flétrit les faux. La supposition de l'honnête indifférent d'après Pascal s'est élargi et a marché" (*Port Royal*, III [Paris, 1860], p. 222).

Cléante's skepticism does not rule out respect for true piety, but it rules out any total confidence in the authenticity of others. Cléante knows there is a difference between true and false piety; what he distinguishes among the actual manifestations of piety, however, is not the true and the false; it is the obviously false and the possibly true. It happens that he discerns the imposture of Tartuffe, but he has and seeks no assurance that those whom he admires for their "real" piety—Ariston, Périandre, Oronte, Alcidamas, Polydore, Clitandre—are genuinely pious. Tartuffe's active desires are so patent that it is impossible for anybody with the slightest discernment not to recognize that they are incompatible with the image of saintliness that he presents to the world. There is no assurance, however, that the Aristons and the Périandres are genuinely pious. All one can tell is that their appearances are not contradictory. No one can be sure that their apparent piety is real. It may simply be a convenient public image behind which they are in reality skeptics. Even if this were so, it would still be virtually impossible ever to detect their imposture, for as long as they do not actively deceive people with their mask, as long as their actual behavior is not in contradiction with it, no one will ever know what lies behind it, and to all intents and purposes it is not necessary or desirable to know what lies behind it. No human being can or need see into the innermost heart of another. On the other hand, these apparently real *dévots* may simply be cleverer imposters than Tartuffe. In that case their imposture will be known to those whom they have deceived, since the latter will have observed contradictions in their actual behavior.

Cléante is not concerned to know whether a man is truly pious or not. He does not consider that another man's inner life is his business. He is concerned only with the actual behavior of men in society, that is with their behavior toward others. It is for this reason that the true *dévots* for him are those whose piety "est humaine, est traitable," those who do not wield the sword and whose judgments are mild:

> Jamais contre un pécheur ils n'ont d'acharnement;
> Ils attachent leur haine au péché seulement . . .
> (I, 5, 399–400)

Cléante is shocked and distressed by the impropriety of reaching out to the individual (*le pécheur*) rather than to the abstract generality (*le péché*). While it is true that the real task of the Christian is to save the sinner, it is also true that Cléante is less interested in this truly Christian mission than in keeping religion at a distance and preserving the inner liberty of the individual. In the end he stands for a kind of liberal and tolerant humanism that demands of the individual no more than that his actual behavior should not infringe on any of the rules established to maintain the equilibrium of society. He respects religion—nothing in the world, he holds, is nobler than "la sainte ferveur d'un véritable zèle" (I, 5, 358). He does not admit, however, that it has the right to lay rough hands on the individual soul, for a man's inner being, in Cléante's philosophy, is sacrosanct. No one must try to penetrate to it; any attempt to see into the soul of another is the beginning of tyranny. Molière's ecclesiastical critics, however wrong their total assessment of *Tartuffe*, were right when they argued that what Cléante advocates is really respectful indifference to religion. Cléante's position is not fundamentally different from the one Kierkegaard complained of in his *Journals* when he wrote that "faith has simply become a fig-leaf behind which people skulk in the most unchristian way" (1849).[6]

The source of Orgon's errors, in Cléante's view, is his failure to accept and maintain a certain distance between himself and the world around him, and to recognize that we can judge only actions, not persons. After the exposure of Tartuffe, Orgon launches into a loud profession of misanthropy, asserting that all appearances are deceptive and all *dévots* impostors. Not so, protests Cléante:

> Vous ne gardez en rien les doux tempéraments;
> Dans la droite raison jamais n'entre la vôtre,
> Et toujours d'un excès vous vous jetez dans l'autre.
> Vous voyez votre erreur, et vous avez connu
> Que par un zèle feint vous étiez prévenu;   `
> Mais pour vous corriger, quelle raison demande
> Que vous alliez passer dans une erreur plus grande,
> Et qu'avecque le coeur d'un perfide vaurien
> Vous confondiez les coeurs de tous les gens de bien?
>   (V, 1, *1607–16*)

It is because Orgon is always trying to see what lies behind appearances, to pry into the inmost heart of others, to *know* their real being, that he falls into error, in Cléante's view. In the end he fails to give to appearances the consideration that they deserve. If Orgon was duped by Tartuffe, it was because he was obstinately blind to what was obvious to others, and if he now denies the piety of all those who appear pious, it is once again

---

[6] Cf. Alfred Simon's intriguing little study *Molière par lui-même* (Paris, 1957), p. 100: "La *Lettre sur l'imposteur* précise la position de Cléante en affirmant que 'la religion n'est qu'une raison plus parfaite.' C'est éliminer la Foi, avec ses paradoxes, ses déchirements et le mystère de la relation de Dieu à l'homme et à l'histoire."

Cf. also the "petite question impertinente" asked by Sainte-Beuve in a footnote to the passage quoted above in the text: "Ce Cléante fait-il encore ses Pâques? Je le crois. Certainement, cinquante années plus tard, il ne les fera plus" (*Port-Royal*, III [Paris, 1860], p. 222).

because, refusing to accept the limitations that are set to our knowledge of others, he rejects at the same time the only source of knowledge that we have. Excessive zeal, says Cléante, is always dangerous. By trying to know too much, we end by making mistakes about everything. In general we must rely on appearances to tell us about others, but we may at any moment have to revise our judgment if new evidence comes to light. We must therefore maintain a salutary skepticism, accepting without demur that we do not have the absolute knowledge or insight of God. "Ne hasardez jamais votre estime trop tôt," he tells Orgon (V, 1, 1623). The only way to avoid serious error is to keep "le milieu qu'il faut" (ibid., 1624). One cannot help thinking, as one reads Cléante's lines, of those prudent empiricists who opposed the science of Descartes, of Gassendi's objections to the Cartesian search for absolute and total knowledge, of Mersenne's argument that though the world as it is to the eye of God may be very different from the world as we see it, the only world we can have any knowledge of at all is the world that we see.

Cléante's position, in other words, is resolutely nominalist. He accepts the radical nominalist separation of things as they appear and as we describe them and things as they are in themselves. To the honnête homme of the seventeenth century it was important to act in accordance with the rules of the social game. It was nobody's concern what a man actually thought in his secret heart, provided he conformed in his actual conduct to the standards that he expected others to observe and that they expected him to observe. To play the game with conscious intent to play it well means to have a perspective on it, to stand at a certain distance from it, so that one can judge and evaluate one's performance. The honnêteté of Cléante depends entirely on the maintenance of this distance between the individual and society.

It is striking, but not unexpected, after our insistence on Orgon's bad faith, to find Cléante saying to his brother-lin-law of the latter's infatuation with Tartuffe:

C'est de fort bonne foi que vous vantez son zèle;
Mais par un faux éclat je vous crois ébloui.
(I, 5, 406–7)

Cléante knows that the alienation from society which is the basis
of *honnêteté* and moderation is also the basis of hypocrisy. The
hypocrite in the seventeenth century is like a man who cheats at
cards. If there is no game, however, there can be no cheating. No
one need be amazed that the age of *honnêteté* is also the age of
hypocrisy or that hypocrisy is such a recurrent theme in the literature of the seventeenth century, not least in the comedies of
Molière. Hypocrisy was in fact the clearest threat to the formal
social structure of Molière's time, for this social structure could
do what it was intended to do—combine freedom with order—
only if all its members played fairly. That is why Tartuffe and
not Orgon is punished at the end of the play. To the average
spectator as well as to Cléante, Tartuffe was the wicked seducer
and Orgon the victim. Molière's *raisonneur* cannot see the de-
linquency of Orgon because he sees Orgon's behavior as a phenomenon of innocence. He identifies it with the behavior of the
man who has not yet learned to live with forms and conventions,
who has not yet grasped and understood his alienation, and fails to
see that it is the behavior of a man who *refuses* to live with forms
and conventions, who *rejects* his alienation and seeks to overcome
it by acquiring absolute possession and control of others. In Prévost's
Manon Lescaut, Des Grieux's father makes the same mistake when
he tries to deal with his son's infatuation with Manon by offering
him a mistress. It is in a way Cléante who is "old-fashioned" and
Orgon who is "modern," not the other way round. In a rather similar way, it was the Gassendists who after all were old-fashioned and
Descartes who was modern. And just as the Gassendists did not
properly appreciate the tremendous significance and modernity of
Descartes, Cléante and the Cléantes could not appreciate the significance and modernity of Orgon. Cléante cannot persuade Orgon

to play the game like everybody else, because Orgon has already
rejected it.

Standing in large measure outwith society, having therefore no
one to present themselves to, Molière's family servants are in certain respects the closest of all his characters to nature. They are
uncomplicated, healthy in their judgments, concrete in their
thinking, and untempted by what is not clearly and immediately
desirable. They have no desire to enter society and no wish,
consequently, to be recognized as anything other than what they
are.

It is because of her very simplicity and directness that Dorine
immediately spots the inauthenticity of those who loudly proclaim their distaste for the desires and pleasures of ordinary
mortals. She is not taken in by Tartuffe and easily sees through his
affected prudishness. To his "Couvrez ce sein que je ne saurois
voir" she answers tartly:

> Vous êtes donc bien tendre à la tentation,
> Et la chair sur vos sens fait grande impression?
> Certes je ne sais pas quelle chaleur vous monte:
> Mais à convoiter, moi, je ne suis point si prompte,
> Et je vous verrois nu du haut jusques en bas
> Que toute votre peau ne me tenteroit pas.
>   (III, 2, 863–68)

The envy, resentment, and frustration in the hearts of the prudes
who criticize her mistress do not escape her. Of Orante, who, according to Madame Pernelle, "mène une vie exemplaire," Dorine
comments crudely but perceptively:

> L'exemple est admirable, et cette dame est bonne!
> Il est vrai qu'elle vit en austère personne;
> Mais l'âge dans son âme a mis ce zèle ardent,
> Et l'on sait qu'elle est prude à son corps défendant.
> Tant qu'elle a pu des coeurs attirer les hommages,

Elle a fort bien joui de tous ses avantages;
Mais, voyant de ses yeux tous les brillants baisser,
Au monde, qui la quitte, elle veut renoncer,
Et du voile pompeux d'une haute sagesse
De ses attraits usés déguiser la foiblesse.
Ce sont là les retours des coquettes du temps.
Il leur est dur, de voir déserter les galants.
Dans un tel abandon, leur sombre inquiétude
Ne voit d'autre recours que le métier de prude;
Et la sévérité de ces femmes de bien
Censure toute chose, et ne pardonne à rien;
Hautement d'un chacun elles blâment la vie,
Non point par charité, mais par un trait d'envie,
Qui ne sauroit souffrir qu'une autre ait les plaisirs
Dont le penchant de l'âge a sevré leurs désirs.[7]

(I, 1, *121–40*)

Likewise Dorine has no time for the abstract considerations of
pride and dignity that torment Mariane. When Mariane declares
that she has made up her mind to kill herself if her father forces
her to marry Tartuffe, Dorine is taken aback by the extravagance
of such an absurdity:

Fort bien: c'est un recours où je ne songeois pas;
Vous n'avez qu'à mourir pour sortir d'embarras;
Le remède sans doute est merveilleux. J'enrage
Lorsque j'entends tenir ces sortes de langage.

(II, 3, *615–18*)

She is equally impatient of the inappropriate vanity of the young
lovers in relation to each other. When Mariane explains that she
can scarcely refuse Tartuffe openly for fear of exhibiting too much
love for Valère ("Et veux-tu que mes feux par le monde étalés?"

---

[7] This speech makes quite clear the *historical* significance, referred to above,
of the rejection of society by the Orgons and the Madame Pernelles.

—II, 3, 635), she reveals that the real motive for her passivity
is not so much the "devoir de fille" she talks about, as her concern
not to give Valère an advantage over her. The following scene
(II, 4) shows Valère obsessed by the same concern. Dorine is
exasperated by the "extravagance," as she calls it, of the lovers'
indulging in chimerical conflicts of vanity at a time when their
future union is only too really imperiled. "Vous êtes fous tous
deux," she concludes. But she is amused and soon appeased: the
lovers finally show a certain amount of common sense when their
desire for each other proves stronger than their vanity.

Despite her success with Mariane and Valère, the effectiveness
of Dorine is as limited as that of Cléante. She can bring Mariane
round from her ridiculous pride by reminding her in no uncertain
terms what being married to Tartuffe will actually be like:

> Monsieur Tartuffe! oh! oh! n'est-ce rien qu'on propose?
> Certes Monsieur Tartuffe, à bien prendre la chose,
> N'est pas un homme, non, qui se mouche du pié,
> Et ce n'est pas pèu d'heur que d'être sa moitié.
> Tout le monde déjà de gloire le couronne;
> Il est noble chez lui, bien fait de sa personne;
> Il a l'oreille rouge et le teint bien fleuri:
> Vous vivrez trop contente avec un tel mari.
>   (II, 3, 641–48)

She can reduce the poor girl to despair with the concreteness of
lines like "Tartuffe est votre homme, et vous en tâterez" (II, 3,
672) or the marvelously suggestive "Non, vous serez, ma foi!
tartuffiée" (ibid., 674). She cannot, however, deal with the problem
posed by Orgon. She mocks and protests and advises Mariane to
tell her father:

> Que vous vous mariez pour vous, non pas pour lui,
> Qu'étant celle pour qui se fait toute l'affaire,
> C'est à vous, non à lui, que le mari doit plaire,

Et que si son Tartuffe est pour lui si charmant,
Il le peut épouser sans nul empêchement.

(II, 3, 592–96)

It is not hard to remind Mariane of what she already knows, to
bring her back to a reality that she has never totally abandoned.
Orgon, however, is not susceptible to the kind of argument that
Dorine brings forward. She appeals to his "true nature"—his
paternal love for his daughter—but without success. Nature seems
quite dead in Orgon. She appeals to his sense of social propriety
and to his material interest, objecting realistically that Tartuffe is
a poor investment and a degrading match for a girl of good family:

Et puis, que vous apporte une telle alliance?
A quel sujet aller, avec tout votre bien,
Choisir un gendre gueux? . . .

(II, 2, 482–84)

But Orgon does not respond to considerations of social standing,
good husbandry, and financial gain.

Dorine's effect on the action is in the last analysis as weak as
Cléante's. Her natural spontaneity, which is the source of her
sympathy with Mariane and the cause of her intervention in a
matter that is no direct concern of hers, is in fact preserved in her
by her very freedom from society and her lack of concern with
what other people think. The very force that binds her to others
—her natural sympathy with them—is paradoxically possible only
to the extent that she remains free of them. Dorine can speak
to Orgon with crude frankness precisely because, being a servant,
she knows her words will carry no more weight with her master
than he chooses to put upon them.

The spontaneity of such relations as those between Dorine and
her employer is lost when the respect and authority which men
have hitherto believed they enjoyed, in virtue of having been
born the persons they are, is seen as only a matter of convention.

Others can henceforth no longer be treated with easy naturalness; they are feared and resented, and they have to be manipulated and impressed, so that they will grant the individual the recognition he needs. At this point a man ceases to behave freely as the person he is and begins to behave in a constrained way as the person he wants to present himself as to others. After the individual, even the group or caste loses confidence in its own inherent authority and seeks to ground it in the recognition of lower castes which are thereby integrated into the ever-expanding vortex of "society." The relations of masters and servants become as formalized at this point as the relations of the masters among themselves had become previously. The formalization of relations between masters and servants during the Restoration (that is after the radical questioning of all hierarchical relations by the Revolution) is beautifully illustrated in several places in the work of Stendhal. In *Le Rouge et le Noir*, Madame de Fervacques is shown to be anxiously concerned with the impression she makes on her servants. In *Lamiel* the hyperconsciously noble Duchesse (ex-marquise) de Miossens is described as deeply distressed because "dans le premier moment de terreur que les pétards lui avaient causé, elle avait dérangé un faux tour destiné à cacher quelques cheveux blancs, et, pendant une heure, elle avait été vue en cet équipage par tous les paysans du village et par ses propres domestiques que surtout elle voulait tromper" (Chap. 2). The *bosse* of the witty and ironical Dr. Sansfin is the brilliantly imagined symbol, in the same novel, of the obsessive preoccupation of each individual, however "superior," with the judgment of every other individual, however "inferior," of the anguished awareness in each of the fatal inferiority which he is constantly afraid others will detect behind his façade of superiority. Sansfin cannot hide his hump as well as the duchess can hide her white hairs. It is not, however, the hump itself which is the source of Sansfin's torment. He is obsessed by the humiliation he receives at the hands of the washerwomen of Carville; but it is not his hump, it is his concern to be superior that gives the women the power to humiliate him.

Dorine speaks naturally to Orgon, without constraint and without resentment, for the very reason that she is not a member of his society and therefore not in competition with him—not even in the underhand way that Sganarelle is in competition with Dom Juan—but it is for this reason too that her words and opinions make no impression at all on him. Dorine is an outsider, an "old-fashioned" character who, because of her status, has managed to preserve a fairly direct relation to people and to things. She can have no influence on a "modern," completely mediated character such as Orgon. In the subsequent evolution of the theater the naturalness of the Dorines could be more and more a stage convention, with little or no reality in contemporary society. In the English drawing-room comedies of the early twentieth century, for instance, the hearty, healthy, plain-thinking, and plain-speaking servant had to be imported from outlandish environments like the Highlands of Scotland, the West Coast of Ireland, or deepest Cockney London, which still remained untouched by the patterns of ordinary "middle-class" behavior, and she became progressively more stereotyped and lifeless. In our own time there are virtually no such outlandish areas left, and even as a stage convention the good, trusty servant has had to be virtually abandoned. There is already about Dorine a strong suspicion of the theatricality that stamps these later and inferior stage characters, but because she still did represent in Molière's time a real, if already ineffectual and obsolescent, mode of being, Molière's servant retains a certain living concreteness which these later characters no longer possess. Like the stock character of the old nurse in the Russian writers of the nineteenth century, from Pushkin to Tolstoy, the stock character of the family servant in Molière is real enough to make a meaningful comment on the follies and excesses of her masters old and young, even though this comment is made from a position that is historically backward and doomed. For we should not forget that Dorine more than any other character in the comedy stands up not only for "nature," but for the status quo, for the maintenance of old hierarchies and proprieties as well as of old freedoms. The practical common sense and the natural compassion of Dorine emphasize both the moral and spiritual decadence of her masters and their loss of control of reality. But Dorine is not to be thought of as the real alternative to Orgon. That is Cléante's role. Only on the eve of the Revolution does Dorine suddenly blossom forth as Figaro.

Elmire is able to achieve more with Orgon than either Cléante or Dorine. Of all the characters in the play, however, she is the most distant and enigmatic. Her behavior is at all times reserved and conventional. We do not know what she really is. It has even been suggested that we cannot be absolutely certain of her fidelity to Orgon. How indeed can we be certain? Molière presents Elmire to us exactly as she would appear to any spectator. She herself argues that a good woman keeps and ought to keep many things to herself, and it is disturbing to find this argument taken up again with only slight verbal modifications by the hypocritical Angélique of *George Dandin*. There is every reason to believe that Molière wanted us to feel relatively uncertain about Elmire. One of the main themes of *Tartuffe* is that no one can *know for sure* what lies behind the appearances of another person's behavior, and that the attempt to obtain such knowledge is an act of violence toward another, which results not in enlightenment but in darkness and error.

A certain degree of trust in others is indispensable in any human relations. It was relatively easier, however, to have and maintain this trust as long as there was little or no separation in people's minds between formal and substantial relations, as long as the name and the thing were held to be indissolubly bound in a single unity. No one suspected in the Middle Ages, for instance, that a host or a guest would act otherwise than as the names host and guest implied. Even by the Renaissance this situation had changed. What happened at the Massacre of Saint Bartholomew,

when the hosts violated the laws of hospitality and murdered
their guests, was only a particularly scandalous manifestation of
a schism between names and things, which had doubtless always
been present to some degree (men had behaved before in ways
that their rank and position should have precluded and even the
philosophical expression in nominalism of the separation of the
name and the thing was not new in the Renaissance and post-
Renaissance periods), but which was becoming characteristic of
larger and larger areas of thought and behavior. The struggles of
this period of anarchy and willfulness were resolved, or rather,
brought under control in the new formalism of the Court and
the absolute monarchy in the seventeenth century. The behavior
of each individual was rigorously prescribed for him by a code
which he had to accept if he wanted to be accepted, in turn, into
the society of his fellows.[8] There was, however, no knowing or
controlling what a man was beneath the mask he wore. Indeed,
cheating became harder to detect as more attention was paid to
the punctilious observation of outward forms of behavior. Hypocrisy, as we have already suggested, was never more prevalent
than in the age of strict convention. Confidence in others was
consequently more difficult than ever before, since no one could
be sure that the mask was genuinely the man. And yet, at the same
time, confidence was more indispensable than ever before, since
no human relation was now possible without it. In an age of
complete awareness of the breach between names and things, appearances and realities, naïve confidence in names and appearances
is no longer possible. Trust cannot any longer be a matter of
ignorance, and yet it cannot be a matter of knowledge either, since
full knowledge of another human being cannot be had. The look
that I train on the other is met by the look that the other trains
on me. The eye of the other becomes glassy as I probe it and re-

[8] The social contract theory, which began to achieve popularity around this
time is not exclusively democratic in origin: it is as implicit in the protocols
and conventions of courts as it is explicit in the projects for regulating com-
munities.

flects only the eye of the beholder. The real nature of trust thus becomes clear; it is a matter not of ignorance and not of knowledge, but of love and faith.

In so far as she plays a conventional role in society, keeping her inner being free of it, Elmire stands, like Cléante, with one foot in the social world and one foot out of it. She is even more *unknown*, however, than Cléante or Dorine. By the very nature of their roles Cléante and Dorine have little depth of existence. We scarcely ask ourselves what they are, behind what they say, for they are in the comedy only to say what they say. Elmire, however, is Orgon's wife. The contrast between her and Tartuffe is set up immediately on Orgon's entry on the stage in the famous Act I, scene 4, where Orgon responds to each of Dorine's comments about Elmire with some comment or question concerning Tartuffe. Inevitably we must wonder if Elmire is truly Tartuffe's opposite number, if she is indeed authentic, faithful, and loyal in contrast to the inauthenticity, faithlessness, and hypocrisy of the *dévot*. Yet just where it is very important that we should know, we find that we know very little, and it is this very lack of knowledge about someone of whom we want to know a great deal that gives to the character of Elmire her extraordinary depth. Elmire resembles the great portraits of the seventeenth century, clean, well-composed, and simple, and at the same time suggesting depths of being which remain forever beyond our certain grasp.

Between the character of Elmire and the purely theatrical characters who followed her in eighteenth-century literature, there is the same gulf that we find in painting between the portraits of the seventeenth and those of the eighteenth century. Art and nature, appearance and reality were known to be separate and distinct in the seventeenth century. The aim of Classicism was to restore the link between them, not by denying the rift, but by suggesting an underlying unity. Form and content, appearance and reality were to be harmonized in a noble art which would combine ease and elegance with originality and profundity, convention and form with freedom and truth. This ideal was indeed only partly realized and too often it degenerated into rhetorical pompousness. Its inherent instability, which in the seventeenth century was the very thing that made it esthetically meaningful and fruitful, caused its collapse in the course of the eighteenth century: form absorbed content, convention absorbed truth, and the mask absorbed the man in a Rococo world which could no longer maintain the tensions of the previous age. Looked at through the eyes of the Rococo, Elmire must appear a purely theatrical character, a mask without a face. From Molière's point of view and from the point of view of the culture to which he belonged, however, Elmire cannot be so simplified and flattened. She appears before the world in a conventional role and participates appropriately in its activities, but she also has an inner being which she preserves from it. And if she hides her innermost being from the world, it is not necessarily because she wants to be judged as something that she is not. It may be simply because she does not seek the world's judgment of her inner being at all. Her *pudeur* and reserve can be equally a sign of authenticity or of inauthenticity. There is more to Elmire than what we see; but what lies beneath need not be contradicted by what appears on the surface. In the absence of any contradiction in her observable behavior, the casual onlooker has no reason to suppose that Elmire has deliberately chosen a mask in order to present a totally false image of what she really is.[9] Admitting her right

---

[9] In his *Descartes par lui-même* (Paris, 1961) Samuel de Sacy points out that Descartes' aim was not to deceive others, but to preserve an inward freedom. His mask was consequently neutral, mediocre, banal, rather like that of Monsieur Teste (or of Mallarmé!). Baillet tells that he dressed, kept house and table and bore himself in a manner entirely befitting his station, no more, no less. There is no need, therefore, de Sacy argues, quite properly as it seems to me, to suppose with Maxime Leroy (*Descartes, le philosophe au masque*, [Paris, 1929]) that the mask of Descartes must hide its opposite. On the contrary, Descartes' concession to his own historical and temporal existence is at the same time a radical devaluation of it. Descartes did what he could to escape the world and others; he had, as he said, a foot in two countries and a home in neither. In so far as he had to recognize that he was

to be free, he therefore accepts the image that she gives of herself in good faith. To the *look*, in the Sartrian sense, however, the look that seeks to know in the sense that "knowledge is power," the line of the surface at which public and private personality are separated presents itself as the line that separates appearance and reality. The boundary of its knowing is the source of its anguish and torment, for to the *look*, the unknown and the unseen is the free and the unpossessed, the limit to its power and the source of unbearable apprehension. The look invariably suspects fraud where it cannot see, and if it persists, it ultimately finds it, for it creates it. The limit of public and private being, which marks the freedom of the individual, becomes a wall only to whoever would violate it. The tyrant's violence transforms conventional masks into real ones and forces hypocrisy on its victims. Thus Dandin finds in Angélique exactly what he expects and deserves. Similarly Tartuffe discovers a hypocrite in Elmire.

There is nothing in the actual behavior of Elmire to cast doubt on her authenticity. This woman finds the assumption of a role with deliberate intent to deceive distasteful, even when she assumes the role in order to save her family. "C'est contre mon humeur que j'ai fait tout ceci," she says to Tartuffe; "Mais on m'a mise au point de vous traiter ainsi" (IV, 7, *1551–52*). The would-be absolutist who can never be satisfied until he has won complete control of the other, will, of course, ask himself whether this diffidence in the matter of unmasking Tartuffe is not itself part of a cleverly conceived and skillfully acted comedy. This is precisely the sort of question that is asked by the Orgons of the world, for they know only one way of bridging the gulf between the self and the other: the way of total domination and pos-

---

a part of the world of others, that he had a social existence, Descartes chose to give himself the most ordinary, the most *non-committal* existence possible. His recognition of his dependence on the world was thus at the same time an affirmation of his inward independence of it. Sacy's penetrating and intelligent portrait of Descartes can help the reader a long way to understanding characters in Molière such as Elmire.

session. The freedom of the other is experienced by these persons as a constant menace. Devoured by fears and suspicions as indefinite and as infinite as their ambitions, they believe, in their madness, anything that seems to confirm these fears and suspicions.

It is Orgon's distrust of his family, his fear of them and his lack of love for them that causes him to be taken in by the wiles of Tartuffe. His desire to enslave his family enslaves him to Tartuffe. Inevitably when he is warned by his wife and children of Tartuffe's falseness, he does not believe them. Their warnings only confirm his fear and distrust of them and throw him even deeper into the clutches of Tartuffe. Orgon's love of Tartuffe is in inverse ratio to his love of his family; his absolute and unquestioning faith in the impostor corresponds exactly to his distrust of his wife and children. Elmire can therefore release her husband from his subjection to Tartuffe only by becoming, like Tartuffe, the instrument of his hidden fears and of his desire for power over another. She succeeds where Dorine and Cléante have failed only because she is in a position to let Orgon *know and see* the traitor. "Mais que répondroit votre incrédulité / Si je vous faisois voir qu'on vous dit vérité?" she asks (IV, 3, 1339–40). Orgon's hidden rivalry with the instrument in which he has vested such enormous power has been referred to already. The fact that he hesitated, albeit momentarily, when Tartuffe was accused by Damis in Act III ("Ce que je viens d'entendre, o Ciel! est-il croyable?"—III, 6, 1073) is a sign that his fear of his family can at any moment be transferred to his idol, for Orgon must fear and resent whatever escapes him, whatever is not himself. He accepts his wife's suggestion, not because he wants to be reasonable and just or because he rediscovers his trust in her, but because it will provide him with the opportunity *to see at one and the same time* the two beings whom he experiences alternately as his rivals and whom he plays off one against the other: his wife and his friend. As he crouches under the table listening to the conversation of Elmire and Tartuffe, Orgon comes as close as he ever does or can do to the absoluteness he aspires to. Significantly, the moment of his "triumph" is also the moment of his deepest humiliation. It is as a grotesquely impotent eavesdropper that Orgon achieves the conquest he has always dreamed of.

At once in the world and out of it, both bound and free, revealing and at the same time concealing her innermost being, Elmire represents a way of life, which Molière seems to have considered the most decent and honest open to human beings in the modern world. Orgon, Tartuffe, and Madame Pernelle are far more tied to the world and far more concerned with others than Elmire is, despite the criticisms of Madame Pernelle in Act I, scene 1. It is they, in fact, who are the predominantly social characters in the comedy and not Cléante, Dorine, and Elmire. At first sight this does not seem to be the case. Society seems to be represented by Dorine, Cléante, and Elmire, while the other trio seems to be extraordinary and exceptional. Molière deliberately presented his characters in this light. He wanted his public to look on the impostor and his two patrons as freaks and to share the standpoint of the more restrained and reasonable characters. In fact, however, it is the impostor and his patrons who prefigure the most powerful forces operating in society. Their passions are social passions —vanity, resentment, ambition—and if their activity appears profoundly *anti-social* (and in a sense it *is* anti-social), this is, paradoxically enough, because they are so obsessed by society. Against them the combined forces of Elmire, Cléante, and Dorine turn out to be completely inadequate. Elmire succeeds in making an impression on Orgon only when she adopts methods that are entirely opposed to her ordinary behavior. When Mariane, who, significantly, is not her own child but a *step*-child, is about to be sacrificed, she can no longer look on from the outside at the painful and distasteful spectacle presented by her husband's ridiculous infatuation with an impostor. She intervenes to protect a helpless and innocent girl, but she can fight her opponents only with their own weapons: deceit can be unmasked only by deceit and fraud overcome by fraud. The dilemma of simple and modest people in a world of lunatic megalomaniacs is that they cannot protect themselves without resorting to the very means that they would like to avoid. Those who do not resort to such means in Molière, the pure and the young, are saved from disaster only by those who do. Were it not for the wile of servants and the cunning of lovers, the world of Molière's comedies would be littered with innocent victims. It is a sign of the enormous power of tyranny, egoism, vanity, and deceit in modern society that even the servants and lovers are not always able to resist them. Many of the comic situations are resolved only by a happy accident. In *Tartuffe*, Elmire's willingness for the sake of her family to descend to measures that are repugnant to her is not enough to stave off disaster. Louis himself has to intervene to save Orgon and his family from ruin at the hands of Tartuffe.

All's well that ends well, and the comedy of *Tartuffe* ends happily for all except the impostor. But Orgon has not been cured. There is something "temperamentally" wrong with him, as Cléante had already warned us. Orgon is undeceived about Tartuffe at the end of the play, but his nature, his desires, his ambitions, all the profound sources of the disruption that have taken place, these are no more changed in him than they are changed in Harpagon, in M. Jourdain, in Arnolphe, in Alceste, or in Argan. The plant has been cut down, but the seeds of anarchy lie deeply embedded in men's consciousness. Those who are relatively free of the ills that beset the comic heroes are powerless in the end to change much. The King alone, from his superior vantage point of power and justice combined, can save Orgon's family from disintegration. Everything depends on his authority and judgment, as the final scene makes clear:

> Nous vivons sous un prince ennemi de la fraude,
> Un prince dont les yeux se font jour dans les coeurs,
> Et que ne peut tromper tout l'art des imposteurs.
>
> (**X**, 7, *1906–8*)

The brilliant rays of light and truth that emanate from the monarch allow him to penetrate, God-like, to the darkest recesses of the human spirit. Thus Louis discerns immediately the treason and deceit of Tartuffe:

> D'abord il a percé, par ses vives clartés,
> Des replis de son coeur toutes les lâchetés.
> (*ibid.*, 1919–20)

The image of the Sun-King, drawn by Molière at the end of *Tartuffe*, is the one that was current among the writers of the age. Louis appears as a supreme being in whom are vested all the qualities usually associated with God: omnipotence, omniscience, justice, and mercy. The last lines of the play announce a general exodus of all the characters to prostrate themselves at the feet of this adored and adorable idol.

The defeat of the false idol thus goes hand in hand with the triumph of the true one. As far as it goes, this is a satisfactory way of looking at the conclusion of *Tartuffe*, and it is doubtless how the King himself saw it. It was probably also Molière's intention that it should be understood in this way. At the same time the intervention of the monarch would never have been necessary had it not been for the folly of Orgon; the triumph of the "true" idol would never have occurred had it not been for Orgon's infatuation with a false idol. In a world possessed by vanity, the worship of idols seems inevitable, and it is doubtless better to worship a Louis than a Tartuffe. But we should not overlook the fact that the characters in the play with whom Molière seems to have been most in sympathy—Cléante, Dorine, Elmire—have no need of idols, royal or otherwise. Molière distinguished between the different idols that men can worship. He saw that some are better than others, but one cannot help thinking that he smiled inwardly at the human folly which makes any worship of idols necessary. We saw earlier that, whether he intended it or not, Molière created in Tartuffe the type and the caricature of all human idols, and that in the relation of Orgon and Tartuffe he drew a prophetic sketch of one of the fundamental structures of human relations in modern society. The grotesque caricature of the *faux dévot* makes the Sun-King seem even more brilliant by comparison, but at the same time it casts a disquieting shadow over him. Likewise the worship of kings, flags, and other symbols of distinction is at once enhanced and rendered suspect by being set alongside Orgon's infatuation with Tartuffe. Relatively the worship of kings may be better, but it is a phenomenon of a disturbingly similar sort.

Molière's conscious purpose had been to satirize the negative forces of opposition to absolutism. By the eighteenth century, the absolutist compromise itself was in full dissolution and many of the satirists of that age directed their barbs at it. Nevertheless, the respect in which Molière was held by a brilliant satirist such as Diderot is an indication of the fruitfulness and continued relevance of Molière's comic practice. When Diderot observes in the *Paradoxe* that satire to be effective must be directed not at individuals but at types or classes, it is the example of Molière that he invokes to support his point. Indeed, the satire of the degenerate aristocracy which was supported by absolutism in the eighteenth century is implicit in many respects in Molière's satire of the early conservative opponents of absolutism. The world of Rameau and Bertin is as theatrical and as subjective as the world of Molière's own comic heroes.

5

GEORGE DANDIN

"Le vide fascine ceux qui
n'osent pas le regarder
en face, ils s'y jettent
par crainte d'y tomber."

Bernanos, *Journal d'un
Curé de campagne.*

IN THEIR DEVIOUS WAYS Orgon and Alceste both seek to win the recognition of others by dissociating themselves from their fellow-men and affirming their superiority to them. Both are members of an elevated social group; both seek to found their superiority in transcendence, not of their particular social stratum—they realize that this can never provide them with ultimate and final superiority—but of *all* social strata, of all other men. Dandin, on the other hand, stands like Monsieur Jourdain, outside and below the social group from which he desires recognition. He does not yet know that the Sotenvilles have their superiors, who despise them. For him the Sotenvilles are God, absolute transcendence, beyond which there is no higher form of being. Recognition for him is therefore a matter of being admitted to society, not of transcending it and condemning it.

Dandin thought at first that by marrying Angélique he could buy the Sotenvilles' recognition of him. But matters are not so simple. If recognition can be bought, it loses its value. Money corrodes all values and reduces them to quantities, "worth so much." The nobleman understands this perfectly well and he strives to maintain an edge of superiority over the rich man whom, parodoxically, he seduces precisely by despising him. Thus when Dandin addresses Madame de Sotenville as "belle-mère," she quickly reminds him that

il y a fort à dire, et les choses ne sont pas égales. Apprenez, s'il vous plaît, que ce n'est pas à vous à vous servir de ce mot-là avec une personne de ma condition: que tout notre gendre que vous soyez, il y a grande différence de vous à nous et que vous devez vous connoître. (I, 4)

What Dandin wants, of course, is precisely the opposite, not that *he* should know who he is, but that *she* should recognize him. Dandin's passion to be recognized grows, in fact, it does not diminish, with the realization that he has failed to buy recognition. The more aware he becomes that recognition by the Sotenvilles eludes him, the more value it acquires in his eyes. In his very first speech we find him grumbling that "l'alliance que (les nobles) font est petite avec nos personnes: c'est notre bien seul qu'ils épousent" (I, 1). The object of his longing is to be recognized by his superiors as their equal, and it is in the light of this longing that we must interpret the hair-splitting and bickering about names and titles in Act I, scene 4. When Dandin calls Madame de Sotenville "belle-mère," this is not a sign of simple earthy belief in the equality of man. Within the framework of Dandin's theology, a theology in which the Sotenvilles are God, this "belle-mère" is a blasphemy and Madame de Sotenville rightly scolds him for it, insisting that he address her as "Madame" and show his reverence for her as an immeasurably different and superior being. Likewise Monsieur de Sotenville is not to be called "beau-père," or even "Monsieur de Sotenville" (de Sotenville as distinguished, for instance, from de la Dandinière?) but simply "Monsieur" (I, 4). Sotenville is like Jahweh, the name that is too holy to be uttered, and Dandin knows that in uttering it he is blaspheming, tempting the wrath of his God, trying to set himself on an equal plane with him. Even Angélique is not to be referred to as "ma femme." She too belongs to a different and higher order of being.

Yet Dandin had married her precisely in order that she should mediate between him and his gods. Faced with the failure of this project, Dandin complains that he is dissatisfied with his marriage. Madame de Sotenville protests: "Quoi? parler ainsi d'une chose

dont vous avez tire de si grands avantages?" (I, 4). In his reply
Dandin reveals the true cause of his dissatisfaction: "Et quels
avantages, Madame, *puisque Madame y a?*" (italics added). The
trouble is not that Dandin doubts the reality of the distinction
between himself and the Sotenvilles. *Quels avantages?* is a specific,
not a general question. He complains only that he has not in
fact been permitted to enjoy the advantages of being allied to the
Sotenvilles. He has not been recognized by them, and since there
is still this *Madame* between him and Madame de Sotenville, all
the profit of his marriage is lost. She remains an unattainable
absolute for him and he remains a mere object for her. In his
vexation, Dandin reminds the Sotenvilles that if they have the
nobility, he holds the moneybags, but it is clear that he himself
is not convinced of the superiority of moneybags over nobility:

> L'aventure n'a pas été mauvaise pour vous, car sans moi vos affaires,
> avec votre permission, étaient fort delabrées, et mon argent a servi
> à reboucher d'assez bons trous; mais moi, de quoi y ai-je profité,
> je vous prie, que d'un allongement de nom, et au lieu de George
> Dandin, d'avoir reçu par vous le titre de 'Monsieur de la Dan-
> dinière'? (I, 4)

To give a radical, Voltairean meaning to Dandin's complaint is
to miss the whole point of Molière's irony. The Voltairean meaning is there all right, but not quite as the radical himself finds it.
Dandin is not an exposer of illusions, he is the victim of them. He
himself does not see that the "advantages" he complains of not
having found in his own case cannot be acquired in any case,
that they have no reality apart from the reality he agrees to give
them. Dandin is the very opposite of egalitarian. As the only
reality he knows lies in names and opinions, he cannot believe
in equality. He believes inevitably in the inequality that the
Sotenvilles impose upon him. This inequality can become equality
only when they recognize it as such. In the end, therefore, Dandin
must uphold the very system of names and opinions which

makes him inferior to the Sotenvilles, since it is only within this system that he can *acquire* the equality he *desires*, but *does not*, in his own view, as in that of the Sotenvilles, *possess*. By accepting the system of the Sotenvilles, however, Dandin effectively precludes the possibility that he will be regarded by them as an equal. In making the Sotenvilles the gods on whose recognition of him he founds his being, he at the same time attributes to them an inalienable superiority, for it is of the very nature of gods that they cannot alienate their absolute qualitative superiority without ceasing to be gods. While upholding the system of the Sotenvilles, therefore, Dandin must also try to destroy it. The Sotenvilles are at one and the same time the source of and the obstacle to his "equality" with them.

When Dandin complains that all he has got out of his alliance with the Sotenvilles is a vain "allongement de nom," what he is really saying is that he wants to *be* Monsieur de la Dandinière. Unfortunately this can mean only one thing for him; namely, that he be recognized by the Sotenvilles as Monsieur de la Dandinière. But this, as he himself admits, is not possible, *because they gave him the title,* and the act by which they gave him the title confirms their superiority. They know he is "really" George Dandin. As their creature, Dandin remains dependent on the Sotenvilles and their superiority is inexpugnable. In his vexation Dandin has only one recourse. He can kill his gods. By doing so, however, he must inevitably destroy the power in whose recognition of him he founds his being. The dilemma of the peasant hero of *George Dandin* is not very different in the end from that of the elegant suitors in *Le Misanthrope*.

For Dandin, as for Sotenville himself, the name of Sotenville is sacred, unutterable without blasphemy by ordinary creatures. To the audience, however, Sotenville and La Prudoterie are as ridiculous as La Dandinière. To the perspective of Dandin Molière adds the perspective of Clitandre. The domesticated, polished, urbane society of Louis XIV looks on its country cousins with their memories and nostalgias of bygone heroism and chivalry as anything but divine. *Sots* and *prudes* they appear to the new aristocracy of Paris and Versailles. Clitandre has only ironical contempt for Sotenville. Naïvely the latter supposes he is known to and recognized by all noblemen because he once distinguished himself at Nancy and because his fathers and forefathers fought gallantly in the service of the King. To Clitandre all this is stuff and nonsense, "old hat." No one who is anyone believes any more in the "voyage d'outremer" or the "grand siège de Montauban." The battles and jousts of the nobility and their victories and distinctions are won in the antechambers and reception rooms of Versailles and Paris.[1] Sotenville seeks recognition from Clitandre, but he suffers the same fate that Dandin suffers at his hands. He is an object to Clitandre, not Sotenville, but *Sot-en-ville*. Molière does not examine the charmed circle of the Court in this play. He does not show here, as he did in *Le Misanthrope*, that the world of Clitandre is upheld by a similar structure of vanity to that which upholds the world of Dandin and Sotenville. He merely provides a new perspective from which the vanity and folly of the cloddish peasant and the equally cloddish nobleman can be easily discerned. Clitandre's mockery of the Sotenvilles discloses that the real vanity and folly of Dandin is his attempt to achieve being in the eyes of others by giving value to what in itself has none. It is not relevant to the comedy of *George Dandin* that Clitandre and the courtiers of Versailles, with their adoration of

[1] It is also possible to look on Clitandre as a seducer in the style of Dom Juan. I find this characterization of him less satisfying, however. Sotenville's name itself suggests that the man who mocks him should be a man of the city and the court, a man who will see him as *sot-en-ville*. Likewise the name Clitandre evokes not a Baroque grandee, but a member of the society of Paris and Versailles. Clitandre, moreover, has none of Dom Juan's brave rhetoric. He behaves not with the gusto and brilliance of a Dom Juan or a Jupiter, but with the sly coldness of the Acaste and the Clitandre of *Le Misanthrope*. He does indeed recall Dom Juan in certain respects, for there is a Dom Juan in him. As we saw earlier, the marquesses of *Le Misanthrope* are themselves latter-day versions of Dom Juan, Dom Juans who have adapted their manners to the conventions of an urbane and courtly society.

the quasi-divine figure of the monarch, are themselves caught up in a similar spiral of vanity and illusion.

Lacking even the relative lucidity of Clitandre, Dandin never sees the hollowness of his idols. Like the slave he is, he apes them. "Les Dandins ne sont point accoûtumés à cette mode-là," he says to Angélique when she argues that an *honnête homme* should be glad to see his wife admired by others (II, 2). "Si je ne suis pas né noble," he had already pronounced, "au moins suis-je d'une race où il n'y a point de reproche; et la famille des Dandins . . ." (*ibid*). Dandin's pride of race is even more grotesque than that of the Sotenvilles. It is the copy of a fake, like the superciliousness of servants and lackeys. There is a hint of much that is to come in Dandin's insistence on virtue and probity as the source of nobility rather than the consequence of it, as Madame de Sotenville holds (I, 4). An old theme to be sure, but it is clear that what matters in the present context is not virtue and probity but the superiority they provide. Virtue and probity are means; superiority is the end. With Molière this early expression of middle-class morality is still a debased self-righteousness. It has none of the vibrating pathos it was to receive later in characters like Laclos's Madame de Tourvel or Lessing's Emilia Galotti. For while the values of these later characters stand in absolute opposition to the moral and emotional bankruptcy of the aristocracy and imply a revolutionary rejection of a degraded and degrading social order in its entirety, the protest of Dandin is not against the Sotenvilles' order but against their refusal to let him participate in it.

Vanity and resentment are not only the determining marks of Dandin's relation to the Sotenvilles. They are the main source of his difficulties with Angélique. Dandin married Angélique not because he loved her, or, as people used to do, because she was chosen for him by his parents or a matchmaker, but because he wanted her to mediate between himself and the Sotenvilles. Like the sacrificial animals of old, Angélique was a mere object to Dandin, a means not an end. He does not understand, however, that no object, only a subject can mediate for him. Only through love could Angélique intercede for him and win for him the recognition of her parents. From the beginning such mediation is ruled out. In the first place Dandin is incapable of love. He does not love persons; they have no reality for him. He loves only the signs of rank; only these meta-physical entities are real in his eyes. Thus he does not seek to be recognized as a person, as George Dandin, but as Monsieur da La Dandinière, and he does not revere the Sotenvilles for what they are, he reveres only their name. In the second place the Sotenvilles are in the same position. They are no respectors of persons. Angélique for them is an object whose entire value lies in her pedigree, and they barter her, like a cow, for money. If there is no love between Dandin and Angélique, there is no love either between Angélique and her parents.

The marriage that results from the deal between Dandin and the Sotenvilles is itself an image, not a reality, a purely formal bond without content. As a subject Angélique escapes Dandin completely, as she herself asserts in her outburst in Act II, scene 2:

> Comment? parce qu'un homme s'avise de nous épouser, il faut d'abord que toutes choses soient finies pour nous, et que nous rompions tout commerce avec les vivants? C'est une chose merveilleuse que cette tyrannie de Messieurs les maris, et je les trouve bons de vouloir qu'on soit morte à tous les divertissements, et qu'on ne vive que pour eux.

With his money Dandin has bought only an object. Instead of his money's acquiring, as he intended, the characteristics of an active and real subject, the active subject takes on in Dandin's hands the characteristics of money—it becomes a formal object. Angélique the subject lies out of reach, and if Dandin possesses her formally as an object, she also sees him and tries to govern him as an object. This is the source of all Dandin's anguish.

Although when the play opens Angélique has not yet "deceived" him, he lives in constant fear and anticipation that she will. Technically she never does, in the play at least, yet in another sense she constantly deceives him, from the very beginning, because she never recognizes him as her husband: "(Elle) se tient au-dessus de moi," he complains, "s'offense de porter mon nom, et pense qu'avec tout mon bien je n'ai pas assez acheté la qualité de son mari" (I, 1). Indeed in the first scene in which Angélique confronts Dandin (I, 6), she addresses not a single word to him, referring to him, as to some object, only in the third person, and in the second of the scenes in which they appear together (II, 2), her replies to his long complaints and reproaches are curt and cold. When she does appear to recognize him as her husband, the recognition is hypocritical; in reality he remains an object for her.

Unlike Dandin's possession of her, which is purely formal, her deception of him is real, but for him the act of physical infidelity, the formal deception, which will mark the end of his formal possession of her, is the real one, and it is this deception that he both desires and dreads. Living as he does in a world of vain forms and unreal values, he confuses the shadow with the substance, tyranny with possession through love. That Angélique does not love him causes him no pain, only that she does not recognize him as her master. Like all tyrants, he concentrates his efforts on converting a subjectivity he cannot possess into an objectivity which cannot satisfy him. He dreams of achieving through tyranny over an object what can only be achieved through communion with a subject, through love. Hence his brutal fantasy in Act I, scene 3: "Si c'étoit une paysanne, vous auriez maintenant toutes vos coudées franches à vous en faire la justice à bons coups de bâton," he says to himself, regretting that he ever took a girl of noble birth to wife. This dream of brutalizing the other is in fact an expression of Dandin's own slavishness. If Dandin aspires to leap out of the category of the slave, it is only into the category of the master. He cannot conceive of true equality and love, and in his hypothetical peasant-wife it is his own inferiority that he longs to punish.

Dandin is indignant at Angélique's non-recognition of him, at her treatment of him as an object-in-the-world. But Angélique rightly points out that it was Dandin himself who established their relationship on this footing. When Dandin invokes the holy bonds of matrimony, the faith that she solemnly swore to him, Angélique has her answer ready:

"Moi? Je ne vous l'ai point donnée de bon coeur, et vous me l'avez arrachée. M'avez-vous, avant le mariage, demandé mon con-sentment, et si je voulais bien de vous? Vous n'avez consulté pour cela, que mon père et ma mère: ce sont eux proprement qui vous ont épousé, et c'est pourquoi vous ferez bien de vous plaindre toujours à eux des torts que l'on pourra vous faire. Pour moi, qui ne vous ai point dit de vous marier avec moi, et que vous avez prise sans consulter mes sentiments, je prétends n'être point obligée à me soumettre en esclave à vos volontés" (II, 2).

This is an accurate diagnosis of Dandin's behavior and it reveals the inner contradiction in the position of this rich peasant who, at one and the same time, proclaims in theory and denies in practice the dignity and value of the individual. It was indeed not Angélique who married Dandin, but her father and mother, and it is not Angélique whom Dandin desires, but her father and mother. Sotenville, not Angélique, is what he "loves." This ex-plains why he constantly seeks out the parents and complains to them, and why he fears and at the same time desires Angélique's infidelity. Dandin is painfully aware that the Sotenvilles have not really recognized him. If he can prove to them that their daughter is a baggage, he thinks, if he can make them recognize that, he will get at the very heart of their aristocratic pride; he will bring them down from the heights where they do not see him. If they can be made to recognize that Angélique de Sotenville has wronged him, George Dandin, they will at the same time recognize him as her husband, not as a money-object. In this very act of achieving recognition, however, Dandin will have deprived it of its value for him, because he will have deprived the Sotenvilles of value. Instead of bringing about his own promotion, his marriage, by its very failure, will bring about the demotion of the Sotenvilles. This accounts for Dandin's *dread*. He fears Angélique's unfaithfulness and tries to prevent it, and at the same time he desires it and—unlike ordinary cuckolds—wants it to be *known*. Somewhere in his tortured mind he is dimly aware that he cannot really win. If Angélique is technically faithful, or if her unfaithfulness cannot be *shown*, then he remains a thing, and the whole object of his marriage is unfulfilled; if, on the other hand, Angélique is unfaithful and if her unfaithfulness is shown, his victory is a hollow one, a victory in which all are defeated and humiliated. Dandin's aims are thus revealed in their true light as profoundly nihilistic. He cannot really fulfill the object of his marriage, he can only destroy it; he cannot really win the recognition of himself as an equal by his superiors, he can only destroy their superiority.

It is not surprising that Angélique is a hypocrite. She sees that the world she lives in is a world of lies and fraud and that to defend oneself in such a world one must adopt its weapons and use them cleverly. This she does. But the Sotenvilles themselves are largely responsible for the hypocrisy of Angélique. She cannot be expected to have respect for values that her parents do not respect, and it is they, in the first instance, who derogated from the very nobility they lay so much store by when they married her to a commoner. Angélique knows that in effect her parents sold her to Dandin, that with all their prattle about nobility they are in practice as *commerçants* as he. In fact they do speak of her as though she were a piece of merchandise carrying a guarantee. "Nous l'avons élevée dans toute la sévérité possible," Madame de Sotenville assures Dandin (I, 4). "Si vous dites vrai," Sotenville adds, "nous la renoncerons pour notre sang, et l'abandonne-

rons à votre colère" (II, 7). Angélique is an object for her parents
just as she is an object for Dandin. That is why she lumps them
together in her disavowal to Clitandre of any sense of obligation
to either: "Pensez-vous qu'on soit capable d'aimer de certains
maris qu'il y a? On les prend, parce qu'on ne s'en peut défendre,
et que l'on dépend de parents qui n'ont des yeux que pour le bien"
(III, 5).

The contempt in which Angélique holds her pompously noble
parents comes out clearly in the malicious humor with which she
practices her deception of them. Like Tartuffe, Angélique takes
delight in presenting the truth to those whom she is confident
will not recognize it. After the little scene in which she upbraids
Clitandre for the benefit of her parents, protesting in almost the
very words used by Elmire in *Tartuffe* that she has said nothing
to her parents about the insult to her virtue because "une honnête
femme n'aime point les éclats" (II, 8), Sotenville urges Dandin
to thank his wife for "l'amitié que vous *voyez* qu'elle *montre*
pour vous" (italics added). But Angélique interrupts: "Non, non,
mon père, il n'est pas nécessaire. Il ne m'a aucune obligation de
ce qu'il vient de *voir*, et tout ce que je fais *n'est que pour l'amour
de moi-même*" (italics added). Angélique knows that her mother
and father will interpret her words, as they interpret their own
actions, in the light, not of the simple truth the words convey,
but of the same bad faith which protects them from the truth
about themselves.

Like Molière's other hypocrites, Angélique is presented without
pathos, neither from the point of view of romantic sympathy with
the rebel, nor from the point of view of outraged morality. The
garden scene in Act III is a striking illustration of the ruthless
objectivity of Molière's comic vision. Angélique is caught by
Dandin in an extremely compromising situation. At first she tries
to deny everything ("Hé bien! quel grand mal est-ce qu'il y a à
prendre le frais de la nuit?"), but as soon as she realizes that
the comedy of outraged innocence will not extricate her from her

predicament she alters her tactics. She strikes an attitude of noble truthfulness ("Mon intention n'est pas de vous rien déguiser. Je ne prétends point me défendre"). When this too fails, she wheedles, acting the part of the loving wife ("mon pauvre petit mari"—"Mari" is the word Dandin likes to hear), the wayward but innocent young woman whose extravagances are to be pardoned as part of her very youthfulness ("mais enfin ce sont des actions que vous devez pardonner à mon âge; des emportements de jeune personne qui n'a encore rien vu, et ne fait que d'entrer au monde: des libertés où l'on s'abandonne sans y penser de mal . . ."). As Dandin remains inexorable she tries another tack. His forgiveness will make her truly love him:

> Si vous m'accordez généreusement la grâce que je vous demande, ce procédé obligeant, cette bonté que vous me ferez voir, me gagnera entièrement. Elle touchera tout à fait mon coeur, et y fera naître pour vous ce que tout le pouvoir de mes parents et les liens du mariage n'avoient pu y jeter. En un mot, elle sera cause que je renoncerai à toutes les galanteries, et n'aurai de l'attachement que pour vous . . .

But Dandin is not to be taken in by this. It is not that he understands that love cannot be bought and that, on the contrary, Angélique would only detest him the more for being indebted to him. Quite simply Dandin does not understand love at all and is not tempted by it. All he understands are the crassest forms of dominion and subjection. Finally Angélique resorts to the ultimate commercialization of human relations: blackmail. She will kill herself, and he will be accused of murder. At first Dandin scoffs: "Bagatelles, bagatelles. C'est pour me faire peur." But as Angélique goes on with the act he becomes alarmed: "Ouais! seroit-elle bien si malicieuse que de s'être tuée pour me faire pendre? Prenons un bout de chandelle pour aller voir." It is perfectly consistent that Dandin, having resisted all the other ruses of his wife, should bite at this one. This kind of nihilistic vengefulness is the one thing he himself understands and is capable of. He goes out into the garden, and at that moment Angélique slips in. The tables are turned. At no point in this scene is the audience intended to take pity on Angélique or to believe a word she says about her youth, her innocence, her willingness to love Dandin truly, etc. She is bluffing all the time and her attitude to Dandin in the moment of her triumph ("D'où viens-tu, bon pendard . . .") is the attitude she really has throughout the scene. Nor are we to feel sorry for Dandin in his final discomfiture. He is only being paid in his own coin. There is no injustice and no pathos in this clash of two equally selfish and egoistic natures, only a struggle for domination in which each party regards the other as an object, in which ruse is pitted against ruse, wile against wile, resentment against resentment.

On the one hand the Sotenvilles with their bad faith; on the other hand Angélique with her hypocrisy. Dandin alone, it would seem, is committed to revealing the truth. But not for any love of truth. The truth is Dandin's instrument in his struggle with others, just as Angélique's instrument is falsehood. Dandin is not interested in the truth for its own sake, or in the truth about himself. That is why he never catches a glimpse of the real nature of his own situation. All he sees and wants is the truth of the law court. "Il s'agit seulement de désabuser le père et la mère," he declares (I, 7). "O Ciel," he cries, "seconde mes desseins, et m'accorde la grâce de faire voir aux gens que l'on me déshonore" (II, 8). He himself tells why he wants his dishonor to be known: "Pour avoir raison aux yeux du père et de la mère, et les convaincre pleinement de l'effronterie de leur fille" (II, 6). When at last he thinks he has caught Angélique in the act, he cannot restrain his joy at finding himself dishonored: ". . . c'est que je vais être vengé, et que votre père et votre mère seront convaincus mainte-nant de la justice de mes plaintes, et du dérèglement de votre conduite" (III, 6).

In the final scenes of the play, bad faith and hypocrisy triumph over truth. Dandin's story is not believed. "Vous voyez quelle apparence il y a," Claudine mocks (III, 7). Thus reality passes for appearance and appearance for reality. The Sotenvilles are easily persuaded that their daughter has been wronged and insulted. Angélique makes the most of the opportunity. She asks to be separated from such a husband. But the Sotenvilles do not want to go so far. They are glad to see Dandin put in his place, but they cannot afford to let him go. Quite apart from the question of a financial settlement, they need Dandin because it is by perpetually affirming his inferiority that they establish and experience their own superiority. Sotenville and Dandin live in the same charmed circle; each upholds the other and neither can do without the other. If the rich peasant resents the rank of the poor nobleman, the poor nobleman resents the wealth of the rich peasant. Sotenville must constantly seek to be reassured about his superiority by humiliating Dandin. "Vous devez vous montrer plus sage que lui, et patienter encore cette fois," he urges his daughter (III, 7). Angélique protests that "après tant d'indignités" she cannot remain with him. "Il le faut, ma fille, et c'est moi qui vous le commande," Sotenville rejoins, playing up to Angélique's comedy of the obedient daughter with his own comedy of the solicitous father. Angélique submits to the voice of the venerable author of her days. Claudine applauds the scene and the actors, and the final comment on it is this appreciation by another mistress of hypocrisy. "Quelle douceur!" "Pauvre mouton!" she sighs. Dandin is made to repeat after Sotenville a humiliating apology to Angélique. Thus Angélique's virtue is justified, while the way is deftly prepared for further "galanteries." (Having destroyed Dandin's credit, Angélique is careful to point out that the same situation is bound to recur.) The Sotenvilles, for their part, succeed in upholding both their profitable bargain with Dandin and their immeasurable superiority over him. Nothing remains for Dandin but to "s'aller jeter dans l'eau la tête la première" (III, 8).

The denouement of *George Dandin* recalls in many respects the denouement of *Le Misanthrope*. Dandin is right and yet he loses his case. But just as Alceste was himself the victim of the very ills he condemned, so Dandin is full of the very evils he complains of and accuses others of. Both seek to assert their superiority by destroying the world that they still accept as their final judge. Neither is truly free of the values he rejects. For this reason both attain only to half-truths. They do not see the truth about themselves, they do not see that they are not outside the situations they try to expose, but part of them. The astonishing scenes in which Dandin is made to repeat the apologies dictated to him by Sotenville reveal both the insubstantiality of the old order and the complete involvement in it of those who are criticizing it, the underlying identity of Sotenville and Dandin, despite their differences, the utter interdependence of the master and the slave. In his humiliation at the hands of the Sotenvilles Dandin finds the confirmations of their superiority and the justification of his ambition to be one of them. He must constantly seek his own humiliation, and the Sotenvilles must constantly seek to inflict it on him in order that the illusory values on which the existence of both is grounded may be upheld. Dandin's aping of the Sotenvilles is the very image of his real degradation, for he is not really forced to be Sotenville's ape, he chooses to be it. The muttered aparte in Act III, scene 7—" 'L'extravagance que j'ai faite' (à part) 'de vous épouser' "—is not a rejection of the Sotenvilles, it expresses only a resentment of them which is inseparable from his acceptance of their superiority. It is because he accepts this superiority that he resents it, and it is because he resents it that he accepts it. Dandin is completely trapped inside the vicious circle of idolatry and resentment. His degradation at the hands of the Sotenvilles confirms their superiority and the desirableness of being like them; this in turn confirms his failure to be like them, which in turn confirms their superiority, which in turn confirms his failure, etc., etc. Dandin's whole behavior is marked by this dual attitude of love and hate, of self-love and self-hate. He must inevitably seek to be humiliated by his idols in order that their divinity be upheld, and he must inevitably resent this divinity because it is the obstacle to his own. His strangely contradictory attitude to Angélique depends directly on his contradictory attitude to her parents. Only here the positions are reversed. It is his resentment of his idols that causes him to seek humiliation at the hands of Angélique, and it is his worship of them that causes him to dread it.

The curious *dédoublement* of Dandin, in many asides and monologues throughout the play, corresponds exactly to the duality of his aspirations. He is constantly telling himself that he is only getting what he asked for: "Vous l'avez voulu, vous l'avez voulu, George Dandin, vous l'avez voulu, cela vous sied fort bien . . ." (I, 7). It would be incorrect to imagine that of the two Dandins in these speeches one stands outside the situation commenting on the other. Both are in it. The George who comments is the resentful George—it is he who seeks to "désabuser le père et la mère"—and the George who is commented on is the idolatrous George. At no time does George Dandin really see all of himself, and he remains comically blind to the—rather bitter—end. What he says to himself in his final speech—that all his troubles come from having married a "méchante femme"—marks very little progress over what he says in his first speech—that it was a mistake to marry a person of noble birth who "pense qu'avec tout mon bien je n'ai pas assez acheté la qualité de son mari." To the very end Dandin sees himself as responsible only externally for his difficulties.

There really is "plus de remède" for Dandin's troubles. He hates himself because he is not Sotenville and he hates Sotenville because he is not Dandin. Irremediably caught up in the spiral of his own false aspirations, totally unable to disentangle himself, George really has only one way out—"de s'aller jeter dans l'eau la tête la première."

To the public that watched the play, Dandin and Sotenville are equally comic figures. Their little feudal world—the world of the small country nobility impoverished after the *Fronde*—is an anachronism, a world without reality and without future. What real substance is there to the nobility of a Sotenville? What real place does he occupy in society when, too poor and too weak to fulfill any useful social function, he is forced, in order to survive, to make shameful deals with his better-off peasants? Sotenville's nobility is seen as an empty form that conceals—though not very well—his real degradation. His whole being is a shadow, and it is Dandin's error that he believes in this shadow and seeks to share in its "glory." As Molière's audiences laughed at the illusions and vanities of the petty feudal world of Sotenville, as they applauded the satire of a meaningless "nobility," they adopted, consciously or not, the standpoint of the absolute monarchy and of its bourgeois allies, the standpoint of realism and of practical common sense; they recognized perforce that the true value of a man lies not in his name and pedigree but in the concrete services he renders to the state as a whole, be it as a merchant, as an administrator, as a soldier, or as an artist. In this sense the success of *George Dandin* marks, as do most of Molière's comedies, a victory for the ideology on which the alliance of the King and the bourgeoisie in the seventeenth century was founded. In this sense alone can it be considered "revolutionary" or "progressive." Dandin's speeches in themselves do not carry the meaning of the comedy.

6

MOLIÈRE IN HIS OWN TIME

"Pour moi, (. . .) je trouve que toute imposture est indigne d'un honnête homme."

Molière, *Le Bourgeois Gentilhomme.*

"Je crois vous avoir déjà dit autrefois, que cet air [de Paris] me dispose à concevoir des chimères, au lieu de pensées de philosophe."

Descartes, Letter to Chanut, May, 1648.

"Il est donc vrai de dire que tout le monde est dans l'illusion: car, encore que les opinions du peuple soient saines, elles ne le sont pas dans sa tête, car il pense que la vérité est où elle n'est pas. La vérité est bien dans leurs opinions, mais non pas au point où ils se figurent. Ainsi, il est vrai qu'il faut honorer les gentilshommes, mais non pas parce que la naissance est un avantage effectif, etc."

Pascal, *Pensées.*

THE FOREGOING CHAPTERS have brought to light a number of themes which seem to be common to all the plays we have looked at. In the present chapter it is proposed to examine these same themes as they appear in the work of other writers and thinkers of Molière's time, in Descartes, in Corneille, and in Racine. By comparing Molière with his two great fellow-dramatists, in particular, we shall try to elucidate what special qualities, what unique privilege, allowed him to see in a comic light situations which they saw in a dramatic or even a tragic light. We shall find ourselves forced to distinguish between an authentic tragic situation in the seventeenth century and a pseudo-tragic situation, which is the one that Molière himself invariably presents as *comic*. We shall also extend the relatively detailed examination of individual plays that we have pursued hitherto to the body of Molière's work in general, and we shall attempt to show that the themes and structures we have found in the plays which we have examined in detail are characteristic of all Molière's major comedies.

Following this, we shall devote a final chapter to showing, very sketchily indeed, that the basic structures of Molière's comedies are deeply relevant to the whole of modern life and literature. As in Molière's time, they have not always been discerned as comic. Indeed the comic perspective seems to have become progressively more difficult for writers to attain since Molière's time. Why this should have been so and what special objective conditions seem

to favor the writing of comedy are questions that we shall also
attempt to deal with in this final chapter.

⁑⁑⁑

Violence that concealed weakness, willfulness that concealed
despair and fear, order that concealed anarchy, these are characteristic manifestations of the world of the early and mid-seven-
teenth century in Europe. This is the age of civil wars and of
absolutism, the age in which a king was beheaded by his subjects,
and the age in which a subject made himself absolute master of
a kingdom. "Il s'agit pour Descartes et ses précurseurs," writes M.
Perelman, "de remplacer la force par un autre impérialisme qui
serait l'impérialisme de l'ordre, et de l'ordre de la vérité" (in
Descartes, Cahiers de Royaumont [Paris, 1959], p. 322). But the
order even of truth can be imposed only by violence and tyranny.
The Inquisition is simply the most notorious of efforts to impose
the order of truth. And what truth? Whose truth? Is the measure
of truth the strength of will and the power behind it? Questioned
about the polygamy of the Patriarchs, Mersenne replied that God
is free to define virtue and sin as He wills (cf. Robert Lenoble's
contribution to *Descartes, op. cit.*, and the same author's *Marin
Mersenne ou la naissance du mécanisme* [Paris, 1943]). The good
which the scholastics, as well as the humanist theologians had
placed in the understanding of God becomes with Mersenne a
free and gratuitous creation of the divine will. In creating the
universe God did not follow the logic present in His understanding; He acted freely and gratuitously by fiat of His divine will:
"Omnia quaecumque voluit fecit, sit pro ratione voluntas"
(*Quaestiones in Genesim*, quoted by Lenoble in *Descartes, op.
cit.*). If he were to give the palm to any of God's attributes, says
Mersenne, it would be to His will (*Impiété des déistes*, quoted by
Lenoble, *loc. cit.*). It is not surprising that the good father, who
said of the *De Cive* of his atheist friend Hobbes that it should

be printed in letters of silver, extended the pre-eminence of will over reason in a God *cujus unica ratio est voluntas* to man or at least to certain privileged men. The prelates of the Church, God's ministers on earth, have the right, says Mersenne, in the interest of order, to exercise a dictatorial power over moral and even over scientific truth. In this they resemble monarchs, who are likewise to be considered divinely appointed. They may, for instance, prohibit books which in effect contain no falsehood "comme le Roy peut justement deffendre les jeux de chartes, de dez, d'echets, de paume (. . .) s'il juge que ces deffences soient necessaires pour maintenir son royaume (. . .) encore que le jeu ne soit pas mauvais de soy-mesme" (*La Vérité des sciences* [Paris, 1625], pp. 111–12).

In Mersenne, however, as in Hobbes, there is little attempt to fuse the two realms of God and of man. On the contrary, Mersenne's vision tends to be as realistic as Hobbes's. Mersenne may well consider all customs and social orders, however different they may be from each other, as so many institutions of God's will for the maintainance of order in society (cf. Lenoble, *Marin Mersenne, op. cit.*, pp. 266–72, 542–43)—this indifferentism places God at such a remove from the world that it is easy for the divine guarantee to disappear altogether without anybody's noticing. Social order becomes a human affair and the justification of any particular order becomes a practical one, as it is for Hobbes, or for that matter for Pascal. Mersenne's ideas about scientific knowledge continue the separation of the divine and the human. Most of the scientists in his circle—Gassendi, Boulliau, Roberval —readily accepted that man can know neither essences nor the true nature of the physical world, these remaining the secret of God. Man's truth and man's science are thus entirely his own work and they need not correspond to absolute truth or to the real nature of the world. "Je ne doute pas," Mersenne writes, "que nous pourrons voir le contraire de ce que nous disons ici en matière de philosophie, quand le voile sera tiré, et que la lumière du Ciel nous éclairera" (*Impiété des déistes*, quoted by Lenoble, in *Descartes, op. cit.*). Mersenne goes so far as to say that if we could create an automaton which would fly exactly as a "real" fly does, it would matter little that there are other beings created by God that are "real" flies. The true for us is as valid for us as the true in itself, which cannot be known (*Harmonie universelle*; cf. Lenoble in *Descartes, op. cit.*).

The separation of God and the world, of reason and will, of nature and Grace, is by no means a purely Pascalian invention. Pascal's two radically distinct orders are characteristic of a whole current of Baroque thought and experience. Naked force, emptied of all reason, impenetrable to the understanding, unquestionable, and intolerant, rules over both orders, the divine and human. Separated by a chasm that no one can bridge except by the forceful annihilation of his own will, the divine and the human are alike in that both are equally marked by power and violence. Everywhere there is conflict of wills, within society between individuals and in the universe between man and God, and nowhere is order maintained except by the violent annihilation of one will by another or by the violent sacrifice of one will to another. Order in the relations among men or in the relation between man and God is achieved not by co-operation, not by a reaching out of one toward the other, not by love (love on the human level, in the order of nature, is never more than desire for dominion), but by violence, the violence of empire or the violence of sacrifice. The dialectic of the Baroque is resolved—if it is ever resolved— not in harmony but by the forceful imposition of one of its terms on the other.

The work of Descartes, of Leibniz, of Spinoza, each in its own way, represents an attempt to find an alternative to this solution of violence. Spinoza saw very well that the vision of God as pure *voluntas* mirrors the violence in the heart of the beholder. Nothing in God's creation is arbitrary, according to Spinoza, ". . . all things follow from the necessity of the divine nature; so

that whatsoever (man) deems to be hurtful and evil, and whatsoever, accordingly, seems to him impious, horrible, unjust, and
base, assumes that appearance owing to his own disordered,
fragmentary, and confused view of the universe." Despite all the
differences that separate them, Descartes, Leibniz, and Spinoza
are all concerned to heal the wounds that have opened up between
power and truth, between will and reason, to substitute the im-
perialism of truth, in Professor Perelman's words, for the im-
perialism of force. All the new orders, however, carry marks of
blood. Every one of them participates in the tensions it is supposed to overcome, and in the end there is no closing of the
wound. The forms of monism evolved by Spinoza and Leibniz
do not really resolve the dualism they seek to replace, and it is
no accident that in the following century Voltaire, who owed
much to the humanist education he received from his Jesuit
teachers, took issue with both Pascal and Leibniz. As for Descartes,
whose work Molière can scarcely have ignored, the failure of the
attempt to close the breach is most obvious in his case.

We saw that Mersenne found no need to reconcile the true
nature of the universe, known only to God, with the nature of
the universe as it was constructed by the mind of man. There is
truth for God and there is truth for man; truth for man is not
absolute truth, just as Hobbes's sovereign has no inherent claim
to sovereignty but only a practical claim. Whereas in practical
politics, however, human freedom splits and creates further problems (who is free, the individual or the group, in a society that
is free to create its own destiny and its own justice?) in the realm
of science, freedom is relatively unproblematic. Disagreements are
not conflicts of will and desire. Each scientist can thus easily accept the coexistence along with his own of the world-order created
by other scientists. Indeed these creators of worlds are fully aware
that their world-order is at the same time their liberty and they
do not seek to destroy the liberty of their neighbor. It is at this
point that Descartes appears as dictatorial on the level of truth

as Hobbes on the level of practice and utility. Descartes will admit of no rival to his world-order. It is the only true one. And it is the only true one because it claims to be not a free creation but a discovery of the true world-order, the world-order of God. Precisely because he posits that each individual is his own liberty, Hobbes is forced, in order to maintain order in the practical area of social relations, to require the annihilation of this liberty for the sake of peace. Peace and order are founded not in any objective limitation to human liberty but in the imposition of an arbitrary limitation, which this liberty wills upon itself. Descartes' insistence that his science is the only true science, on the other hand, rests on the claim that it is objectively true, not on any criterion of convenience. In political terms this would be equivalent to saying that the sovereign must be obeyed because he is divinely appointed, because he is in his very nature just. Descartes' science claims to be as divine as the Right of Kings.

Descartes' problem is to reconcile the independence of his own mind and will with the omnipotence and omniscience of God. The difficulties that Henri Lefebvre pointed out in the Cartesian doctrine of will and freedom (cf. his *Descartes* [Paris, 1947]) have been explored again by Kemp-Smith and Father Lenoble. It is in virtue of our will that we can refuse our assent to the evidence of mere sense, according to Descartes, but, as Father Lenoble properly asks, "l'envers de la liberté de douter n'est-il pas nécessairement la liberté de dire oui?" (*Descartes, op. cit.*, p. 320). When he finds the truth, Descartes tells us, he feels liberated, that is his own will finds itself in accord with the will of God, source of all truth. Descartes is sparing, however, of information as to how this accord takes place. "A fréquenter Descartes," Father Lenoble writes, "on se demande si, même pour lui, les choses se passaient aussi simplement qu'il le dit. Il me semble que sa *pratique* de l'adhésion au vrai nous montre, beacoup mieux que sa théorie—élaborée, encore une fois, avec de très gros plans—qu'il n'a pas oublié aussi complètement qu'on pourrait le croire son volontarisme" (*ibid.*, p.

318). Lenoble draws attention to the confidential and intimate utterances of Descartes the seeker, rather than to those of Descartes the theoretician, utterances which show him groping toward the truth by a series of practical decisions, just as in ethics he felt his way toward the Good. The abyss that is supposed to exist between the Cartesian search for the Good—a slow approximation—and the search for the True—a series of illuminations—is an invention of Descartes' scoliasts, Lenoble contends, though in this respect Descartes may well have been, as Lenoble wittily puts it, the first of his scoliasts. Henri Gouhier ("Doute méthodique ou négation méthodique," *Les Etudes philosophiques*, 1954, No. 2) had already indicated that Descartes' confident statements about the irresistible force of truth are complemented in his actual work by a very prudent understanding of the real difficulties in the way of any discovery and recognition of truth. The difficulty of assenting to evidence is admitted by Descartes himself in several places. Gouhier quotes a passage from the Replies to the Sixth Objections where, having applied his method to the distinction of body and mind, Descartes adds: "Toutefois je confesse que je ne fus pas pour cela pleinement persuadé." He felt rather like those astronomers "qui, après avoir été convaincus par de pressantes raisons que le soleil est plusieurs fois plus grand que toute la terre, ne sauraient pourtant s'empêcher de juger qu'il est plus petit lorsqu'ils jettent les yeux sur lui."

Assenting to the truth, it would seem, thus involves an act of will similar to that involved in assenting to Grace in Thomist theology. Truth liberates, according to Descartes, and man is not free until he possesses it. But he already has a kind of freedom, in virtue of which he can will to be free. For Pascal and the anti-Cartesians, God's knowledge and man's knowledge are separated by an abyss, just as the realm of nature and the realm of Grace are. To be united with God, to share with Him, to enter into His will and His understanding requires a complete break with the self, a total annihilation and transmutation of the natural man. Since man's will never leads him to the Divine but always away from it, this will must be destroyed and completely absorbed by the divine will. For Descartes, on the other hand, knowledge of the truth involves the acquiescence of man's will, its active assenting as human will to the truths created by the divine will. Man submits to God, in Descartes, without thereby losing or denying his own will. On the contrary his will is elevated by being identified with that of God.

The ambiguity in Descartes' doctrine of knowledge pointed out by Lenoble and Gouhier is a crucial one. The fact is that Descartes must maintain both that man finds his own way to truth and that this truth is a divine illumination. Man's freedom, the independence of his will, and the validity of his thought must be maintained; man is not to be the slave of God; he is to be himself capable of raising himself to the divine. At the same time only the divine sanction can guarantee the objective and universal validity of the knowledge he thus discovers for himself.

It is significant that a similar ambiguity to that discovered in Descartes' scientific method by Lenoble and Gouhier was discovered in the *cogito* itself and discussed by Ginette Dreyfus in an article published a decade or so ago ("Discussion sur le *Cogito* et l'axiome 'Pour penser il faut être,' " *Revue Internationale de Philosophie*, 6, 1952, pp. 117–25). Descartes maintains that the validity of the *cogito* rests on the axiom "to think it is necessary to be." [1] But what is the validity of the axiom? Is it valid in the way mathematical principles are? If so, then its validity must be subjective until the hypothesis of the *malus genius* has been overcome, for the *malus genius* puts in doubt not that $2 + 3 = 5$ or that a square has no more than four sides in my mind, but that these truths are

---

[1] Cf. *Discours de la Methode*, 4 partie: "Il n'y a rien du tout en ceci: *Je pense, donc je suis* qui m'assure que je dis la vérité sinon que je vois tres clairement que, pour penser, il faut être"; also *Principes*, I, 10: "Lorsque j'ai dit que cette proposition *Je pense, donc je suis* est la première et la plus certaine à celui qui conduit sa pensée par ordre, je n'ai pas nié qu'il ne fallût savoir auparavant ce que c'est que penser, certitude, existence et que pour penser il faut être;" also "Replies to Sixth Objections."

valid for things considered as independent of my mind. I may, to
be sure, when I apprehend myself thinking, apply the axiom to
my thinking and postulate in consequence that I exist, but if the
necessity of the axiom is only a subjective one, the necessity of the
link between my thinking and my existing can also be only subjective. Similarly, while it is true that the axiom finds an application through the *cogito* to the real world, it is not clear how this
confers an objective validity on the axiom or on the necessity it
pretends to. The fact that my experience provides the opportunity
to apply the rule to a real datum does not suffice to found the objective validity of the rule. One might, on the other hand, choose
to consider the axiom as being discovered immediately in those
things (*res*), which, unlike mathematical things, are not subject to
doubt. If the *res* are in doubt, the axioms they contain are in
doubt: this is what happens to the axioms of mathematics as soon
as the fiction of the *malus genius* puts mathematical propositions
themselves in doubt. But if the *res* are not doubtful, the axioms
they contain are not doubtful either. As my thinking is not in
doubt and as I perceive in the reality of this *res* that it is necessarily bound to a being, the axiom "to think it is necessary to be"
cannot be in doubt either. The necessity of the axiom in this interpretation is that of a rational truth and of a rational truth which
is not to be thought of as a law that thought imposes on things,
but rather as imposed on thought by things themselves. In short,
the necessity of the axiom "pour penser il faut être" is not purely
subjective; it is objective, being the direct expression of a necessity
written into the existents that are given me in direct apprehension.
In the *cogito ergo sum*, thought and being are thus two sides of the
same medal and it is impossible to think the one without thinking
the other. For this reason, so this argument would conclude, it is
easy to understand why Descartes could affirm that the axiom "to
think it is necessary to be" escapes the doubt introduced by the
hypothesis of the *malus genius*, whereas the axioms of mathematics
do not. Descartes himself, however, explicitly states not that the

axiom is derived from the *cogito*, but that the axiom is prior to the *cogito* (cf. note 1, *supra*). Furthermore Descartes preserves the axiom from the doubt introduced by the *malus genius*, not by supposing it contained in any indubitable *res*, but by arguing that it does not involve the affirmation of any *res*, of any actual existence at all. Again if the necessity of the axiom rested on the intuition of certain *res* that contain it, the axiom would be subject to doubt for as long as I had not obtained through the *cogito* the intuition of these indubitable *res*. It would therefore be doubtful from the outset in exactly the same way as the axioms of mathematics. The difference between the two kinds of axioms would become apparent only at a later stage: in the case of the axiom "to think it is necessary to be," I would always be able to call up the indubitable existents which contain it and make it itself indubitable, whereas in the case of the axioms of mathematics I would not be able to do this, and the *res* which contain them remaining doubtful, the axioms would also remain doubtful, until such time as I had proved the existence of a truthful God to replace the hypothetical *malus genius*. But Descartes himself declares that the axiom "to think it is necessary to be" is *ab initio* free of all doubt, even that brought on by the *malus genius*. When Descartes states that the axiom "to think it is necessary to be" is not one of those eternal verities which the hypothesis of the *malus genius* puts in doubt, he is distinguishing between the absolute objective necessity of this axiom and the subjective necessity of those axioms—the axioms of mathematics for instance—which become objective only after the arguments derived from the *cogito* have disposed of the fiction of the *malus genius*. (The hypothesis of the *malus genius* in no way destroys the subjective necessity of mathematical propositions and axioms, as Kemp-Smith and others have properly insisted: $2 + 3$ still $= 5$ for me, even while the hyperbolic doubt introduced by the *malus genius* is in operation. It is only the objective necessity of the propositions that is suspended.) Now it does not seem that a subjectively necessary axiom acquires the quality of objective necessity merely by being applied to a concrete datum. The axiom "to think it is necessary to be" does not *acquire* objective necessity by being applied to the concrete datum: *cogito*. On the contrary, the *cogito* supplies only one indubitable term: I think. If I then affirm, as Descartes does, not only that I am, but that, in virtue of the axiom "to think it is necessary to be," I am necessarily, this necessity of my being can be affirmed objectively only in so far as the axiom itself is objectively valid. It seems, therefore, that the *cogito* provides the axiom with an application, but does not give it its objective validity, whereas, on the other hand, the axiom, when applied to the *cogito*, provides it with an objective validity which it does not have in itself. The objective necessity of the axiom must therefore rest, several commentators have concluded, on the eternal necessities contained in the notion of the power and immensity of God. These commentators argue that the certainty of the axiom "to think it is necessary to be," like that of the causal axiom, derives not from any *res* which may be shown to be indubitable as a result of the *cogito*, but from an absolute impossibility pertaining to the "exigencies of existence" in Gouhier's phrase, which are founded directly in God. According to this argument, the axiom "to think it is necessary to be" derives its objective necessity and certainty, its impermeability even to the doubt introduced by the *malus genius*, from God himself, from the act by which God is His own cause. It does not rest on the *cogito* but on the immanent presence in us of the idea of God. The fact that the certitude of the axiom is not only prior to but the condition of the certitude of the *cogito* thus corresponds directly to the fact that God is prior to my own existence, of which He is the condition. The necessity of the axiom "nothing has no properties" being derived directly from the nature of God comes and consecrates from above, so to speak, by way of the axiom "to think it is necessary to be," my intuition of my own thinking. In this way it imposes a necessary link between thinking and being which does not derive directly from any thinking, but from God himself imprinting His idea in us.

Summing up these arguments we find that from the outset there is a strange duality in the *cogito*. It contains two elements, each of which is indispensable to it: the direct intuition of my own thinking, and a necessary principle, the foundation of which must be looked for in God. For Descartes, however, and this is vital to the meaning which the *cogito* had for him and for most rationalists, this duality of self and God remains internal to the subject and does not deprive the *cogito* of its intrinsic rationality or of its validity as a first principle. With Malebranche, for instance, the tension of the duality is broken by the exteriorization of one of its terms, and the consequent recognition that the certainty of my own existence is dependent on an existence beyond me. Malebranche seems to be faithful to Descartes in deducing the *cogito* from the principle "nothingness has no properties," but this principle is known in Malebranche only by being seen in God, by being situated outwith my consciousness, and not, as in Descartes "senti en moi-même." The *cogito* becomes thereby a mere empirical fact, not a rational truth or a first principle of philosophy. Rationality and necessity reside in the divine reason, and the *necessary* connection between thinking and being is not in the *cogito* itself but is explicitly conferred upon it *from outside* the self, by our applying to it a necessary truth which resides in God and which it cannot contain within itself. While it is true that for Descartes the axiom "to think it is necessary to be" seems to be founded in God through the axiom "nothing has no properties," it nevertheless resides in me, in my innate understanding, and I know immediately that it is true and objectively valid without needing to know what I can know only later, viz., that it is founded in the immensity of God's omnipotence. It is enough that I perceive it to be evident immediately·in myself, and that I find that the *malus genius* cannot put it in question, since it contains no actual affirmation of existence. The evidence and necessity of the relation which is established for me between my thinking and my being thereby appears to me as entirely interior to my consciousness and the *cogito* can thus claim to be both a rational truth and a direct intuition, which does not require to be demonstrated by any express appeal to God.

The difficulty of the *cogito*—as well as its historical significance —lies precisely in this union of self-sufficiency and duality. On the one hand its immediacy and rationality, which assure its independence, imply a necessity that seems to have only a subjective foundation—the directly experienced impossibility of denying myself in the act of affirming myself. On the other hand the necessity of the *cogito* is objective and immediately so, because it comes not from myself but from elsewhere, being imposed on myself by God. An objective idealism thus lurks behind the apparent subjective idealism of the *cogito*, and in fact the Third Meditation does seek to found in something other than myself the necessity I discover in myself.

Just as truth for Descartes is at once a divine illumination and a result independently arrived at and freely assented to by the human mind, so the certainty of my own existence is at once self-contained in me and objectively validated by something beyond me. With Malebranche's version of Cartesianism, God is restored to His position as the unique source of all certain knowledge. The innate qualities of the human understanding thereby cease to provide the foundation of science and philosophy. This is the cost of Malebranche's greater coherency. As in so many other cases (the pineal gland, for instance), Descartes prefers an uneasy reconciliation of opposites to strict coherency, and it is precisely in these uneasy reconciliations that the greatness and historical significance of his thinking lies. The deep underlying tendency of Descartes' thought, as his opponents clearly recognized, is the deification of man, the attribution to him of that absolute autonomy, certainty, and self-sufficiency that belong traditionally to God. Concealed within this claim to autonomy and absoluteness, however, is the secret poison that transforms them into total dependence and contingency. No one expressed the duality lurking in the apparent unity of autonomous rational man better than Valéry. In the

"Lettre d'un ami" appended to the *Soirée avec M. Teste*, Valéry writes : "J'imagine qu'il y a dans chacun de nous un atome important entre nos atomes, et constitué par deux grains d'énergie qui voudraient bien se séparer. Ce sont des énergies contradictoires, mais indivisibles. La nature les a joints pour toujours, quoique furieusement ennemies. L'une est l'éternel mouvement d'un gros *électron positif*, et ce mouvement engendre une suite de sons graves où l'oreille intérieure distingue sans nulle peine une profonde phrase monotone: *Il n'y a que moi. Il n'y a que moi. Il n'y a que moi, moi, moi* . . . Quant au petit électron radicalement *négatif*, il crie à l'extrême de l'aigu, et perce et reperce de la sorte la plus cruelle le thème égoiste de l'autre: *Oui, mais il y a un tel* . . . *Oui, mais il y a un tel* . . . *Tel, tel, tel*" (*Monsieur Teste*, 23rd ed. [Paris, 1946], p. 84). By surreptitiously introducing God as the objective guarantor of the autonomy of the self—in such a way, to be sure, that this autonomy seems in no way compromised—Descartes succeeds in holding together the two aspects of the self, its consciousness of itself as utter absoluteness and its consciousness of itself as utter contingency, its apprehension of itself as a plenitude of being and its apprehension of itself as constantly dissolving into nothingness, its desire to realize its own total independence and its need to found itself objectively in something transcending its own self-awareness, its assertion of its complete freedom and its experience of its complete subordination. One of the main themes of Molière's comedy, as we saw in the foregoing analyses of individual plays, is the falseness and imposture of the self that proclaims its independence of and indifference to others. Whereas Descartes is arguing for the autonomy of a universal self, however, the subject of Molière's comedies is an historically concrete self, which in its general form becomes not universal, but a social type. The question of autonomy is raised and answered in Molière only in concrete social terms. At the limit, the problem of the autonomy of Descartes' self is the problem of the autonomy of Molière's *honnête homme*, who, like Descartes himself, accepts his social role as a role, while remaining free of it as a mind. The *honnête homme*, however, is not the central figure of Molière's comedies. It is the false independence of the Dom Juans and the Sotenvilles that Molière laughs at, discerning clearly the contradictions in the pretensions of these outmoded and impoverished grandees.

In Corneille, on the other hand, although some of his heroes have a fairly obvious historical relevance, there is still a tendency toward abstraction, which may partly account for the attempts of literary historians to discover a similarity between the playwright and the philosopher. The self in Corneille, the *moi* of which he writes so generously, is often conceived abstractly in typical Baroque style. This *moi*, however, seeks to incarnate itself historically, and it is in this attempt to achieve a concrete form that its double aspect is clearly visible, as Rousset and Starobinski have amply demonstrated.[2] At the very moment it proclaims: "Je suis maître de moi comme de l'univers," the *moi* is the supreme technician of its own theatricality. "La maîtrise de soi," writes Starobinski (p. 47), "est une activité réfléchie qui suppose le dédoublement de l'être entre une puissance qui commande et une nature réduite à obeir, entre une autorité hégémonique (. . .) et des parties subordonnées. Cette force hégémonique n'est pas tout l'être; pour qu'elle règne, il faut qu'elle réduise au silence d'autres forces, ou du moins qu'elle les cache aux regards du dehors. Ce qui fait la grandeur ostentatoire du héros est aussi ce qui l'engage à dissimuler l'appétit inférieur qu'il refrène en lui-même. Ainsi en va-t-il des rois, lorsque l'amour vient contredire leur passion de régner. S'ils ne parviennent à détruire en eux cet amour, leur souci est alors de le refouler consciemment au plus secret d'eux-mêmes, pour n'en rien laisser paraître au-dehors."

[2] Jean Rousset, *La Littérature de l'âge baroque en France: Circé et le Paon* (Paris, 1954); Jean Starobinski, *L'Oeil vivant* (Paris, 1961). I am particularly indebted for the following remarks on Corneille to the brilliant essay of Starobinski. I agree entirely with Starobinski's analysis of the structures of Corneille's plays. I disagree with him, to some extent, if I am not mistaken, as to the significance of these structures. I have consequently allowed myself to give some of his insights a meaning that he does not give to them.

The heart of the problem of the self in Corneille is not to be looked for among those characters who are satisfied with appearances.

> Il faut (. . .)
> Trouver à ma disgrâce une face héroique,
> Donner à ce divorce une illustre couleur
> Et sous de beaux dehors dévorer ma douleur

says Irène in *Pulchérie* (IV, 1, 1109–12). These lines strikingly recall certain lines spoken by Molière's Amphitryon. They indicate acceptance of a total split between the reality and the appearance of the self. Far more significant are those characters, like Cornélie in *La Mort de Pompée* or Auguste and Emilie in *Cinna*, for whom the task is to be truly that which they present themselves as and to present themselves as that which they truly are ("dissimuler l'appétit inférieur qu'il *refrène en lui-même*"). In fact this involves their shaping themselves according to an ideal model which is no longer appropriated from the outside world of others, but invented by the character himself. "L'on peut croire," says Starobinski (p. 55), "qu'il s'est fait lui-même à partir d'une libre affirmation de ce qu'il veut être. *Etre* et *faire* se répondent à la rime: '*Ce que vous faites / Montre à tout l'univers, Seigneur, ce que vous êtes!*" [3] At the same time this supreme independence must be recognized by others in order that the hero can recognize it himself. The fatal flaw of the hero, the crack in his absolutism is the need he has in order to take cognizance of his absolutism, of the eye of the other. The axiom which in Descartes' *cogito* guaranteed the objective validity of the self that takes cognizance of itself becomes, in Corneille, the world, which in its admiration of the hero and its recognition of his absoluteness guarantees the self-awareness of the hero. In both cases, however, there is equivocation. Descartes interpolates the axiom surreptitiously, without justifying it or explaining its provenance,

---

[3] *Sertorius*, I, 3, 297–98.

in order to preserve the autonomy of the self; Corneille presents the awed admiration of the world as the consequence of his heroes' absolute independence and superiority, whereas in fact it is the *condition* of it.

In his early comedies, Corneille presents his young heroes as completely dazzled by the blinding glory of some supreme beauty. The word *éclat* which recurs so frequently in his works expresses the power of these splendid visions. These beauties do not have to do anything in order to overwhelm all who see them, their victories are effortless and immediate, due only to the inherent power of their presence. In similar fashion, the victories of Louis XIV are almost magical: "Louis n'a qu'à paroître" ("Sur les Victoires du Roi en l'année 1677," *Oeuvres complètes de Corneille*, ed. Marty-Laveaux, Les Grands Ecrivains de France, Vol. X, p. 323, l. 3). For the beholder the danger is great, however, that the fascination of which he is the victim may become a veritable death. Confronted with the plenitude of being of the "God," he himself may easily shrink into nothingness like the moth that burns in the flame. Thus the *éclat* of the beloved, by its very excess, threatens the lover with annihilation. The beauty of Mélite is such, thinks Tircis, that the entire universe is at her feet. And if this is so, where does he stand, obscure and insignificant as he is? Others may well be more favored than he and he has no real assurance that he is loved. The beloved becomes an enigma that he cannot penetrate. "L'objet admirable, dans l'exacte mesure où il est fascinant," writes Starobinski, "ne peut être possédé: il s'impose sans se laisser saisir. Offerte aux regards, mais rendue lointaine par l'intensité même de son éclat, la figure séductrice échappe à l'amour que sa présence enflamme" (*op. cit.*, p. 40). The ruses of his rivals—lies, counterfeit letters, impostures of all sorts—are immediately believed, because the lover is so overwhelmingly convinced of his own nothingness and of the beloved's absolute indifference, but far from removing him from the competition, as they are intended to do, and so freeing him from his fascination, they succeed only in intensifying his obsession with the beloved. Starobinski has drawn attention to the struggles of these early Cornelian lovers to assert their independence of the beloved, and to their failure to do so:

"Un moment vient où la raison se ressaisit et regimbe. Il y a quelque chose d'inacceptable et de dangereux dans ce bouleversement soudain. C'est une faiblesse inavouable, qui livre l'âme sans défense à l'éblouissement. Et pourtant, il est difficile de renoncer aux plaisirs de la lumière: quelle joie d'être illuminé par la beauté! quelle joie plus grande encore d'être source de lumière! D'où la singulière ambivalence de tous les personnages corneliens à l'égard de l'éblouissement. Ils veulent être fascinés et s'en défendent; ils veulent admirer, et ils déclament contre le 'faux éclat':

> Et les dehors trompeurs (. . .)
> N'ont que trop ébloui mon oeil mal éclairé
> (*Toison d'Or*, V, 2) [4]

Ils veulent se protéger, préserver leur indépendance, comme si l'éblouissement risquait de la consumer. Mais ils sont invinciblement attirés par l'éclat de la beauté ou de la gloire; ils ne peuvent renoncer à adorer ce qui resplendit. Alors ils y mettront certaines conditions: il faudra faire en sorte que l'éclat ne puisse plus être suspecté d'être 'faux,' il faudra trouver des gages suffisants qui permettent d'accepter les dehors sans redouter qu'ils soient trompeurs. Il faudra lier la vérité à l'éblouissement" (Starobinski, *op. cit.*, p. 36).

In this extremely acute passage several things remain unexplained. Why is it a *joie* to be illuminated by beauty? In fact it is a *joie* only in so far as this illumination distinguishes the lover from all his rivals. And this also explains why to be illuminated is also a source of anguish and why the greatest joy is in fact to illuminate. As long as he is not himself the source of light, the lover is dependent on the caprices and whims of the beloved; he must con-

---

[4] Aaete to Hypsipyle in *La Toison d'Or*, V, 2, 1904–5.

stantly seek to please her in order to attract to himself that light that marks him out from all his rivals. His insecurity and dependence are such, however, that he lives in perpetual dread of losing or not having the light, of being deceived and thus reduced to total obscurity and nothingness. He is always ready to believe what he fears most: that the light has been withdrawn from him. In his anguish he will often turn against the beloved herself, the cause of all his suffering, or so he imagines. He will lend a willing ear to those who defame and denigrate her or charge her with imposture. As it is not, however, the beloved herself whom he really desires but the superiority over others which he acquires when her light is shed on him, he will not cease to worship her in his heart, whatever appearance of indifference he may assume, as long as others—his rivals—recognize her magic power. For in herself the beloved has no real power. The power she possesses is that which is invested in her by the admiration of the universe; she herself is not the cause of his anguish, since she does nothing to arouse it. The cause of his anguish, *which he places in her*, is in fact in himself. Unable to ground the autonomous being he lays claim to in himself, dependent on the recognition of it by others in order to recognize and experience it himself, he is torn between desire to win this recognition and refusal to admit, even to himself, that he needs it.

Corneille himself makes it clear that rejection and defamation of the idol is mere resentment. Suspicion and calumny are the servile characteristics of valets and weaklings. A truly noble soul having nothing to fear never suspects imposture around him. But this is the case only among equals. Thus Chimène's father recognizes immediately the nobility and generosity of Rodrigue. The moment there is inequality, however, the moment the greatness in the other reduces the self to the status of an inferior, this recognition is withheld and the greatness of the other put in doubt, for the inferior will not avow his inferiority. The refusal to recognize greatness or superiority thus becomes itself the mark of inferiority, of *bassesse d'âme*. The ultimate triumph in Corneille is the triumph of generosity, of a generosity that recognizes the superiority of the other, beloved or prince; and paradoxically this act of generosity restores the admirer to equality with the object of admiration, the lover to equality with the beloved. "La 'reconnaissance' qui survient au dénouement est le résultat d'une désillusion, d'un désabusement. Où donc était l'illusion? Non pas dans l'éblouissement initial, mais dans les soupçons suscités par le rival malveillant . . . la désillusion cornélienne n'est jamais la destruction d'un éclat, elle est l'abolition de l'ombre jetée pas la calomnie sur cet éclat; elle est passage à un éclat supérieur" (Starobinski, *op. cit.*, p. 41).

The political significance of this victory of generosity will be apparent. As long as the hierarchies among men were founded in the mists of antiquity and heredity, as long as each could feel that his place and his dignity were secure and unquestioned, as long as no one felt himself the rival either of his superiors or of his inferiors, the recognition of greatness in another was natural and easy and it implied no derogation for the admirer. The collapse of this traditionally and, as most thought, divinely structured world amid the struggles of individual ambition and acquisitiveness provided the occasion for the substitution of a new structure. The monarch stepped into the chaos and imposed a new order, of which he himself was the summit and the foundation, no longer *primus inter pares* but absolute master and supreme architect of his own universe. Confronted by the dazzling light of this new apparition men could question it, cry imposture, revolt against the absoluteness that reduced them to utter dependency and that seemed to have the power to annihilate them completely. But in the end they did not really want to destroy their idol-rival, for in their struggle with each other he constituted a necessary umpire, a judge capable of distinguishing them by his favors from their rivals. The anarchy of their own passions, their covetousness and greed secured the monarch on his throne and their vanity invested him with absolute power over them. Since they could not accept a fixed place, since each of them coveted the place of his neighbor and contested every superiority, all became equally courtiers, wooers of kings, seekers of favors.

Corneille saw clearly that those nobles who refused to recognize the monarch, who accused him of imposture and fraud and who revolted against him, were simply resentful of a superiority which they in fact recognized by the very fury of their hatred. Cinna's attitude to Auguste is a curious mixture of awe and of resentment. What Corneille did not perceive—or could not perceive—however, was the objective rightness of an accusation that was grounded in the basest of emotions. Corneille does not admit either in the early or in the later plays that the idol, beloved or prince, is nothing in himself, that his prestige rests on the vanity of his idolators and that his supposed absoluteness is itself a myth which he can sustain in his own consciousness only by reading it in the eyes of his subjects, and which he can sustain in the consciousness of his subjects only by carefully and cunningly manipulating their vanity and rivalry. It is because he did not see this that Corneille's comedies remain comedies of intrigue, courtly exercises, while his "tragedies" are never more than heroic dramas. When the idol himself becomes false, the situation that forms the groundwork of Corneille's plays becomes the vast comedy that it is in Molière or the tragedy of wasted and self-consuming passions that it is in Racine.

Corneille constantly maintained, as Starobinski rightly insists, the inherent value of his idols. "L'aveuglement, chez les personnages de Corneille, n'est pas un égarement total, mais une connaissance provisoirement obscurcie, qui retrouvera toute sa clarté dans une illumination instantanée (. . .) L'illusion laisse le monde intact (. . .) Toujours la pièce évolue vers ce moment où les personnages sont vus dans leur vérité, et voient la vérité (. . .) Alors il n'y a que des regards éblouis. Cet éblouissement final est tout différent de l'éblouissement initial (. . .) De l'illumination première à l'illumination dernière, une action a été parcourue: c'est le chemin qui va de la séduction à la vérité, du saisissement instantané à la gloire immortelle" (Starobinski, op. cit., pp. 43–44). For Cor-

neille there are genuinely superior beings, sources of light for all
those around them, deriving their luminosity from no source other
than their own inherent grandeur. More and more Corneille's
characters will aspire to be one of these beings. They will not be
content to be dazzled, they will seek to dazzle; they will strive to
be no longer the spectators of a blinding light, but themselves the
source of blinding light and spectators of their own glory.
"L'éclat," writes Starobinski (*op. cit.*, p. 56), "ne sera plus le
privilège inexplicable qui s'attache à la beauté d'un être, mais la
lumière qui environne les actes et les décisions." The Cornelian
hero comes to assume many of the characteristics associated with
an important current of the Baroque. With respect to the early
plays, his *éclat* will lose some of its mystery. It will cease to be
gratuitous and unexplained, it will be motivated rationally, having
its source in the acts of the hero's own consciousness. At the same
time it will preserve a quality of magic in that these acts of consciousness will emerge suddenly upon the world transforming it
from top to bottom. And instead of acting directly on the world
and on others, this magic power will be only indirectly concerned
with others, by refraction, as it were. Praising the glory of the monarch in his palace of Versailles, Corneille compares him to God
who

> (. . .) jouit dans le ciel de sa gloire et de soi,
> Tandis que sur la terre il remplit tout d'effroi.
>   ("Vers présentés au Roi sur sa campagne
>   de 1676," *Oeuvres complètes*, ed. cit.,
>   Vol. X, p. 305, ll. 23–24)

The quasi-divine figure of the monarch is completely independent
of and indifferent to the effect of his glory on others, nor does he
seek to create any effect. On the contrary his absoluteness is such
that he is his own judge and his own spectator. If his glory fills the
universe with awe, this is merely an indirect by-product of an ac-

tivity that is completely self-contained, self-determined, and self-directed. The monarch-God exults in his own glory and in his own self *tandis que*—quite incidentally and without his even being aware of it, so absorbed is he in the contemplation of his own glory —the mass of trembling mortals looks up in awe.[5] Those heroes whom we have come to regard as typically Cornelian are their own creations, absolute and autonomous products of their own will, having neither father nor mother nor image in which they are formed. They are what they want to be:

Voilà quelle je suis, et quelle je veux être,

says Sophonisbe to Massinisse (*Sophonisbe*, II, 4, 695).

Je suis maître de moi comme de l'univers,

Auguste pronounces (*Cinna*, V, 3, 1696).

[5] Corneille's portrait of the monarch can be compared with Bernini's St. Teresa group in the Cornaro Chapel in the church of Santa Maria della Vittoria in Rome. While the ecstasy of St. Teresa has an audience in the eight members of the Cornaro family whose busts appear behind priedieus arranged along the side walls of the chapel, the ecstasy itself is set on a kind of stage which is *partly protected* by the marble columns supporting the framing aedicula. "When standing on the central axis opposite the group of St. Teresa," writes Rudolf Wittkower (*Gian Lorenzo Bernini*, London, 1955, p. 29), "it becomes apparent that the chapel is too shallow for the members of the Cornaro family to see the miracle on the altar. For that reason Bernini has shown them arguing, reading and pondering, certainly about what they know is happening on the altar, but which is hidden from their eyes." Professor Wittkower emphasizes the relevance of this architectural arrangement, which he considers characteristic of Bernini's work, to the Christian notion of the "mystic hierarchy of things"—man, Saint, and Godhead. "The connection across space between praying figures and the altar," he writes (p. 32), "had (. . .) a specific and intensely religious meaning, and even the counterfeiting of priedieus had originally nothing in common with theater boxes." Bernini's idea, it seems to me, must have been not, indeed, to create a simple theatrical effect, but to avoid creating one, to preserve the St. Teresa group from theatricality. If the saint's ecstasy is being "acted" for our benefit, it cannot be real and authentic. It must therefore be only "incidentally" or "accidentally" visible to the spectator. It is tempting to discern a parallel here between this architectural form and the myth by which the great, while absorbed in their own activity and self-contemplation, are yet "accidentally" the object of the admiration and awe of the universe.

And yet there is a crack in the superbly confident absolutism of these supermen and super-women. They do expect recognition from others and they do expect to arouse fear and respect in others. Their name, the very image of their power, is presented to the world, and it is in the act of presenting it that the supposedly indifferent and self-sufficient hero seeks the confirmation in the eyes of others of the absoluteness to which he lays claim:

> *Le Comte*
> Sais-tu bien qui je suis?
> *Don Rodrigue*
>
>   Oui; tout autre que moi
> Au seul bruit de ton nom pourroit trembler d'effroi.
>   (*Le Cid*, II, 2, 411–12)

Likewise Cornélie will advance toward her interlocutor, bearing her name before her like a flaming shield by which all must be blinded:

> Souviens-toi seulement que je suis Cornélie.
>   (*Mort de Pompée*, III, 4, 1026)

Without the recognition accorded to his name the Cornelian hero is nothing; his absoluteness fades into utter contingency and the plenitude of being he claims for himself shrinks to a terrifying absence of being. *L'infiniment grand* becomes suddenly *infiniment petit*. There are lines in *Suréna* which open up frightening abysses of nothingness:

> Que tout meure avec moi, Madame: que m'importe
> Qui foule après ma mort la terre qui me porte?
> Sentiront-ils percer par un éclat nouveau,
> Ces illustres aieux, la nuit de leur tombeau?
>
>   .   .   .   .
>
> Quand nous avons perdu le jour qui nous éclaire,
> Cette sorte de vie est bien imaginaire,

Et le moindre moment d'un bonheur souhaité
Vaut mieux qu'une froide et vaine éternité.
(I, 3, 301–304, 309–313)

Commenting on these lines Starobinski writes: "Ce qui triomphe maintenant, c'est l'envers de la gloire; la nuit (. . .) Tout se passe alors comme si la vérité dernière n'appartenait pas à l'éblouissement, mais au fond nocturne sur lequel l'éblouissement avait choisi d'apparaître. Quand se taisent l'artifice et la fiction, quand l'imaginaire est dénoncé, quand la volonté n'invente plus ses décrets absolus, seule demeure cette obscurité confuse: un froid mortel se produit. Qui veut vivre doit produire de grands actes, et leur donner force de vérité. C'est-à-dire ne jamais cesser de faire la guerre au vide nocturne (. . .) la muer en lumière éclatante. Encore faut-il que cet éclat soit accueilli et soutenu par le regard complice des peuples et des générations prises à témoin. L'individu a beau déployer la plus surprenante énergie, il n'est rien sans l'écho que lui renvoie l'admiration universelle. Que l'assentiment extérieur lui soit refusé, que le secours du spectateur ébloui vient à manquer— reste alors une ombre qui s'agite vainement sur un tréteau ou seule la mort est certaine" (*op. cit.*, p. 68). In the end the Cornelian hero is as dependent on his admirers as they are dependent on him. The other is the unavowed condition of the hero's "absolutism," just as God is the unavowed condition of Descartes' absolute ego. When Descartes went on to deduce from the imperfection of his being the existence of a perfect being, he was merely making explicit an assumption that in fact underlay the initial and supposedly autonomous affirmation of his own being. No man can lay claim to absoluteness without falling into an imposture that appears grotesque as soon as it is perceived. If nowadays we find the solemnity with which Don Diègue or Cornélie brandish their names a trifle ridiculous, it is because we perceive the weakness behind the apparent power, the petty feudal reality behind the Baroque mask. These superb heroes reveal the chasm of nothingness behind them each time they ask "Sais-tu bien qui je suis?" We need only take the question literally in order to prick the bubble. The flaming shield of the name becomes a piece of limp cardboard; "Cornélie" turns out to be no better than "Mamamouchi."

Descartes and Corneille seek to stave off the void that threatens to engulf them by proudly and confidently asserting their autonomous existence. The strained quality of the self-assertion itself betrays the inward terror that provokes it. Yet there is a significant difference between these two affirmations of self. While neither the philosopher nor the dramatist openly admits the dependence of the self, the unavowed guarantor is different in each case. For Descartes it is God himself; for Corneille it is other men. In his ethical writings Descartes does take account of others, and quite a few articles in the *Traité des passions de l'âme* concern the effect of our behavior on others and the manner in which we can construct a certain appearance of ourselves (e.g., articles 180–81). On the whole, however, Descartes distinguishes carefully between the judgment of others and actions that are right and good in themselves. He himself warns against confusing *orgueil* and *générosité*, *gloire* and the *satisfaction intérieure* of having acted rightly (157–58). The soul finds true peace, he insists, only if its resolutions are founded on the knowledge of truth (49). Though it is not easy to acquire certainty in moral matters, we do our duty if we act as best we can in any given circumstance. There is no sign in Descartes of any need of grace to accomplish the good, no sign of any awareness of original sin; a man can feel confident in judging his own actions and his own self. His own approval is tantamount to divine approval, and he finds peace and security in the consciousness that he has acted for the best. Once again in Descartes, consciousness is assumed to be the impartial spectator and judge of its own acts; once again, however, this judgment can acquire objective validity only if we grant the co-presence alongside and in some manner within the individual consciousness of the divine mind. Just as the ego cannot found itself objectively without an axiom that in itself rests on God, so the moral life can be given no objective validity, even though Descartes does not avow this openly, without the final judgment of God.

In Corneille's case there is obviously no room for any real distinction between *gloire* and *sentiment intérieur* or between *orgueil* and *générosité*. The unavowed presence which gives objective value to the hero's contemplation of his own triumphant being is no other than the world itself. Even a supremely wicked and evil person, provided he commands the admiration and awe of the universe, can experience a divine plenitude of being which raises him beyond all judgments of a moral nature. Many of Corneille's heroes are in fact of this sort; he himself even took the trouble to justify theoretically the irrelevance of moral judgments to heroic greatness.

It is clear from our brief analysis of Descartes and Corneille, however, that individual man is never absolute and autonomous, whatever he may claim for himself. He must constantly seek to ground his being objectively in something beyond himself, and he cannot find in his own self-transcendence the objectivity he requires, for consciousness of self transcends itself as consciousness of consciousness of self, and so on in an infinite spiral. In despair the individual consciousness attempts to appropriate the alien consciousness which alone has the power to assure its objectivity, believing that through the possession of this alien consciousness it will avoid both the Scylla of skeptical solipsism and the Charybdis of utter dependence on others, and so resolve the contradiction of objectivity and autonomy that is so intolerable to it. Thus Descartes injects into consciousness the axiom by which alone the *cogito* becomes not an experiential truth but a rational and objectively necessary one. In fact, however, as we argued earlier, the validity of the axiom rests on the nature of a God independent of and distinct from the self-conscious self. Likewise the Cornelian hero is often presented to us as exulting in the spectacle of his own glory. "Sa grande âme s'ouvroit à ses propres clartés," Corneille will write of Louis XIV ("Vers présentés au Roi sur sa campagne

de 1676," *Oeuvres, ed. cit.,* X, p. 306, l. 40). This pure self-sufficiency is a myth, however, for the universal audience before which
the hero stands and which he seems to subsume in his own self-
contemplation is in fact the unavowed and independent ground
of this self-contemplation.

The autonomous, quasi-divine self of Descartes and of Corneille
is an imposture, for it rests on a fundamental contradiction. Self-
awareness has an empirical but not an ontological priority. In so
far as Descartes can be said to "find" God in himself, God ceases
to be the transcendence in which alone the self discovers its objective ground, and in so far as he finds himself in God he loses the
absolute autonomy of existence to which he lays claim. The attempt to appropriate others into the self is equally futile. Once
appropriated, the consciousness of the other loses its power to
ground my being, which it had when it was free and which was the
very power I wished to appropriate. If I am to find a foundation for
my being, I must allow the independence and absoluteness of other
consciousnesses, so that I may see myself reflected in them; thereby,
however, I cease to be absolute and autonomous myself and I fall
into dependence upon them.

If the non-autonomous nature of the self be admitted, it becomes
folly to ground my own existence on other selves, since they are as
dependent and contingent as I am. Many of those who took this
position in the seventeenth century envisaged God rather as their
contemporaries envisaged the King. Like the courtier who longs
for and is elated by a sign of recognition from the monarch, the
Jansenists of Port Royal longed for and were elated by tangible evidence of God's favor (*miracle de la sainte épine*, etc.); and as the
courtier lives in constant fear of not being noticed by the King, so
Pascal is terrified by "le silence de ces espaces infinis." In the God
of Pascal and the Jansenists, power and will have completely over-
shadowed love. This God is unmistakably Baroque. To be ignored
by Him is to be in dis-grace and to sink, abandoned to oneself,
into utter nothingness. The significance of the Jansenist attack on
the Thomist doctrine of sufficient grace as well as of Arnauld's at-

tack on frequent communion becomes apparent. "Turn ye unto me, saith the Lord of hosts, and I will turn unto you" (Zechariah, 1:3). The Pascalian and Jansenist position reduces me to nothing before the Lord. I may turn to Him and He may not turn to me. I may look and there will be only emptiness, I may hearken and there will be only silence. *Vere tu es Deus absconditus*. The awareness of himself as *derelict*, abandoned of God, is the deepest and most anguished experience of seventeenth-century man. The silence of God, that God on whom alone all his being rests, is the condition of seventeenth-century tragedy.

The comic equivalent of the silence of God is the indifference of the world. In the universe of comedy it is not God whose recognition of us has to be elicited and whose non-recognition of us reduces us to anguish and fear of being swallowed up in nothingness. The other becomes the God in whom all power is invested.

Corneille sous le masque de Molière is the title of a recent work that takes up once again Pierre Louys's attempt to show that Corneille was the author of Molière's comedies.[6] More accurately we might argue that Molière's comedies are an unmasking of Corneille.[7] The exploding of the Cornelian myth of the autonomous and proud hero leads directly to the comedy of Molière, on the one

[6] Henry Poulaille, *Corneille sous le masque de Molière* (Paris, 1957).
[7] Cf. on this topic J. D. Hubert, "L'Ecole des Femmes, tragédie burlesque," *Revue des Sciences Humaines*, 97, 1960, pp. 41–52; and P. H. Nurse, "The Role of Chrysalde in L'Ecole des Femmes," *Modern Language Review*, 51, 1961, pp. 167–71. Nurse points out that "even Chrysalde's long stoic-inspired discourse in Act IV on the importance of controlling the will can be justified for its esthetic impact in heightening the comedy, for it emphasises the basic comic incongruity between Arnolphe's assumed *persona* of a masterful mind, shaping his own destiny, and his real impotence in the face of adversity. It is highly significant in this respect that Molière puts into Arnolphe's mouth, at the end of Act II, a line taken from Corneille's play *Sertorius:*

C'est assez.
Je suis maître, je parle: allez, obéissez.

Arnolphe is comic precisely because his 'Cornelian' postures are unmasked as false; the authoritarian masquerade collapses whenever it is put to the test, and he who preaches to Agnès an ascetic *morale* based on the repression of instinct can only grimace with helpless rage when Chrysalde later turns the argument of rational self-discipline against him."

hand, and to the tragedy of Racine, on the other, though of course
it is not suggested that either Molière or even Racine deliberately
set out to "debunk" Corneille.[8]

The order and harmony of the French classical universe is constantly being threatened by the tensions of unresolved conflict. The
supreme art of the period rests on an infinitely subtle tension between form and content, and within the form itself, among its different elements. The finely molded Alexandrines of Racine express terrifying forces of passion and willfulness which constantly
threaten but are always contained by the structure that at once
conceals and manifests them. The brutal willfulness of Pyrrhus,
the sadistic sexuality of Nero, the scheming and desperate power
mania of Agrippine are concealed and at the same time revealed
by the noble Alexandrines in which they find expression. The ceremonial of the verse, like the courtly ceremonial introduced into
France by Louis XIV, conceals and reveals a secret world of anguish and violence. Even the wild cries of Hermione, the dark
despair of Phèdre, the nihilistic voluntarism of Athalie do not break
the formal pattern of the verse. Yet within this formal pattern, betraying what at first sight seems so well hidden, what movement
and disturbance there is, what swellings and retractions, what swift
rises and falls from overwhelming passion to constrained and icy

---

[8] On the contrary, Molière's predilection for Corneille is well known. It
might in fact be appropriate to insist here that the discussion of Descartes and
of Corneille (particularly of the latter) in the preceding pages was in no
way intended to be exhaustive of those writers. Certain elements that are
only implicit in the work of Corneille, for instance, were emphasized because
of their relevance to the situations that I believe to be fundamental to
Molière's comedy. A very serious distortion of Corneille's work as it is in itself
inevitably results, however, from emphasizing elements in it that are significant above all retrospectively and in the light of subsequent developments.
We should never overlook, for example, the historical interval between Corneille and Racine. Corneille in his time saw that the rebelliousness of the
nobility was a mark of its weakness and inferiority as well of a certain heroism,
and he enjoined on it the generosity of recognizing the monarch in whom the
hope and the future greatness of France lay, while at the same time enjoining
on the monarch that he show magnanimity toward his brave and rebellious
subjects. The artist's vision, it seems to me, was correct. Corneille's royalism

politeness! The universe of Racine is the universe of the seventeenth-century Baroque, but it is a revelation as well as an expression of this universe, of the violence and imposture on which it is built. The quasi-divine mask of the great is removed and no illusions are left. Nero replaces Caesar Augustus as the type of the superior hero. No longer "masters of themselves as of the universe," no longer presented as indifferent to and incommensurably superior to the universe that surrounds them, the heroes of Racine must extract by violence from their "subjects" the recognition of that power and absoluteness which they desire but do not possess. The Racinian passion is invariably the desire to obtain the recognition and submission of the other. This passion arises out of the indifference of the other and feeds on it. The celebrated ladder structure of *Andromaque* reveals this with striking clarity. Every one of the characters, with the exception of Andromaque who is at the top of the ladder, turned to her dead husband, seeks to attract the recognition of a being who ignores him. "Me cherchiez vous, Madame," asks Pyrrhus as Andromaque walks by without deigning to notice his presence. In the midst of an anguished confession, Hermione suddenly sees that Pyrrhus is not even listening to her, that his attention is elsewhere:

---

expresses the highest truth of his time: his presentation of the sovereign is not a lie, not at least in the earlier dramas. Indeed it is a mark of Corneille's great honesty that he does reveal the ambiguity of motivation of a hero such as Auguste. (Does Auguste pardon out of inward *générosité* of soul or out of concern for his appearance and public image? The text itself is not clear on this score.) By Racine's time the experience of absolutism and of courtly society was sufficient to make a deeper understanding of the nature of the monarch-idol and his relation to his worshipers possible. Racine would have fallen short of truthfulness if he had continued along the lines of Corneille. We cannot expect an author to have an experience and understanding of the world that the historical limitations of his existence inevitably place beyond his reach. We can expect him only to strive toward the greatest possible understanding of his world and its problems within the historical conditions of his experience. I am keenly aware that without the corrective of this historical perspective my own pages on Corneille might well give the impression that this great artist was in some sense more obtuse than his successors. This, I would like to emphasize, was not my intention.

Vous ne répondez point? Perfide, je le voi,
Tu comptes les moments que tu perds avec moi!
Ton coeur, impatient de revoir ta Troyenne,
Ne souffre qu'à regret qu'un autre t'entretienne.
Tu lui parles du coeur, tu la cherches des yeux.
                    (*Andromaque*, IV, 5, 1375–79)

The "désir curieux" of the emperor Nero for the captive Junie is likewise excited by the latter's indifference to him:

Quoi, Narcisse? tandis qu'il n'est point de Romaine
Que mon amour n'honore et ne rende plus vaine,
Qui dès qu'à ses regards elle ose se fier,
Sur le coeur de César ne les vienne essayer:
Seule dans son palais, la modeste Junie
Regarde leurs honneurs comme une ignominie,
Fuit, et ne daigne pas peut-être s'informer
Si César est aimable, ou bien s'il sait aimer?
                    (*Britannicus*, II, 2, 419–26)

She too passes by without noticing the emperor, full of thoughts other than the thought of him, while he, fascinated by this indifference to him, watches for her:

Cette nuit je l'ai vue arriver en ces lieux,
Triste, levant au ciel des yeux mouillés de larmes [9] . . .
                    (*Britannicus*, II, 2, 386–87)

We are far from Corneille's hero, lost in rapt contemplation of his own glory while the world looks on in irrelevant admiration. On the contrary, it is the hero who is here obsessed by the world and the world that is indifferent to him. Nero retires to his room, but he is haunted by the image of this girl who is hardly aware of his existence:

[9] As Andromaque looks up to Hector, ignoring Pyrrhus, Junie looks up to heaven, ignoring Nero.

Je l'ai laissé passer dans son appartement.
J'ai passé dans le mien. C'est là que, solitaire,
De son image en vain j'ai voulu me distraire.
> (*Britannicus*, II, 2)

The humiliation of the hero is intensified when he finds himself
the rival of his "inferior." "Xipharès mon rival?" exclaims Mithridate (*Mithridate*, III, 4, 1009), as he ruminates on the relations of
his wife and his son. "Dis-moi: Britannicus l'aime-t-il? (. . .) Que
dis-tu? Sur son coeur il auroit quelque empire?" Nero inquires
(*Britannicus*, II, 2, 427, 435) and discovers himself the rival of his
weak and despised half-brother. Hermione is the rival of a foreign
slave, that *Troyenne* for whom, daughter of Helen and princess of
Greece, she has such contempt.

The hero's attempt to extract the other's recognition of him fails
to the very degree that it succeeds and reveals his utter impotence
in the measure that it manifests his power. The lover finds himself
recognized in the tears and anguish which he provokes in the beloved. Pyrrhus sees Andromaque seek him out and fall finally at
his feet, but he cannot escape the fact that in recognizing him she
at the same time affirms her withdrawal from him, for it is
Astyanax-Hector, and not Pyrrhus himself who has provoked this
recognition. "Ah! je n'en doute point: c'est votre époux, madame, /
C'est Hector qui produit ce miracle en votre âme," Céphise exclaims on learning of Andromaque's decision to accept Pyrrhus'
terms (IV, 1). In Act II, scene 6 of *Britannicus*, Junie has to reject
coldly the young man she loves in order to save his life. Nero's
blackmail of Junie repeats Pyrrhus' blackmail of Andromaque.
Nero watches the scene secretly: he can observe in the tortured
eyes of Junie that constant presence of himself to her, even in physical absence, that marks her final recognition of him. At the same
time, however, as the tears and suffering of Junie satisfy him at last
that he exists for her, they also mark her rejection of him, a rejection that is now irrevocable. The victim recognizes her torturer.

only to reject him, and the torturer must continue his torture in order to enjoy his recognition by his victim. Nero is not present in absence to Junie as Hector is present in absence to Andromaque. He has to watch her through a crack in the curtains and force the awareness of his presence on her. The furthest extreme of a passion that expresses itself in sadistic violence is murder, the annihilation of the beloved whose existence is a constant denial of the lover's autonomy and absoluteness. In desperation Hermione plans the assassination of Pyrrhus, but her rapid *volte-faces* confirm the contradictoriness we mentioned earlier. The success of her enterprise must also be its failure, the exercise of her power must also be the avowal of her impotence. While violence and sadism, contradictory as they are, sustain the lover in a constant agony of frustration, death marks not only the annihilation of the beloved but the annihilation of the lover. Humiliated by the beloved's refusal of him, the lover can still find himself reflected in the tears which he causes to flow from the eyes of the beloved. But once he has destroyed the beloved, the beloved has escaped him for ever. The lover finds himself reduced to nothing, unrecognized, bereft even of his anguish and frustration. Hermione expresses this absolute emptiness of all her being in the short, dying phrases of her final lines to Oreste:

> Adieu. Tu peux partir. Je demeure en Epire:
> Je renonce à la Grece, à Sparte, à son empire,
> A toute ma famille;
> > (*Andromaque*, V, 4, 1561–63)

Hermione's physical suicide simply incarnates the metaphysical suicide she had already committed when she had Pyrrhus assassinated. Filled with what Malraux calls the *volonté de déité*, the characters of these early tragedies of Racine transfer the divinity they desire for themselves to whoever, by resisting or ignoring them, proves his superiority to them. This "superior" being becomes thereby the source of their own being. By killing Pyrrhus Hermione at the same time destroys herself. The independent and autonomous hero of Corneille is unmasked completely in this Racinian vision, for we are all seen to be dependent on others. The hero, the "superior being," is himself never absolutely and objectively superior. Hermione herself invests Pyrrhus with his superiority. Objectively he is enslaved to Andromaque. The autonomy of the Cornelian hero and the admiration, of which he is for Corneille the just object, peter out in the plays of Racine in the impotent sadism of a Nero, the humiliating jealousy of a Roxane or a Mithridate, the pathetic despair of an Hermione. We may feel compassion for these victims of human vainglory; we cannot think of them as quasi-divine.

Goldmann has pointed out that in both *Andromaque* and *Britannicus* the tragic character is peripheral.[10] He does not consider the worldly characters who occupy by far the greater part of these two early plays to be tragic. For reasons which will shortly become clear, I think Goldmann is right. The tragic character occupies the center of the Racinian stage for the first time with *Bérénice* and achieves fullest expression only in *Phèdre*. What we observe in the early plays is the unmasking of the heroic imposture. Racine moves only gradually toward the tragic catastrophe, which he realizes most successfully with *Phèdre*. The tragic character in Racine knows that all worldly desire is corrupt. He rejects the world in which the Neros and the Hermiones pursue their goals of desire and destruction. This world hardly even figures in *Bérénice*, for instance. It does not constitute a temptation for the tragic hero. What may tempt him is the achievement of value in the world. Desiring to fulfill their love in marriage, Titus and Bérénice are pursuing a goal which is a value in itself. Likewise, Phèdre chooses in Hippolyte a being who by his purity seems to her to offer the possibility of a true relation in the world. If Phèdre's interest in

[10] Lucien Goldmann's brilliant study of Pascal and Racine, *Le Dieu caché* (Paris, 1955), will be alluded to frequently in the following pages.

him had been no more than a desire to overcome a resistance, as
"love" is for the characters of the early plays and as it might, at
first sight, appear to be for her, the discovery of a rival would have
excited her passion still further. Instead, Phèdre's discovery of
Hippolyte's love for Aricie dashes her hopes and reveals to her the
enormity of her error and illusion. After an initial outburst of rage
and jealousy, she immediately returns to consider herself:

> Que fais-je? Où ma raison se va-t-elle égarer?
> Moi jalouse! Et Thésée est celui que j'implore!
> .   .   .   .
> Misérable! et je vis? et je soutiens la vue
> De ce sacré soleil dont je suis descendue!
> (*Phèdre*, IV, 6, 1264–65, 1273–74)

Filled with horror at her *faute*, she sees herself condemned without
hope of pardon:

> Où me cacher? Fuyons dans la nuit infernale.
> Mais que dis-je? Mon père y tient l'urne fatale;
> Le sort, dit-on, l'a mise en ses sévères mains:
> Minos juge aux enfers tous les pâles humains.
> Ah! combien frémira son ombre épouvantée,
> Lorsqu'il verra sa fille à ses yeux présentée,
> Contrainte d'avouer tant de forfaits divers,
> Et des crimes peut-être inconnus aux enfers!
> Que diras-tu, mon père, à ce spectacle horrible?
> Je crois voir de ta main tomber l'urne terrible;
> Je crois te voir, cherchant un supplice nouveau,
> Toi-même de ton sang devenir le bourreau.
> (*Phèdre*, IV, 6, 1277–88)

Unlike the Cornelian hero, the Racinian hero is anything but
master of himself and of the universe. He is weak, seeking at best
the right and the just, listening for the voice of God, but not always

hearing it distinctly, nor sure that he will have the inward strength
to execute what he takes to be God's will. Titus continually asks
himself whether it is truly the will of the gods and of the people
that he send Bérénice away:

> Je viens percer un coeur qui m'adore, qui m'aime.
> Et pourquoi le percer? Qui l'ordonne? Moi-même.
> Car enfin Rome a-t-elle expliqué ses souhaits?
> L'entendons-nous crier autour de ce palais?
> Vois-je l'Etat penchant au bord du précipice?
> Ne le puis-je sauver que par ce sacrifice?
> Tout se tait; et moi seul, trop prompt à me troubler,
> J'avance des malheurs que je puis reculer.
> Et qui sait si, sensible aux vertus de la Reine,
> Rome ne voudra point l'avouer pour Romaine?
> Rome peut par son choix justifier le mien.
>   (*Bérénice*, IV, 4, 999–1009)

In *Bérénice* the word of the gods does come through clearly. Titus
does not distort the signs he has received in an effort to bend them
to his own will. The sacrifice of their happiness by Titus and Bérénice is not, however, as it is in Corneille, a triumph of human will
over human passion, a drawing together of the entire personality
in an act of will, an affirmation of self. On the contrary, it is a victory of divine will over human will, of piety over love. Far from
affirming the unity of the personality, this victory tears it asunder
in bitter anguish. For these two lovers there is no home and no
repose apart from each other.

> Depuis cinq ans entiers chaque jour le la vois,
> Et crois toujours la voir pour la première fois,

says Titus simply (II, 2, 545–46). Stunned by the very thought of
separation from her lover, Bérénice stretches out her hands toward
him and asks:

> Dans un mois, dans un an, comment souffrirons-nous,
> Seigneur, que tant de mers me séparent de vous?
> Que le jour recommence, et que le jour finisse,
> Sans que jamais Titus puisse voir Bérénice,
> Sans que de tout le jour je puisse voir Titus?
>   (IV, 5, 1115–18)

Bérénice ends with a victory, but a victory that is one of under-standing, renunciation, and suffering, that shows the hero not in the light of regal glory and majesty, but in the heaviness and soli-tude of his heart.

To Phèdre the voice of God speaks as clearly. She bears from the beginning the full weight of the knowledge of her guilt. Even before she appears on the stage we learn from Théramène that she is

> (. . .) atteinte d'un mal qu'elle s'obstine à taire,
> Lasse enfin d'elle-même et du jour qui l'éclaire
>   (*Phèdre*, I, 1, 45–46)

and her own first words are an avowal of her weakness and dere-liction:

> Je ne me soutiens plus: ma force m'abandonne.
> Mes yeux sont éblouis du jour que je revoi,
> Et mes genoux tremblants se dérobent sous moi.
>   (I, 3, 154–56)

With great delicacy of insight Goldmann draws attention to the stage direction that follows: "Elle s'assied." Weary, sick at heart, oppressed with guilt and shame, Phèdre is the very opposite of the proud heroes of Corneille. Where they seek the full light of day and the admiring gaze of the universe, Phèdre cannot bear the light:

> Dieux! que ne suis-je assise à l'ombre des forêts!
>   (I, 3, 176).

The report of Thésée's death seems, however, to indicate that the gods do not frown on Phèdre's love for her step-son. Titus in his weakness could speculate on the will of the gods, but there was nothing at all except the voice of his own desire to still the voice of conscience. With the report of Thésée's death, the silence of the gods becomes terrifying. How to interpret this news? Does it mean that Phèdre can declare herself to Hippolyte, that she can legitimately seek to realize in the world the pure love for which she longs? The voice of Oenone, of convenience and everyday commonsense, the voice of a world ignorant of all piety and value provides an interpretation that seems to justify Phèdre's love:

> Vivez; vous n'avez plus de reproche à vous faire:
> Votre flamme devient une flamme ordinaire.[11]
>
> (I, 4, 350)

Phèdre weakens and succumbs to the temptation of Oenone. Constantly, however, she is reminded of her guilt, even though she is now embarked on a journey from which there is no going back. The humiliation she experiences at Hippolyte's indifference to her is in itself a sign of her guilt:

> J'ai dit ce que jamais on ne devoit entendre.
> (III, 1, 742)

The awareness of guilt in these words overshadows the shame of pride.

The moment she allows the hope that she can reconcile justice and piety with her own desire to enter her heart, Phèdre finds herself surrounded by enigmatic silence. The gods no longer speak. All the signs become subject to endless interpretation, sources of innumerable errors. But this silence is one only for the heart that

[11] Note the subtle and cruel irony of "flamme ordinaire." The moment she tries to realize the pure love she envisages with Hippolyte, this love becomes impure and Phèdre's "flamme" becomes a "flamme ordinaire."

will not hear. In her innermost soul Phèdre knows that if she cannot read the signs or hear the word of the gods it is because she is listening to the voice of her own desire. In the great speech at the end of Act IV she asks her father's forgiveness for her sin. At the same time she ponders on the mystery of her fate. Why, she asks, was she abandoned by the gods? Why did they refuse her their clear guidance and the strength to resist the temptations of her own desire?

> Pardonne. Un Dieu cruel a perdu ta famille;
> Reconnois sa vengeance aux fureurs de ta fille.
> Hélas! du crime affreux dont la honte me suit
> Jamais mon triste coeur n'a recueilli le fruit.
> Jusqu'au dernier soupir de malheurs poursuivie,
> Je rends dans les tourments une pénible vie.
> (IV, 6, 1289–94)

The end of every tragedy is a mystery. The tragic hero is at once the most sublime and the most wretched of men, chosen by the gods yet abandoned by them, constantly searching the heavens for a sign from them, and constantly confronted with blank silence. He cannot justify his sin; nor, however, can the world condemn it. Phèdre's repentance and Thésée's banal condemnation of her are separated by an abyss. No one can know what Phèdre's ultimate sentence will be. Certainly it is not for the world to pronounce it. Will she, having lost her life, find it again, and having gone to the end of the night, will she again come out into the light of the sun —that sun which never ceased to haunt her throughout her dark journey? Or will the gods execute the terrible sentence she foresaw with horror in the first act? Why are we so forsaken in our hour of need? Tragedy does not give the answers. It only raises the questions. All or nothing—for the tragic hero this is the only possible choice, and to choose otherwise is to deny his being. He cannot ask the question of the meaning and value of human life in terms of the inessential and the contingent. He can ask it only in the

most radical and absolute terms. Whatever the final answer for
Phèdre, she alone in the play, wretched as she is, experiences the
real mystery of existence, she alone lives the problem of man's fate.
As Goldmann wrote at the end of his short essay on this play:
"Pour les yeux essentiels de la divinité, le cadavre n'est pas derrière
la scène, là où se trouve le corps de Phèdre, mais sur le devant, dans
la personne du roi qui va régner et gouverner l'Etat" (Goldmann,
op. cit., p. 440).

What lies behind the heroic self-sufficiency of the Cornelian
supermen is revealed in those slaves of passion who inhabit Racine's
earlier plays. In *Phèdre* we have his ultimate vision of the tragic
plight even of the just and well-meaning man. Against Auguste's
"Je suis maître de moi comme de l'univers," we can set Phèdre's
pitiful moan:

> Moi régner! Moi ranger un Etat sous ma loi,
> Quand ma foible raison ne règne plus sur moi!
> (III, 1, 759–60)

It seemed to us that Goldmann was right to regard as tragic figures in Racine only those characters who are aware of a world of
value and being *beyond* this world, who found their existence in a
transcendence that is truly objective, even if invisible, and to exclude from the tragic universe those characters who spend their
lives pursuing their own being in another whom they themselves
have invested with absoluteness and divinity. The lives and passions of the latter dissolve in the futility of illusion, wasted effort,
and pride, but the destiny of the tragic character is never futile. It
raises the question of being and value, it does not deny being and
value. No one feels that the passion of Oedipus or Lear or Phèdre
is futile.

The silence of God, in which we find the foundation of the tragic
consciousness of the seventeenth century, is precisely that which
encloses the question of being and value. We have seen how this

silence of God is at the heart of *Phèdre*. Let us now examine how the indifference of the world is, as we argued earlier, the foundation of seventeenth-century comedy.

ᗏ ᗏ ᗏ

We tend, occasionally, to think that some of Molière's comedies are gay and light-hearted, whereas others are more somber and ambiguous. A Jourdain or a Magdelon presents audiences with no problems, but an Alceste leaves them perplexed and uncertain. Jourdain and Magdelon are figures of unalloyed fun, according to this view, pure fools as anyone can easily discern; Alceste, on the other hand, does not seem very funny and to some he even seems almost tragic. Oddly enough, Molière's contemporaries do not seem to have entertained these uncertainties. We hear, of course, of opposition to *Dom Juan* and to *Tartuffe*, but we know that there was also opposition to *Les Précieuses ridicules* and to *L'Ecole des femmes*. Most people appear to have laughed at *all* the comedies. As for ambiguity, there is, as we shall see, a good deal of it in *Le Bourgeois Gentilhomme*. A very sentimental reader might find Monsieur Jourdain almost as pathetic and as misunderstood as Alceste.[12] Romantic interpretations of *Le Misanthrope* can easily be extended to all the plays. While it must be recognized that there is a difference between two types of comedy in Molière, between the comedies of the *Bourgeois Gentilhomme* type and the comedies of the *Misanthrope* type, if we may make a loose initial distinction, this difference cannot be perfunctorily attributed to the fact that one group is funnier than the other or less mysterious and ambiguous. We should rather try to elucidate it by examining the more or less complex form of the comic hero's relation to the world.

The final judge and the transcendence to which the tragic hero

[12] In Pirandello's *Henry IV*, Molière's Jourdain does indeed appear in a new and deliberately tragi-comic guise.

of Racine looks for the ground of his being and the value of his existence is God. The comic hero, on the other hand, looks to others to give him his value and his being. The sign of recognition that Phèdre expects from God, the Jourdains, the Cathoses, and the Alcestes expect from the world. Whereas one group of Molière's characters make no attempt to conceal their idolatry, however, another group of characters affect to despise the idols whose recognition they desire, postulating instead their own superiority and setting themselves up as idols for others to worship.

With the notable exceptions of Dom Juan and Jupiter, the majority of Molière's best known characters are bourgeois of one degree or another. Within this bourgeoisie it is nevertheless possible to distinguish an upper and a lower range. While Alceste obviously belongs to a social class very close to the nobility, perhaps even to a long established family of *noblesse de robe*, Jourdain is a very ordinary, if rather well-off, merchant, the son of a draper. Corresponding to this hierarchy of ranks, there is the hierarchy of Paris and the provinces. While it is not possible, as it would doubtless be in the work of later writers like Balzac or Stendhal, to identify absolutely attitudes and modes of being in Molière with social class, it is broadly speaking true to say that the "open" comic heroes, those who recognize their models and superiors without shame, are characters of the lower bourgeoisie and the provinces. The "closed" comic heroes, those whose resentment of their idols, precisely for being idols, leads them to deny their recognition of them, belong rather to the upper bourgeoisie and the aristocracy, to those groups that are close to social equality or who have social equality with their idols. The vanities and illusions of the first group, being openly avowed, have a quality of naïvety that makes comedies like *Le Bourgeois Gentilhomme* or *Les Précieuses ridicules* hilariously funny. It is not hard for us to discern and transcend the folly of Jourdain. The vanities and illusions of the second group are less easily discerned as comic, for they resemble those we ourselves conceal, those of "in-groups," courtiers, artists, professional people—"tous ces métiers dont le principal instrument est l'opinion que l'on a de soi-même, et dont la matière première est l'opinion que les autres ont de vous," as Valéry describes them (*Teste*, "Lettre d'un ami," *ed. cit.*, p. 82).

In the first case the desire *to be distinguished* is a desire to be distinguished from one group by being recognized as a member of a superior group, the superiority of which the aspirant himself necessarily recognizes. "Mon Dieu! ma chère," exclaims Cathos, "que ton père a la forme enfoncée dans la matière! que son intelligence est épaisse, et qu'il fait sombre dans son âme!" "Que veux-tu, ma chère," Cathos answers contritely. "J'en suis en confusion pour lui. J'ai peine à me persuader que je puisse véritablement être sa fille, et je crois que quelque illustre aventure, un jour, me viendra développer une naissance plus illustre" (*Précieuses*, sc. 5). "Lorsque je hante la noblesse, je fais paroître mon jugement," says Jourdain to his wife, "et cela est plus beau que de hanter votre bourgeoisie" (*BG*, III, 3). A little later he accuses his good wife of having "les sentiments d'un petit esprit, de vouloir demeurer toujours dans la bassesse" (*BG*, III, 12). There is nothing secret about the reverence these characters have for their idols, and they seek quite openly to elicit from their silent or masked or absent divinity the sign of recognition that for them is a sign of salvation. "Pour moi," says Mascarille ironically, "je tiens que hors de Paris, il n'y a point de salut pour les honnêtes gens." "C'est une vérité incontestable," answers Cathos (*Précieuses*, sc. 9). "Est-ce que les gens de qualité apprennent aussi la musique?" asks Jourdain. "Oui, Monsieur," says the Maître de Musique. "Je l'apprendrai donc," Jourdain rejoins without hesitation (*BG*, I, 2).

More complex and less immediately comic in their desire to achieve distinction are those who will not share it with anybody, who refuse the models that everyone else accepts and who, far from recognizing their idols, go to great lengths to conceal their mediation by others. They make a point of loudly scorning the ways of the world, those very ways that a Jourdain and a Cathos revere so unquestioningly. Madame Pernelle in *Tartuffe* refuses the courtesies of her daughter-in-law: "Ce sont (. . .) façons dont je n'ai pas besoin" (I, 1, 4). Harpagon likewise condemns the manners of the world. He reproaches his son with the very imitation that is the butt of Molière's satire in *Le Bourgeois Gentilhomme:* "Je vous l'ai dit cent fois, mon fils, toutes vos manières me déplaisent fort: vous donnez furieusement dans le marquis (. . .) Je voudrois bien savoir, sans parler du reste, à quoi servent tous ces rubans dont vous voilà lardé depuis les pieds jusqu'à la tête, et si une demi-douzaine d'aiguillettes ne suffit pas pour attacher un haut-de-chausses? Il est bien nécessaire d'employer de l'argent à des perruques, lorsque l'on peut porter des cheveux de son cru, qui ne coûtent rien" (*L'Avare,* I, 4). Arnolphe has his own taste in women and it is not that of everyone else:

> Moi, j'irois me charger d'une spirituelle
> Qui ne parleroit rien que cercle et que ruelle,
> Qui de prose et de vers feroit de doux écrits,
> Et que visiteroient marquis et beaux esprits!
> (*Ec. femmes,* I, 1, 87–90)

Sganarelle, like Harpagon, refuses the fashions of his contemporaries. His brother, he complains, would have him ape the manners of the "jeunes muguets." But he will have none of

> (. . .) ces petits chapeaux
> Qui laissent éventer leurs débiles cerveaux,
> Et de ces blonds cheveux, de qui la vaste enflure
> Des visages humains offusque la figure.
> De ces petits pourpoints sous les bras se perdants,
> Et de ces grands collets, jusqu'au nombril pendants.
> De ces manches qu'à table on voit tâter les sauces,
> Et de ces cotillons appelés hauts-de-chausses.
> De ces souliers mignons, de rubans revêtus,
> Qui vous font ressembler à des pigeons pattus . . . etc., etc.
> (*Ec. Maris,* I, 1, 25–34)

No, Sganarelle will follow his own fashion in complete indifference to everyone else—"Et qui me trouve mal, n'a qu'à fermer les yeux" (*ibid.*, 74).

The rejection of society is not, clearly, confined to articles of clothing and a few superficial customs. It is the entire way of life of everybody else that these characters ostensibly reject. People enjoy company, entertainment, balls, receptions, conversations? Madame Pernelle will have none of them. On the contrary she will make a virtue of solitude, abstention, and even brusqueness. Money is spent on carriages, fine clothes, amusements? Harpagon will not spend it at all. Instead he will treasure and revere it for itself. Everybody wants an entertaining, witty, and sociable wife? Arnolphe and Sganarelle will choose a "bête," and they will value precisely that in her which nobody else seems to admire, her ignorance and simplicity. The world is full of flattery and soft with compromise? Alceste will be brusque, frank, and scrupulously uncompromising. Society observes certain codes of behavior, of decency, and of propriety? Dom Juan will flout them and will be blatantly indecent and immoral. These characters—Harpagon, Arnolphe, Sganarelle, Alceste, Dom Juan, Madame Pernelle, Orgon—refuse to recognize that they are mediated by others; the almost childlike guilelessness of Jourdain's fascination with the nobility gives way in them to a subtle concealment by the character of his true desires, and of their source. Far from recognizing their mediators, these characters pretend they have none. Several of them appear to be in thrall to idols; Orgon and Madame Pernelle to Tartuffe, Philaminte and her daughter to their Trissotin, Harpagon to his "*cassette.*" The last example reveals these idolatries for what they are, however. As we pointed out in our chapter on *Tartuffe*, Orgon is bent on using Tartuffe as much as Tartuffe is bent on using him. The *femmes savantes*, like the *dévot*, see in their idols an instrument for asserting their superiority to the world around them, and it is on this world that their eyes are really turned. "Nul n'aura de l'esprit hors nous et nos amis" declares Armande: "Nous chercherons partout

à trouver à redire, / Et ne verrons que nous qui sache bien écrire"
(*FS*, III, 2, 924–26). Likewise Orgon sets himself up *against* society as the only true Christian in it. The function of Tartuffe
is to guarantee Orgon's superiority to *everybody* else. In the case
of Harpagon the idolatry of the instrument has reached its climax
in total alienation and fetishism. In all three plays the idol is
used to assert an opposition to society, a distinction from it and
a superiority to it. Philaminte and her daughters do not really
care about science, Orgon and his mother do not really care
about religion (both texts illustrate this amply), and Harpagon
does not really care about wealth—on the contrary, his wealth
is used to keep him poor. What these characters want above all
is *to be distinguished*, but they refuse to adopt the usual method
of social advancement and privilege, since this method offers only
a *relative* superiority to others, whereas the superiority they desire
is *absolute*. They are comic not only because there is a constant
contradiction between what they are and what they affect to be,
but because their attempt to transcend all social superiorities and
to reach an absolute superiority misfires. *La Cour et la ville* will
not be convinced that stringent devoutness or erudition are more
desirable than social advantage and worldly success. They are no
more envious of the spiritual insights of Orgon and the telescopes
of Philaminte than they are of Harpagon's beloved "*cassette*."
Philaminte, Orgon, and Harpagon do not see this of course.
Harpagon imagines that everyone is after his *cassette*, that there
is a vast plot to deprive him of this mark of his superiority. Likewise Orgon imagines that his whole family is plotting to remove
Tartuffe out of jealousy. Arnolphe and Sganarelle, convinced that
the eyes of the entire universe are upon them and that everybody
desires to corrupt the virtuous young persons, in the possession of
whom they find the mark of their superiority, shut them up and
guard them as jealously as Harpagon guards his *cassette*.[13] While

[13] In the same way Rousseau believed, rightly or wrongly, that all his friends
were trying to seduce Thérèse.

choosing to be *different* from everybody else, while turning away from what they castigate as the vain ambitions of the world in order to devote themselves to "authentic" values, these characters nevertheless have to believe that they are envied by everybody else. Thus while Orgon raves that the world in its corruption does not appreciate the saintliness of his Tartuffe, he also imagines that everyone is jealous of his special relation with Tartuffe; while Arnolphe prefers *une bête*, who will interest no one, to an elegant society girl who would be the object of everybody's attention, he still imagines that the entire universe is pursuing his Agnès.

Underlying the apparent indifference of the Arnolphes and the Orgons there is in reality the same fascination with others that we find among the Jourdains or the Cathoses. Orgon could after all practice his devotions quietly, without ostentation. Arnolphe and Sganarelle could avoid being made cuckold by remaining bachelors. But they never entertain this notion. The true object of their craving is not a faithful wife—or in Orgon's case salvation through Christ—but the recognition by others of their superiority. The goals which they choose to pursue are not after all pursued for themselves, nor do they themselves select them as they imagine they do. They are determined for them by their very opposition to society. Arnolphe and Sganarelle are not content to do without a wife; on the contrary; but she must be the opposite of all other wives. Orgon is not content to withdraw inwardly from public life; on the contrary, he continues to live a remarkably public life, but one which is the opposite of the life everyone else leads. Harpagon is not content to renounce material riches; he continues to pursue them but he gives them a meaning and a value absolutely opposed to the meaning and value they have for everyone else. All the posing of the Orgons and the Arnolphes and the Harpagons —though in this last instance it must be admitted that the pose has become truly the only reality of the man; Harpagon has so completely alienated himself that he can even run after his own body (cf. *L'Avare*, IV, 7)—cannot conceal that they are as

dependent on others and as mediated by them, whatever claims
to independence they may make, as simple fools like Jourdain
and Cathos or Magdelon. Their basic folly is the same and all
their cleverness is used not to eradicate it, but to disguise it from
themselves and others. This becomes particularly clear in *La
Comtesse d'Escarbagnas*. At the end of this play the Countess,
having failed to distinguish herself in her little provincial society
by aping the noble ladies of the Court, decides to distinguish
herself by inverting this imitation, by seeming to reject it in favor
of a superiority all her own. She marries Monsieur Tibaudier just
to prove her absolute superiority to everyone. "Oui, Monsieur
Tibaudier," she says, "Je vous épouse pour faire enrager tout le
monde" (sc. 9). Unable to attract the gaze of the world by acting
with it, the Countess resolves in desperation to attract the attention
she craves by acting *against* it. The world and not Monsieur
Tibaudier remains, however, the object of her fascination.

In fact, of course, the world is not the least bit *enragé*. The play
closes with the Viscount's ironical: "Souffrez, Madame, qu'en
enrageant, nous puissions voir ici le *reste* du spectacle" (italics
added). The countess has failed absolutely to fix the world's attention on herself in the way she wanted. On the contrary, it has
watched her as it would watch a comedy—which the Countess'
behavior *in fact is*—and it is now off to watch another comedy,
another stage play. The truth is that it is not the comic heroes
who are indifferent to the world, it is the world that is indifferent
to them. It is not they who fascinate the world; they are fascinated
by it.

The world, indeed, has to be forced by the hero to give him its
attention. It is only when Harpagon tries to impose the rules
of his crazy universe on others that they begin to be seriously
concerned with him. It is only because Philaminte, Armande, and
Bélise are not content to be "blue-stockings" quietly on their own,
but insist on organizing the lives of Chrysale and Henriette around
their own obsessions that father and daughter find themselves

forced to take note of them. If Arnolphe had not forcibly embroiled Agnès in his plans, Horace and everyone else would simply have regarded him as an eccentric mysogenist and would not have given him a second thought. This seemingly inevitably imposition of themselves on others is a revealing characteristic of the comic heroes of Molière. It confirms that their professed indifference to others is a sham. Far from seeking to live the good life himself, Alceste is concerned only to impress on others that they are not living it and that they do not have his superior moral vision. As we pointed out in our chapter on *Le Misanthrope*, the hero's withdrawal to his desert at the end of the play is itself a *spectacular* gesture, and it is for this reason one that will constantly have to be renewed and revived. It is by no means final. Dom Juan is not simply indifferent to the world: he has to arouse its wrath—and thereby its attention—by perpetually flouting its rules, seducing its virgins and wives, blaspheming against its God. The sadism of Orgon has already been alluded to; it is in no way exceptional in the work of Molière. Orgon's relation to Mariane has its counterpart in the relation of Harpagon to Elise or Cléante, of Argan to Angélique or little Louison, of Monsieur Jourdain to Lucile.

❧ ❧ ❧

In the comedies of Molière the hero's transcendence is the world of others. The silence of this world is intolerable to him, but he is obliged to *force* it to speak and recognize his existence. In the early tragedies of Racine, as we have already suggested, the hero's transcendence is also the world of others and he too has to resort to violence in order to have himself recognized. It is not surprising, therefore, that sadism is a characteristic shared by comic and tragic heroes alike. This parallel of the early Racinian heroes and of the comic heroes of Molière can be pursued in some detail.

Almost all Molière's comedies oppose ruse to ruse, hypocrisy to hypocrisy, violence to violence: how are we to choose between Jupiter and Amphitryon, Alceste and the two *marquis*. Orgon and Tartuffe, Dandin and Angélique, Argan and Béline? Likewise how are we to choose between Pyrrhus and Hermione or between Hermione and Oreste or between Nero and Agrippine? That salvation and purity are impossible in the world forms part of the tragic vision of Racine. In Molière also participation involves compromise. In a world in which fathers brutalize their children, mothers are jealous of their sons, guardians stultify their wards, no one who participates can be innocent. The only weapon against violence and blackmail is ruse and hypocrisy. "La sincérité souffre un peu au métier que je fais," Valère admits; "mais quand on a besoin des hommes il faut bien s'ajuster à eux; et puisqu'on ne sauroit les gagner que par là, ce n'est pas la faute de ceux qui flattent mais de ceux qui veulent être flattés" (*L'Avare*, I, 1). Lamenting the fact that sons have to get into debt on account of "la maudite avarice des pères," Cléante protests: "et on s'étonne après cela que les fils souhaitent qu'ils meurent" (*L'Avare*, II, 1). Covielle in *Le Bourgeois Gentilhomme* mocks his master for the naïve honesty of his dealings with Jourdain: "Ne voyez-vous pas qu'il est fou? et vous coûtoit-il quelque chose de vous accommoder à ses chimères?" (*BG*, III, 13). In a world in which the only law is willfulness and the only authority is tyranny, no one can remain pure without becoming a victim. Elmire, Horace, and Valère do not seek out ruse and hypocrisy, but they cannot escape them either, for these are the instruments of survival. Even little Louison in *Le Malade Imaginaire* has to learn how to deal with her father's tyranny and violence by cunning and deceit. Those who remain pure and innocent risk becoming victims, like Mariane in *Tartuffe* or Angélique in *Le Malade Imaginaire*, and if they escape this fate it is only because someone more energetic and less scrupulous has intervened in their behalf. Sometimes they do indeed become victims, as Alcmène does, and sometimes they preserve their innocence through an enigmatic absence or abnegation of desire which places them outside the world, like Eliante in *Le Misanthrope* or Elvire in *Dom Juan*, after her conversion. These characters are as peripheral in Molière's comedies as Racine's Junie, whom Goldmann adjudges the sole tragic character in *Britannicus*. Goldmann saw—rightly it seems to me—that the *innocent stratagème* by which Andromaque hoped to foil Pyrrhus' attempt at blackmail seriously compromises her tragic stature. A similar problem was encountered by Molière in *L'Ecole des femmes*, where Agnès has to be at the same time desiring, active, and innocent. If we look closely at the text, we find that Agnès never *consciously* disobeys Arnolphe. Both her desire for Horace and her active participation in the plot against Arnolphe are conceived entirely on the level of instinct. Only in this way could Molière preserve the innocence of his heroine, while at the same time allowing her to act in pursuit of her own desires.[14]

In both Molière's comedies and Racine's early tragedies the main characters are moved primarily by their desire to force the world to recognize them. In both, the instruments of this desire are imposture and sadism. In both, the heroes fail to make the world break its silence. Racine's characters find themselves refused in the very suffering they inflict on those whose recognition they demand. The comic hero's victims defend themselves against his tyranny by ruse and hypocrisy, and he thereby becomes for them not the transcendent subject of his intention but an object to be tricked and manipulated. The mock-recognition of Jourdain at the end of *Le Bourgeois Gentilhomme* or of Argan at the end of *Le Malade Imaginaire* has its counterpart in the mock recognition of Oreste by Hermione in *Andromaque* or in the scenes between Nero and Agrippine in *Britannicus*. If we look up the scale in *Andromaque* from Oreste to Andromaque herself we find that

---

[14] This aspect of Agnès' behavior was pointed out to me by Mr. Eugenio Donato in a paper he prepared for one of my graduate seminars. I am very happy to acknowledge my debt to him.

for every character the character above is a transcendent subject who is adored and yet at the same time resented precisely on account of this transcendence, which negates the transcendence that the idolator desires and claims for himself. If we look down the scale, we discover that for every character the character below is an object to be manipulated and used. The refusal of the "upper" character to recognize the "lower" one confirms the "lower" character in his adoration and at the same time intensifies his desire to reverse the positions. The same pattern is found in the comedies of Molière, though in less schematic form. The verbal battles that make up almost the whole of *Andromaque* have their counterpart in innumerable scenes in Molière's comedies.

If we examine some of the structural elements of *Andromaque* and *Britannicus* in particular, it is impossible not to see in them the ingredients of comedy. The celebrated ladder structure of *Andromaque*, to which we have already alluded, is in fact a characteristically and traditionally comic one from Shakespeare to Marivaux.[15] In *As You Like It*, the folly and illusion of love-vanity is emphasized by the travesties: Silvius loves Phebe who

[15] In an interesting paper, "Tragische und komische Elemente in Racines 'Andromaque': eine Interpretation," *Forschungen zur romanischen Philologie*, Heft 3, 1958, Harald Weinrich traces the history of the *Liebeskette* theme and shows that it is traditionally a comic one. Racine, however, "sucht die Tragödie. Trotz der latenten Komik des Handlungsschemas" (p. 13). Weinrich goes on to examine how Racine succeeded, in his view, in shaping this latently comic material into a tragedy. According to Weinrich, the latent comedy in the situation serves to *heighten* the tragic effect. I quote from p. 16 of his paper, where he discusses the character of Hermione in particular: "Die stolze Helenatochter, (. . .) von einem Verschmähten verschmäht, stürzt in einem Abgrund der Schmach. Selbst bei Orest, den sie ihrerseits verschmäht, muss sie ein schadenfrohes Lachen befürchten:

> Quelle honte pour moi, quel triomphe pour lui
> De voir mon infortune égaler son ennui!
> Est-ce là, dira-t-il, cette fière Hermione?
> Elle me dédaignait; un autre l'abandonne! (II, 1)

Hier ist wieder eine Stelle, an der die Liebeskette deutlich sichtbar wird. Die Liebeskette mit ihrer immanenten Komik. Denn in dieser Szene ist das Komische in der Form der Lächerlichkeit, ja der Schmach für Hermione gegenwärtig. Alle Komik der Liebeskette stürzt als Schmach auf sie ein. So

loves Rosalind—Ganymede who loves "no woman," but Orlando. In *A Midsummer Night's Dream*, the illusory prestige of the beloved idol is delightfully exposed by means of the spell which inverts all the previous relations while maintaining and even intensifying the passions that inform them. Helena loves Demetrius who loves Hermia who loves and is loved by Lysander. Under the spell the situation alters: Hermia loves Lysander who loves Helena who loves and is loved by Demetrius. The meaning of the comedy is revealed by the infatuation of Titania, the Queen of the Fairies, for Bottom, the weaver, in his ass's costume. The same structure appears again, much later, in Proust: Saint-Loup loves Rachel who loves the polo player who loves André. (Note

---

steht sie nun im Zentrum der Tragik, einer Tragik als Schmach. Sie ruft Pyrrhus zu:

> Vous veniez de mon front observer la pâleur,
> Pour aller dans ses bras *rire* de ma douleur. (IV, 5)

Diese Worte stehen in dem berühmten *couplet d'ironie*, dem tragischen Höhepunkt des Stückes. Hier ist nicht nur das Schicksal einer Unglücklichen, hier wird die Tragik potenziert durch den ungehemmten Ausbruch der Komik der Liebeskette in Gestalt der Schmach für Hermione, nicht nur verschmäht, sondern auch noch *verlacht* zu werden. Auf dieses Ridikulum antwortet Hermione dann nur noch mit einem abgrundtiefen Hass gegen alle, von denen sie sich verlacht wähnt, gegen Andromache, Orest und den lebenden Pyrrhus." Weinrich concludes that Racine had to struggle to avoid the comic implications of his material ("die drohende Komik zuruckzudrängen") but that he succeeded on the whole in doing this and that one of the means he employed was indeed the utilization of the comic material for the purposes of tragedy. "Die 'Andromaque' ist keine Tragikomödie, sondern eine Tragödie. Und sie ist so tragisch, weil sie so leicht komisch hätte werden können" (p. 18).

Weinrich's argument is extraordinarily interesting and suggestive. One might well wonder, however, whether *Tragik als Schmach* leaves tragedy with any real or objective meaning. What, in fact, has objectively changed to transform a comic situation into a tragic one? Surely it is only that the subjective anguish of the character or characters has been taken seriously and invested by the author with a dignity that it does not have in comedy, since the comic writer takes great care to point out the grotesque discrepancy between objective reality and subjective thoughts and emotions. (It is unlikely, in fact, that Pyrrhus in the arms of Andromaque would give Hermione a thought, not even to laugh at her). The *peur du ridicule* is indeed a highly serious matter and a cause of grave concern—to the courtier. Since his entire existence is a social one and all his being is at the mercy of his worldly judges, the fear of ridicule can be truly the most terrible and powerful emotion he feels.

how the travesty element in Shakespeare is taken up again by
Proust in the last of these relations. The meaning of all the
infatuations is revealed by the homosexual relation that crowns
them just as the key to all the infatuations in A *Midsummer
Night's Dream* lies in Titania's love for an ass, and not even a
real one at that!) Without making his situation blatantly comic,
Proust does emphasize the sameness of these enslavements. They
constitute a tiresome *ronde* of futility and illusion. If we do not
laugh, we can at least smile at the stupidity and blindness of these
characters as they pursue the will o' the wisps that they have
themselves invested with reality. Oreste loves Hermione, who
ignores him and loves Pyrrhus, who ignores her and loves Andromaque, who ignores him and remains faithful to her dead husband.
The situation is strikingly similar to those we find in Shakespeare
or Proust, and Goldmann has rightly underlined the utter futility
and inauthenticity of all these characters:

> Avec Hermione, Oreste, Pyrrhus, nous sommes dans le monde de
> la fausse conscience, du bavardage. Les paroles ne signifient jamais
> ce qu'elles disent; ce ne sont pas des moyens d'exprimer l'essence
> intérieure et authentique de celui qui les prononce, mais des in-
> struments qu'il emploie pour tromper les autres et se tromper lui-
> même. C'est le monde faux et sauvage de la non-essentialité, de la
> différence entre l'essence et l'apparence (*op. cit.*, p. 356).

Now this world is precisely the world of the comedies of Molière,
a world of vain words and names and appearances, a world in
which the characters pursue empty titles and hollow forms.

Instead of bringing out the sameness of the passions in *Andromaque*, Racine expends all his talent on particularizing them, on
giving a highly individual and particular physiognomy to his
characters. To the extent that he succeeds, he saves his play from
degenerating into a ridiculous and empty ballet. Certain criticisms
of the sameness of the characters suggest, however, that he did
not succeed fully. Despite all Racine's talent, Oreste, Hermione,

and Pyrrhus remain as much the same basic character as Monsieur
Jourdain, Cathos, Philaminte, or Argan. Their infatuations, their
constant *volte-faces*, their interminable play-acting for themselves
as well as for others are profoundly ignoble. Only the passion and
solemnity of the verse saves them, but at some cost to the play,
for the contrast between the noble lines and the ignoble and
inauthentic thoughts and feelings they express sometimes brings
the play itself to the brink of ridicule. (Stage performances reveal
this more clearly than a reading of the text.) The imperfection
of this play must be attributed to a lack of vision on the part of
Racine himself. It was certainly not technical or poetic talent that
he stood in need of. He simply did not see that the situation he
was trying to present as tragic was in its deepest nature not tragic,
for there is no tragedy of vanity.

The *coquetterie vertueuse* of Andromaque substantiates our
judgment of this play. Lemaitre was quite right to raise the issue
of Andromaque's relation to Pyrrhus and of her *innocent stratagème*.[16] Let us, however, disregard the rather wild theory according to which Andromaque is actually attracted to Pyrrhus. If we
were to entertain it, the comic structure of the play would be
complete and the entire work would be irremediably frivolous.[17]
Let us rather consider Andromaque's behavior in the way Goldmann and most critics suggest, as an attempt to beat the world
at its own game and so preserve both her son and her fidelity to
her husband. Goldmann argues, once again I think quite rightly,
that the *stratagème* of Andromaque seriously weakens her tragic
stature, transforming her rather into the heroine of a *drama*. "Si
Andromaque devait rester une tragédie," he writes, "il fallait, à

[16] Cf. also Voltaire's comment that Racine's tragedy is "un peu affaiblie
par quelques scènes de coquetterie et d'amour, plus dignes de Térence que de
Sophocle" ("Remarques sur le troisième discours du poème dramatique" (of
Corneille), *Oeuvres*, ed. Beuchot, 36, p. 520).
[17] It is well known that Racine's audience laughed when Pyrrhus uttered
the lines

> Crois-tu, si je l'épouse,
> Qu'Andromaque en son coeur n'en sera pas jalouse?

partir de la scène 4, la traiter en coupable qui finit comme Phèdre par reconnaître sa faute" (*op. cit.*, p. 358).[18] The use of ruse against the world of ruse is characteristic, as we have seen, of the world of Molière's comedy. The dissociation of ends and means is a comic and dramatic motif, however, never a tragic one.

The structure of *Britannicus* recalls in many respects that of *Amphitryon*. The great hero, the proud and mighty monarch-God, is fascinated by the slip of a subject who ignores him and prefers a mere mortal. In the agony of his vanity he becomes the slave of his subject and finds himself obliged to descend from his lofty superiority in order to trick and confound—or murder—his humble rival. In *Britannicus*, as in *Andromaque*, the tragic character—or rather the only character who has any authenticity at all and is susceptible of tragic treatment—is peripheral. Nero, Agrippine, and Narcisse occupy the center of the play, just as Jupiter and Amphitryon occupy the center of Molière's comedy. Junie is only their victim, as Alcmène is the victim of the protagonists of the comedy.

We might well wonder how a structure which in the work of Molière is comic acquires a tragic meaning in the work of Racine. Even if we argue that these early plays of Racine are not truly tragic, we must at least recognize that they are dramas, and the question remains: Why are they not comedies? The answer may be sought, partly at least, in the relation of each of the two authors to the society in which he lived.

Racine was born into a typical family of *robins*. His grandfather was comptroller of the *grenier à sel* at La Ferté-Milon, his father was *greffier du grenier à sel* and *procureur au bailliage* in the same town. On his mother's side, the family held similar positions in the towns of Picardy—Soissons, Crépy-en-Valois, Château-Thierry. Both families were completely won over to Port-

---

[18] The problem of *Andromaque* has been recognized by most academic critics. Mornet judges it "encore une pièce romantique" (D. Mornet, *Jean Racine* [Paris, 1943], p. 108).

Royal and the Jansenists. It was in the home of the Vitarts, relations of the Racines, that Lancelot and later Singlin found refuge from the persecutions of which Port-Royal was intermittently the object. The family seems to have fallen on hard times, for there was no fortune and no situation for the young Racine. He had to make his own way. He first tried to do so without success through his maternal uncle Antoine Sconin, prior of the *chanoines réformés* of the cathedral church of Uzès. While Mornet leads one to believe that Racine knocked at his uncle's door on the instigation of his family, Goldmann suggests that this attempt to make his fortune in the church by drawing on the influence and patronage of his uncle represented a serious betrayal by Racine of one of the cardinal points of Jansenist doctrine, a betrayal which may well have caused him considerable anxiety, especially when it failed to produce any results. "La réaction la plus naturelle à cet état de choses," writes Goldmann, "était un ensemble de sentiments ambivalents, aussi bien à l'égard de Port-Royal qu'à l'égard du 'monde' " (*op. cit.*, p. 448). The failure of the Uzès venture, however he regarded it, did not cause Racine to withdraw from the world. On the contrary, it propelled him further into it. He sought to win his way more directly by acquiring a reputation for wit and by flattering the monarch (*La Nymphe de la Seine*, 1660; *Ode sur la convalescence du roi, Renommée aux Muses*, 1663). This time he succeeded. He received money from the King's chests and by 1663 he was being admitted to the *lever du roi*. The first plays—*La Thébaïde* (1664) and *Alexandre* (1665)—marked a complete breach with his Jansenist family background and education, and a total adherence to the world and the values of the Court. His family and his teachers were horrified. His aunt Agnès de Saint-Thècle Racine wrote in 1663 conjuring her *cher neveu* "d'avoir pitié de votre âme, et de rentrer dans votre coeur, pour y considérer sérieusement dans quel abîme vous vous êtes jeté (. . .) Vous ne devez penser à nous venir voir," she adds; "car vous savez bien que je ne pourrois pas vous parler, vous sachant dans une état si déplorable et si contraire au christianisme" (*Oeuvres de Racine,* Les Grands Ecrivains de France, Vol. VI, pp. 521–23). Racine did not give up the court. Saint-Simon and Dangeau wrote of him as an assiduous and successful courtier. Spanheim said that the King liked him to read to him at his bedside. He was permitted to have the armorial bearings to which the family laid claim—the *cygne* (cyne), minus the *rat!*—painted on his carriage. When the King suffered from insomnia, he asked that Monsieur Racine sleep in his bedroom. He was involved in the biggest scandal of Louis XIV's court, the *affaire des poisons* and la Voisin, in her deposition, accused him of having poisoned Mademoiselle Du Parc. Racine remained a courtier all his life.

At the same time there is no reason to doubt that Racine had a "bad conscience," as Goldmann puts it, about Port-Royal and the Jansenists. Even Mornet who is unfavorable to the idea of a Jansenist Racine admits that "il resta lié d'une étroite affection avec ses amis jansénistes et (. . .) il mit un réel courage à les aider, à les défendre dans les persécutions qui les poursuivaient avec un acharnement sans cesse plus impitoyable" (Mornet, *op. cit.,* p. 204). His final disgrace seems to have been provoked by some act in which he defended Port-Royal and criticized the monarchy.

The case of Racine is not untypical. The Jansenism of his family is fairly characteristic of many families of *robins* at the time, as Goldmann has abundantly demonstrated. Goldmann cites several cases of the dissatisfaction of the *robins* at the progressive diminution of their rights and privileges in favor of the royal officers. Even a non-Jansenist like Omer Talon seems to sympathize with the reaction of a *Premier Président du Parlement* at a *lit de justice* where the King, contrary to all precedent, took the votes of the presidents of the *Parlement* after those of the princes and cardinals: "M. le Premier Président . . . avoit été si fort surpris . . . qu'il fut sur le point de supplier le Roi de le décharger de sa charge, et lui permettre de se retirer" (quoted by

Goldmann, p. 145). Goldmann's findings are by no means isolated. Individual studies of particular provinces, such as Burgundy, furnish similar evidence of the dissatisfaction of the *robins*, of their resentment and their impotent criticism of the monarchy, on which, despite all their discontents, they knew that they depended utterly (cf. G. Roupnel, *La Ville et la campagne au XVII siècle; étude sur les populations du pays dijonnais* [Paris, 1926]). "L'Etat monarchique dont ils (les robins) s'éloignaient progressivement sur le plan idéologique et politique," writes Goldmann, "constituait néanmoins le fondement *économique* de leur existence *en tant qu'officiers*, et membres des Cours souveraines. D'où cette situation paradoxale par excellence (. . .) d'un mécontentment et d'un éloignement par rapport à une forme d'Etat—la monarchie absolue—dont on ne peut en aucun cas vouloir la disparition ou même la transformation *radicale*. Situation paradoxale qui s'est trouvée encore renforcée par une mesure géniale de Henri IV, la Paulette qui, d'une part, renforçait la situation sociale et économique des officiers en augmentant considérablement la valeur de leurs offices qu'elle transformait en biens patrimoniaux, et d'autre part rendait les officiers bien plus dépendants d'une monarchie qui agitait en permanence le spectre du refus de renouveler le droit de l'annuel" (p. 133). It is in this situation that Goldmann sees the "infrastructure" of Pascal's *Pensées* and of *Phèdre*.

The position of Racine was even more acutely contradictory than that of the *robins* who continued to hold office in the provincial cities or who, in the only gesture of revolt that was open to them, retired to Port-Royal. Racine had to bear all the burden of an ambiguous existence in the very heart of the Court itself. By birth, by education, by religious conviction, he was deeply opposed to the life he was leading; but he was ambitious and he wanted to make his way. He must often have thought in the midst of his flatteries and intrigues of the lessons he had learned in his youth from his aunt, from his grandmother, and from his Jansenist teachers. He must have been deeply conscious of his own deg-radation. And at the same time he was so intimately involved in the life of the Court that he must have experienced intensely all the anguish of fear and vanity that the Jansenist in him con-demned and recognized as sinful. In his life Racine never gave up the world of the Court, but his work is a growing rejection of it. He presents the strange picture of a consummate courtier whose literary production is a progressive revelation of the willfulness, the vanity, the cruelty, and the futility of Court life.

Racine's own involvement in the life of the Court, his own experience of pride and vanity, his own desire to conquer, and his own fear of being rejected undoubtedly led him to give to the intrigues of the Court and to the anguish of the courtier a prestige and a dignity which they would not have had for him had he been able to distance himself from the Court and from himself. It was not only the lords and ladies of Louis XIV's Court who saw them-selves reflected in an Hermione or an Oreste, it was Racine him-self. Even while one part of him condemned and rejected the entire mode of existence represented by characters of this kind, his own experience of it was too intense and real, and the im-portance he himself attached to the recognition of the Court was too great for him to see the futility of the fears, desires, and pre-tenses of his princes and princesses. For this reason his early plays present the strange combination, to which we have already drawn attention, of a comic structure and a tragic content. This comic structure is the structure of the Court, from which Racine was able to free himself only slowly and painfully. The Court in *Andromaque* and *Britannicus* occupies the center of the stage while the characters we defined as tragic stand on the periphery. In the course of Racine's literary development, however, as has been pointed out, the Court came to occupy a more and more peripheral position, to assume more and more the character of in-essentiality, while the tragic character moved more and more toward the center. With *Phèdre* this process has been completed.

The long silence that followed *Phèdre* is not an accident. Having written it, Racine had achieved both his own personal liberation and the most perfect expression of his tragic vision.

The development of Racine's theatre gives us a clue to the real meaning of his earlier plays. In fact they do not deal with the same material as the comedies of Molière. The Court is rarely at the center of Molière's work. The comedies almost always deal with what is below it or anterior to it. Usually Molière's perspective —that of *honnêteté*—is equated with that of the Court. The Court is mirrored in the comedies only to the degree that it failed to live up to its own theoretical ideal of *honnêteté*.

The difference between Racine's treatment of the theme of rivalry and Molière's treatment of it illustrates that while Racine's early "tragedies" are *discoveries* of the actual futility of the Court, Molière's comedies are mockeries of that which no one in the society of *la Cour et la Ville* could take seriously any more—the pretensions of provincial noblemen, the excesses of learned ladies, the vanity of wealthy merchants. In *Amphitryon* and in *Dom Juan* the hero's desire is inspired by a rival who is his inferior. Jupiter desires Alcmène because he wants to win her from Amphitryon; Dom Juan desires the young woman of whom he tells Sganarelle because he is jealous of her innocuous and quite ordinary lover. In both cases the "superior" character is *recognized* as dependent on the "inferior" one, and in this way his claim to superiority is exposed and laughed out of court. In Racine the rivalry situation is less clear. Racine had to discover weaknesses which were not generally recognized. The strong and well-established thus *discover* that they have rivals in the weak and dispossessed, and the audience shares in this discovery. Thus Hermione is *confronted* with the rivalry of the despised and captive "Troyenne"; Nero *finds out* that Britannicus is his rival for Junie's favors; Mithridate *learns* that his rival is his son Xipharès.

The obvious fascination that the Court exercised on the *robin* and even, one suspects, on many Jansenists, makes their rejection of it suspect. The dissatisfaction of the *robins* cannot be the *cause*, it can only be the *condition* of a tragic vision of the world. What this dissatisfaction causes is resentment, and the resentful *robin*, while rejecting the Court, is constantly obsessed by it. Alceste, not Phèdre, incarnates this figure. Racine's own development as a dramatist of truly tragic calibre required that he transcend a vision of the world caused by his experience of pride and humiliation and that he attain a superior vision, of which this experience was no doubt the condition, but in which it had been understood and overcome. Before *Bérénice* this has not happened. The opposition of Andromaque or of Junie and the world in *Andromaque* and *Britannicus* is too stark, too violent to be truly tragic; and the predominant role played by the world in these early plays, as well as the strange prestige with which it is invested, demonstrates amply that the author himself was still far more deeply concerned with the world of men than with the world of God. Junie may raise her eyes to heaven, but Racine himself, one feels, saw rather with the eyes of Narcisse than with those of the heroine.

Of the life of Molière we know little. The traditional biography includes many details which modern scholars like Michaut have doubted or rejected as patently false. We do know, however, that Molière's father, Jean Poquelin, purchased the charge of *tapissier ordinaire du roi* from his brother Nicolas in 1631 (cf. Eudoxe Soulié, *Recherches sur Molière* [Paris, 1863], p. 13). Jean Poquelin, of whose marriage with Marie Cressé, the daughter of a *marchand tapissier, bourgeois de Paris*, Molière was the first child, had been apprenticed by his father, Jean Poquelin, to a certain Dominique Trubert, *maître tapissier à Paris*, "demeurant rue Saint Denis" (v. Elizabeth Maxfield Miller, "A document of April 12, 1672, signed by Molière," *Romanic Review*, 47, 1956, pp. 166–78). Molière's family background is thus one of successful and well-to-do artisan-merchants. The list of witnesses of the marriage of Molière's father to Marie Cressé gives a good idea of the kind of milieu from which the playwright emerged. The contract, reproduced in full by Soulié, mentions among others "Daniel Crespy, marchand plumassier, bourgeois de Paris, oncle maternel; Toussaint Perier, marchand linger à Paris, beau-frère à cause de sa femme; honorable homme Marin Gamard, maître tailleur d'habits à Paris, aussi beau-frère à cause de sa femme; (. . .) Claude le Vasseur, veuve de feu Jean Mazuel, vivant violon ordinaire du Roi; (. . .) honorable homme Jean Autissier, juré du Roi en oeuvres de maçonnerie, oncle maternel à cause de sa femme; Noel Mestayer, marchand bonnetier à Paris . . ." Molière's brother Jean, associated in business with his father, shared the title of *tapissier du roi* with him on Molière's abandoning it in 1643. On the death of his brother in 1660, Molière again took over the title, which he retained after the death of his father in 1669. Jal recounts that on the playwright's own death his bier was "couverte du poelle des tapisseurs." Jal also explains briefly what the functions and privileges of the *tapisseurs du roi* were: "Ils faisaient les meubles du Roi, avaient soin du mobilier et faisaient le lit de Sa Maj. au pied, quand le valet de chambre ordinaire le faisait à la tête. Leurs gages étaient de 300 livres auxquelles se joignaient 37 l. 10s. de récompense. A cela s'ajoutaient tous les privilèges accordés aux commensaux de la maison du Roi. Les valets de chambre tapissiers et autres avaient le titre d'Ecuyer." In addition to their connection with the royal household, of course, the Poquelins continued to conduct their own business affairs. In 1633, two years after purchasing the charge of *tapissier du Roi* from his brother, Jean Poquelin the elder bought a house situated "sous les piliers des halles, devant le pilori" (Soulié, p. 148). The family business was conducted from this house. Auguste Baluffe (*Autour de Molière* [Paris, 1889]) claims that the clientele of Jean Poquelin included several of the most noble families in France. There is still some doubt as to the relations, personal and financial, of Molière and his father. Soulié believed that Poquelin senior quarreled with his son over his theatrical career and refused him all financial aid. Auguste

Baluffe took quite the opposite point of view, claiming on the basis of the *Elomire Hypocondre*, which shows the entire Poquelin family present at the early performances of the Illustre-Théâtre, that Poquelin senior did not object to his son's theatrical ventures and that he constantly provided him with financial support. Most recently Miss Miller has found a document substantiating what Soulié had already argued, namely that far from Poquelin senior's helping his son financially, the boot was on the other foot. According to Miss Miller, Poquelin's business activities must have suffered a set-back, for his son was making him loans in the 60's, using his friend the physicist and mathematician Rohault as a blind, in order to spare his father's feelings. Loiselet (*De quoi vivait Molière* [Paris, 1950], p. 79) supports this view. If it is correct, it suggests that Poquelin senior had criticized his son and had not approved of his choice of career—hence the delicacy with which Molière helped his father—though it also indicates that the relations of father and son were by no means as bad as some of Molière's more Romantic biographers have believed.

The many problems and obscurities in Molière's biography need not detain us here. It is enough for us to have established what his family background was. There is nothing in it that resembles the pinched moralism, resentment, and pride that we find in Racine's. There were doubtless occasions when the Poquelins experienced something of Dimanche's exasperation at the charming and condescending evasiveness of noble clients who would not pay their bills, but there is no reason to suppose that they entertained any resentment of the King himself. As respected and respectable artisans and merchants they had none of the courtier's stifled jealousy of the monarch on whom he is dependent for every advancement and distinction, and whose superiority he at once recognizes and denies. The Poquelin family's relations with the royal household were helpful to them both financially and socially. (Molière's daughter Madeleine was to marry an impoverished gentleman, Claude de Rachel de Montalan, and it is interesting to compare the witnesses to this marriage contract, all highly placed or noble persons, with the witnesses to the marriage contract of Poquelin senior and Marie Cressé—cf. Soulié, pp. 327–30.) They had no cause to deny their indebtedness or to resent it. Molière's own relation to King and Court was as different from Racine's as that of the social groups from which they emerged. Racine felt very intensely that his renown as an author—the very means he had used to launch himself on a courtly career—was a handicap to him as a man of the world. "Croyez-moi," he admonished his son Jean-Baptiste in 1694, "quand vous saurez parler de comédies et de romans, vous n'en serez guère plus avancé pour le monde et ce ne sera pas par cet endroit-là que vous serez le plus estimé" (*Oeuvres de Racine, ed. cit.* Vol. VII, p. 142). Racine's literary productions, especially in the earlier period of his career at Court, thus express an ambiguous attitude to the Court: desire and rejection, admiration and resentment, awe and condemnation. Like Racine, Molière cut his links with his social and family background. But unlike Racine he had no courtly aspirations. To the end of his life he bore the title *tapissier du roi*, and it was as an actor and playwright that he sought the favor of the King. He was an actor-author, not a courtier-author. He did not leave one world in order to seek entry into another; on the contrary, he chose to belong to no world, to be an outsider, as possibly all actors must be and as the seventeenth century regarded them officially. Certainly he had to please people and make them laugh; and not only his livelihood but the very possibility of having his works performed depended on his pleasing the great and the powerful. Like Shakespeare's jesters or like the servants in his own comedies, he maintained, as a person, a degree of freedom from his patrons that the courtier does not easily have, but he was as subject as Shakespeare's jesters and his own servants to the caprices and susceptibilities of a powerful and imperious public. "Et pensez-vous que ce soit une petite affaire que d'exposer quelque chose de comique devant une assemblée comme celle-ci, que d'entreprendre de faire rire des personnes qui nous impriment le respect et ne rient que quand ils veulent?" he cries in *L'Impromptu de Versailles* (sc. 1). Molière did run into a great deal of trouble with influential groups at Court: this story is too well known to bear retelling. One can imagine that he often felt bitterly resentful of his dependence on favors which could be withdrawn at any moment as the result of the pressure and the intrigues of men of lesser intellect but higher station than he. He must first have heard in his own heart many of the lines spoken by his servants or by disgruntled heroes like Alceste and Arnolphe. But Molière transcended even his own resentment. For as an actor Molière had constantly to stand back from himself, to transcend every part and every pose. It was his very business to see himself as well as others, to be aware of himself as an actor, and to recognize the determining role and importance of the public, of the world of others.

ooo

The comedy of a situation is always perceived from a vantage point that is superior to that situation. Comedy always implies transcendence. It is from the point of view of *la Cour et la Ville* that most of Molière's comedies must, in the first instance at least, be evaluated. From this vantage point the vanity and folly of all that is below can be easily perceived, the subtle posing of an Alceste as well as the more straightforward imposture of a Monsieur Jourdain. All who turn away from King and Court are seen to be ridiculous. Argan fawning on his doctors, Dandin aspiring to the dizzy heights of Sotenville, Orgon worshipping his Tartuffe, Philaminte enthusing over her Vadius, have each and every one chosen a false exemplar, the only true exemplars being the King, the Court, and the *honnêtes gens*. Likewise the Sotenvilles or the Countess d'Escarbagnas are ridiculous because they turn their gaze downward instead of upward, seeking recognition by their inferiors rather than by their superiors and thus putting themselves, on the same level as their inferiors. None of Molière's comic characters escapes some form of vanity, all seek to be recognized by someone. The universe of comedy is distinguished by its peculiarity, its self-sufficiency. Dandin and the Sotenvilles, Argan and his doctors, Jourdain and his teachers, Chrysale's womenfolk and their scholars and poets all constitute worlds on their own in which the play of vanity and folly is obvious because it is apprehended by the audience from beyond and above. There is a certain real sense in the implication at the end of Tartuffe that the King perceives all imposture and unmasks all fraudulence, for indeed it is from the vantage point of superiority that the petty strutting and posturing of those who do not recognize their own reality can be discerned. From an inferior position this is not possible. Thus Clitandre can see the folly and vanity of the Sotenvilles as well as the folly and vanity of Dandin, but Dandin himself is no more able to distinguish the hollowness of his idols than Jourdain can see that of his *Grand Turc*. In so far as a reader or an audience is unable to rise above the comic hero—which is what happened to the *précieuses*, the *femmes savantes*, and the *dévots* of Molière's own time, which is what happened also to Rousseau and to many modern audiences with respect to Alceste —his deeply comic nature will not be apprehended and only superficially comic elements will be appreciated. There will likewise be uncertainty if the audience is so unsure of its own social coherence that it can adopt the superior vantage point only intermittently, sympathizing at other times with the hero against society. The ambiguity that is attributed to the comedies in these circumstances I would characterize as Romantic ambiguity. Molière was himself deeply familiar with it, but his comedy is achieved precisely in the transcendence of it. The real ambiguity in Molière does not stem from uncertainty as to whether the social or the individual vantage point should be adopted, but from the problematic relation of the ideal of *honnêteté* to the world of the

Court. In those comedies that deal with provincials or petty noblemen the point of view of *la Cour et la Ville* serves as the point of
view of the *honnête homme*. As we saw in the chapter on *Le
Misanthrope*, however, the ideal of *honnêteté* was not always
identical with the real life of *la Cour et la Ville*. From the point
of view of the *honnête homme, la Cour et la Ville* could themselves be discerned as full of vanity to the degree that their reality
did not correspond to the standards they professed in theory. The
two levels on which the comedy is played out are not therefore the
social and the individual—which is an inferior one with respect to
the social—but the social and what for want of a better term we
might call the universal or divine, which is superior to the social.
Court and Town laugh—and rightly—at the antics of the Jourdains and the Dandins, but are they themselves really different?
Are not they too, viewed from a perspective that transcends the
Court and the Town, just as funny as the Jourdains? From one
point of view the laugh is on the Jourdains, but from another point
of view the laugh is on those who imagine that the laugh is on
the Jourdains. The second perspective does not invalidate the
first; it complements it. The imposture of Jourdain, in short, puts
the "real" nobles themselves and all our ideas about nobility in
question. Do not the "real" nobles carry on the same masquerades
as Jourdain? What, in fine, is the difference between the ecstasy
of a Jourdain when he receives the title of *Mamamouchi* and the
ecstasy of a "real" nobleman when he receives the title of *premier
gentilhomme de la chambre du roi*, between the eagerness of
Jourdain to be accepted into the society of a *marquise* and the
eagerness of a "real" courtier to be admitted to the *lever du roi*?
In his desire to acquire the appearance of distinction and superiority to others, Jourdain accepts without question the authenticity of the power that accords this superiority. But the
Grand Turc is only the valet Covielle in disguise. The audience
laughs at Jourdain's folly and the imposture of which he is the
dupe. The audience that laughs, however, has its own *Grand*

Turc, and, as Saint-Simon's *Mémoires* make abundantly clear, the *Grand Turc* of late seventeenth-century France was the King himself. When at the end of *Le Bourgeois Gentilhomme* everyone pretends to enter Jourdain's world and recognizes its validity, the good bourgeois, now Mamamouchi, cries out "Ah, voilà tout le monde raisonnable." The irony here is double-edged. Jourdain confuses an obvious and ridiculous convention with the *raisonnable*, but is the "truly" *raisonnable*—the perspective from which we perceive the folly of Jourdain—not itself a convention? Almost the reverse of Jourdain's words are those of Amphitryon, the great nobleman whose identity has been put in doubt by the imposture of the god: "Tout le monde perd-il aujourd'hui la raison?" The true nobleman, like the false one, appeals to reason, and reason turns out in the end to be nothing more than the set of conventions which condition our performance on the stage of social life. Virtually everyone, in the end, is an actor before others, and when Molière spoke in *L'Impromptu de Versailles* of *acting the parts of actors* he was referring to nothing unusual, but to the ordinary business of his work as a professional actor. Similarly when he observed of actors in rival troupes that their performance is never so perfect that one cannot discern the actor behind his role, he was alluding indirectly to those worldly actors to whom in his plays he gave the names Alceste, Dom Juan, Jupiter, Cathos, Philaminte, Madame Pernelle, as much as to the professional actors who copy their roles *on the stage*. There are very few in the world, however high, however low, he says, "qu'on ne pût attraper, (. . .) si je les avois bien étudiés" (*Impromptu*, sc. 1). The field of the playwright's research is consequently infinite. "Molière aura toujours plus de sujets qu'il n'en voudra," we are told; "et tout ce qu'il a touché jusqu'ici n'est que bagatelle au prix de ce qui reste" (*ibid.*, sc. 4).

Molière's comedy ranges high and low. It can reach the king on his throne as well as the bourgeois in his parlor, for hardly anyone can flatter himself that he is not an actor in some way or another.

The comedy of *Amphitryon*, for instance, mocks the rich and powerful nobles, Louis XIV's erstwhile rivals, who after the collapse of the Fronde, could only sulk in impotent discontent. At the same time, however, the mockery of the *seigneurs* did not spare the monarch himself. Jupiter does not come off much better than Amphitryon. Indeed, as almost all Molière's heroes are tyrants and despots in one way or another, they have a double function. On the one hand their pose is seen through from the superior vantage point of the Court and the *honnêtes gens*; on the other they themselves bear many of the characteristic traits of King and Court. Just as *Le Bourgeois Gentilhomme* is at once the satire of the would-be gentleman and in a more subtle way the satire of the "real" one, so *L'Avare*, *Le Tartuffe*, or *Le Misanthrope*—each in its own way a satirical portrait of the proud and resentful individualist who sets himself above all others—can be applied to the King himself as well as to his jealous and embittered critics.[19]

[19] The reader will have observed how close the interpretation of Molière we are presenting here stands to the *irony* which several critics have emphasized in Pascal's comments on society (cf. *Blaise Pascal, L'homme et l'oeuvre*, Cahiers de Royaumont [Paris, 1956], especially the remarks of Théodule Spoerri and Maurice de Gandillac in the discussion of Spoerri's paper "Les Pensées de derrière la tête de Pascal," and the contributions of MM. Goriely, de Gandillac, and Goldmann to the "discussion générale" at the end of the volume). Fragments 328–38 (ed. Brunschvicg) in particular—"tout le monde est dans l'illusion" etc.—are relevant to our present discussion of Molière. It is equally notable that Pascal's irony, like Molière's, seizes upon doctors, lawyers, courtiers. (If judges really dispensed justice, if doctors really dispensed cures, neither would have need of their robes, etc. Cf. Fr. 307.)

I quote from M. Goriely's remarks (*Blaise Pascal, op. cit.*, pp. 441–42): "Quelles conclusions tirer de ces critiques? Est-ce que l'homme doit se résigner à tout ce que l'Etat représente? Au mal inhérent à cet Etat? Bien sûr, il le dit, mais il ne le dit pas toujours; il y a dans son ironie vis-à-vis de tout ce que représente la loi des hommes qui est l'oeuvre de la force mais non la loi, d'étranges degrés. Il y a de toute évidence des institutions qui l'amusent; tous les appareils dont s'affublent ceux qui représentent la loi, dont s'affuble le roi, dont s'affublent les juges, les médecins: l'ironie est plutôt gaie. Lorsqu'il dit: 'Il a quatre valets . . . ,' l'ironie est amère. Lorsqu'il dit: 'je dois lui céder le pas . . .' il est convaincu, 'parce qu'il me donnera les étrivières' est un maigre argument. Là déjà nous sentons une part de sarcasme et de ricanement. Mais lorsqu'il parle de la guerre (. . .) il a un cri: 'Pourquoi me tuez-vous?' Il n'y répond pas. Il ne pouvait répondre à ce moment, il n'eût pas

In the France of Louis XIV the violence that marked the earlier part of the century—the period of Cromwell or of Richelieu—was superseded by a more concealed and subtle form of dominion. The superiority of the sovereign was not made to rest on mere power, nor was it to be a glorious triumphant victory in the grand manner of the Baroque. To found superiority on violence and force is to admit that it can be questioned. The absolute superiority of the *roi soleil* was therefore to be grounded in the willing and eager submission of his subjects, bourgeois and nobles alike. The absolute superiority of the monarch with respect to the noblemen of the realm was sustained in mid and late seventeenth-century France by the vanities and rivalries of the noblemen among themselves, rather than by naked force, just as the position of Tartuffe in Molière's play is sustained by the vanity and hidden rivalry of Orgon and Madame Pernelle. Louis XIV's move to Versailles was

---

répondu: oui, si mon prince m'ordonne de tuer, je tuerai." These few sentences suggest some of the similarities and some of the differences, as well as the underlying unity of the two visions of Molière and Pascal. Both envisage problems in a strongly dialectical way. Pascal, however, cannot maintain his vision on the level of irony and humor. Reality overwhelms his irony, and this defeat of irony is a mark both of Pascal's great generosity and of his vanity and resentment. When Pascal's humor becomes "sarcasm," as Goriely puts it, it does so in response to an intolerable awareness of objective injustice and evil, to an outraged human conscience, but it does so also in response to a personally experienced humiliation that arises out of Pascal's own social position. (Goldmann has described this position brilliantly in *Le Dieu caché*.) The bitter despair with respect to social life which ultimately overwhelms Pascal and extinguishes his humor is inseparable from his inability to rise above his own situation and his marvelous capacity for conceiving it in the broadest and most universal terms. With Molière the tendency is the opposite one. To the degree that he constantly transcends his own bitterness toward the comic vision, his work tends in the end toward a vision of universal comedy from which those alone escape who become spectators of this comedy, in which as actors, as social persons, they themselves, indeed, also participate. (In the eighteenth century, and especially in the work of Voltaire, this tendency becomes even more marked, although the idea of comedy as a *limited and corrective criticism* has not yet entirely disappeared from Voltaire.)

Neither Pascal nor Molière was able in the end to find a *real* solution to the problems that both experienced and formulated dialectically. For Pascal the "solution" was a tragic vision. M. Goriely—rightly, it seems to me—rejects a too rigorously Augustinian interpretation of Pascal. "En général," he

a stroke of genius. The virtual abandonment of Colbert's plans for the reconstruction of the Louvre and the establishment of the King's residence at some distance from the dwelling-places of his subjects mark the transformation of the monarch from a brutal house-tyrant into a remote and indifferent divinity, full of mysterious power and grace, concerned, again strangely like Tartuffe, not with the activities of mere mortals but with "higher" things. As bourgeois and nobles struggled for his favor and attention, Louis could look out calmly over the otherworldly order and serenity that Le Nôtre had imposed on the mundane world of nature. In this way bourgeois and noblemen were likewise held at arm's length, and the bourgeois could experience some satisfaction at the relative humiliation of his aristocratic rival. Degraded and weakened, the nobleman could feel himself distinguished from the bourgeois and from other noblemen only by being admitted to the

---

observes, "pour rendre plausible l'interprétation de Pascal, on recourt à, je dirai, un augustinisme ou à certains développements de tradition augustinienne; il est difficile de dire que l'Etat est la plus splendide chose et le roi l'être le plus merveilleux que Dieu ait créé. Mais Pascal dit: le mal est de ce monde. Vous connaissez la théorie augustinienne que la cité terrestre est par essence une caverne de brigands, que les deux plus grandes cités de l'histoire—Israël et Rome—sont toutes deux le fait de fratricides et que, néanmoins, elles doivent être voulues, elles sont de Dieu. C'est ainsi qu'on a en général interprété Luther; il n'a jamais dit que l'Etat, c'était à quoi l'homme trouvait la plus haute valeur à laquelle il puisse [se] soumettre. Mais sur le plan terrestre, il doit se soumettre; vous connaissez les conclusions qu'on en a tirées. Est-ce l'interprétation qu'on peut réellement tirer de Pascal? J'avoue que j'en doute" (*Blaise Pascal, op. cit.*, p. 440). Goldmann has stressed elsewhere that the radically unilateral position adopted by his sister Jacqueline was as unacceptable to Pascal as the personalism of Barcos or the moderate political optimism of Arnauld and Nicole. God *and* the world, the profession of truth *and* submission to the Church, divine justice *and* human justice, for Pascal these were not alternatives. Both terms had to be included in a unity. His inability to realize this unity constitutes the tragic ground of all his thinking ("le déplaisir de se voir entre Dieu et le Pape").

Equally unable to resolve his dialectic, Molière by-passes it *at the limit* by emptying it of all content, for the comic transformation of social life in its entirety ultimately involves a schematization of it. In the vast *spectacle* of human folly the reality and significance of human existence is conjured away. Comic schematizations—and it may well be that all comedy implies some degree of schematization—are indeed valid when they are *limited*, and when a

proximity of the monarch in the holy of holies at Versailles; the closer he got to the monarch, indeed, the more distinguished he— and everyone else—considered him to be. The rivalry of the nobles among each other and with the King himself was thus transformed into rivalry for the grace of the monarch. The old paternalism was dead and gone, but the cement of the new order was not naked violence.

Yet, just as in a situation where supremacy is based on force, the ruler is constantly preoccupied with maintaining his power and the ruled are constantly preoccupied with undermining it, so in a situation where supremacy is based on vanity, both parties, ruler and ruled, are obsessed by vanity. The ruled are constantly absorbed in watching for signs of grace or disgrace from the ruler; the ruler, however, while he must appear to be too far elevated above his subjects to care what they think, must nevertheless constantly observe them to make sure that they care what he thinks.

---

real mode of being can be opposed to them. Where this is no longer the case, the comic resolution is a pseudo-resolution, a resolution of impotence concealing the profoundest pessimism and despair. Molière constantly tried to walk along the edge of this abyss without falling over. We have already suggested that figures such as Eliante and Philinte are both real and unreal. In so far as they can be considered real, they *limit* the field of the comedy, and this is what Molière intended them to do. We suggested in the chapter on *Le Misanthrope*, however, that their relative insubstantiality points to a profound pessimism in the mind of Molière as to the possibility of any true social relations or any true communication between people in the *real* world. This question will be further elaborated later in our text. The purpose of this note was simply to point out a striking relationship between Molière's vision of the world and Pascal's (along lines rather different from those followed by Michaut in his *Pascal, Molière, Musset* [Paris, 1942]). The similarities are immediately apparent; the differences (tragedy on the one hand, comedy on the other) then seem overwhelming; but in the end the two lines, parallel as they may be, are seen to converge, after all, at their extreme limit. Goldmann's formulation of Pascal's position could equally well be applied to Molière's— "qu'il faut se soumettre à la loi et aux ordres du prince, non pas parce qu'ils sont bons ou valables, mais parce que nous n'avons aucun moyen de réaliser une amélioration. Il y a là un antagonisme entre les conséquences rigoureuses tirées par un grand penseur de ses positions idéologiques et sa répugnance humaine et affective devant ces conséquences. La conclusion de Pascal? Puisque tout Etat est mauvais et absurde (. . .) accepter sans aucune illusion l'ordre social et politique existant."

The King's superiority is not in doubt: it is recognized by all because it is the source of all superiority among the ruled. The King does not seek the recognition of his inferiors. On the contrary, the face of the monarch is turned away from his subjects. Versailles, as Saint-Simon remarked, looks out over empty space and its back is turned to Paris. The disaffected subject, on the other hand, is ignored by others, since they all have their gaze uplifted toward the Court and the great Sun that shines in its firmament. He has to struggle frenetically and yet always unsuccessfully for recognition by others of the superiority he claims for himself. Thus Alceste, for all he disapproves of the vanity of others, spends his entire time acting and posturing before others. If we adopt Alceste's own perspective, as many audiences do, we fail to see the comic contradiction between what he claims to be and what he is. The comedy of Alceste is perceived only when we look at him from a vantage point external to his own dilemma. Acaste and Clitandre see through him without difficulty.

In a sense, however, Alceste is the inverted image of the King himself. He is the King dethroned, the King whose marble columns have come crashing down and who finds himself no longer on the balcony but with the crowd below. Alceste is not in a position to make others participate in his comedy; hence the flagrant contradiction between the superiority and independence he claims and his actual subservience to the opinion of others. The King succeeds in having his absolute superiority recognized by others because he has the means to nourish and sustain their vanity. But he too, in his own way, must constantly be on the watch for any derogation, while pretending of course to be totally unconcerned. The basic similarity of what are apparently opposites emerges most clearly in *Amphitryon*. The irruption of Jupiter into the world reduces Amphitryon to helpless impotence. His former pre-eminence is no longer recognized, and he has to present himself to others in order to wrest from them a recognition that he believes is owing to him in virtue of his own inherent qualities. Jupiter himself, however, is likewise obliged to present himself in order to win from Alcmène the recognition she reserves for her husband. As long as he remains genuinely indifferent, as long as he really turns his back on mere humans, Jupiter is equally ignored by them, and all their veneration and respect are lavished on a mere mortal. The intervention of the god is thus inspired initially by envy, by his desire to win from his subjects that recognition which is supposed to be given him without his asking for it, as if by a law of nature, but which he does not get from them without effort. It is not an accident that Jupiter's desire is excited by the spectacle of a recently wedded couple. The significance of the piquant eroticism which Mercury sees as the source of Jupiter's interest in the newly-wed Alcmène can be discerned if we compare his situation with the strikingly similar one described by Dom Juan in *Dom Juan*, Act I, scene 2.[20] The god is thus discovered to be in no way indifferent to the opinion of mere mortals. On the contrary, moved by jealousy of the devotion Alcmène has for her husband, he becomes the rival of a being who is ostensibly his inferior. Like Molière's mortal tyrants and would-be tyrants Jupiter needs to have his absolute superiority recognized by others, and he will tolerate no derogation from the respect due to him alone. From his lofty Olympian indifference he is constantly watching out of the corner of his eye to make sure that he is never forgotten. Having found that one of his "inferiors" has usurped his place in a young woman's heart, he swoops down on his rival mercilessly. So did Louis XIV crush Fouquet after the magnificently extravagant fête offered by the superintendant of finances at Vaux-le-Vicomte in 1661. As Tapié remarks: "Ce que Fouquet avait fait ne scandalisait Louis XIV que parce qu'il aurait voulu le faire à sa place. Le coup de foudre de l'affaire Fouquet (. . .) signifiait que la gloire des arts et de la richesse ne devait servir qu'à la réputation du roi" (V. L. Tapié, *Baroque et Classicisme* [Paris, 1957], p. 182).

Molière's comedy is a constant unmasking of imposture, a con-

[20] Cf. supra, pp. 42–43.

stant process of liberation from the slavery and fear of illusion and falsehood. Nothing is spared, not even the monarchy itself. Molière's audiences could enjoy the satire of a Jourdain or an Alceste. They could laugh at the would-be gentleman's fascination with empty names and titles and at the efforts of Alceste to conceal under an affectation of indifference his real fascination with the society he claimed to despise. But if the nobleman thought he was superior, *as a nobleman,* to these characters, he saw only the bones of the comedy and missed the marrow. Like the Sotenvilles who, in their anxiety to affirm their superiority to Dandin, fail to see themselves as others see them, the audience that feels smugly satisfied at its superiority to a Jourdain, that fails to see itself in the grotesque figure of the would-be gentleman, is trapped in the same circle of vanity and illusion, albeit at a slightly higher level, as Jourdain. The audience must indeed be above the particular form of vanity that possesses the hero in order to perceive it, but it must then inquire whether the vanity of the hero is not the image of its own.

@@@

It is well known that Molière found the material for many of his greatest comic creations—for Alceste, for Arnolphe, for Argan—in himself as well as in the world around him. In *Le Malade Imaginaire* he explicitly affirmed his own emancipation from the illusions of his hero. "Il sera encore plus sage que vos médecins," Béralde says to Argan of Molière, "car il ne leur demandera point de secours" (III, 3). But if Molière transcended "ces belles imaginations, que nous venons à croire parce qu'elles nous flattent" (*ibid.*), it was because he knew what it was to have them. It was only because he himself had been and in a sense still was Argan—for what man can be sure of having overcome his weaknesses once and for all?—that Molière could create the comedy of Argan. The writing of the comedy *was* his liberation. Béralde is not exactly Molière's mouthpiece; nor, however, is he simply another point of view. In projecting himself into his work, Molière was obliged to individuate two aspects of himself which in his own being and consciousness were inseparably linked. Argan and Béralde, Arnolphe and Chrysalde are one in the consciousness of their creator: only in the comedy does their inward dialogue receive dramatic expression as a dialogue of two separate characters. By being thus simplified, the folly of the one is more clearly defined, objectified, and exorcised. The wisdom of the other is, however, also simplified. Here we touch on one of the most striking characteristics of Molière's *raisonneurs*. Béralde may well say of the marvelous achievements of medicine: "Quand vous en venez à la vérité et à l'expérience, vous ne trouvez rien de tout cela, et il en est comme de ces beaux songes qui ne vous laissent au réveil que le déplaisir de les avoir crus" (*ibid.*), there is and can be no indication in the play that he ever did or felt tempted to believe them. The same is true of many of the other *raisonneurs*. Cléante (*Le Tartuffe*), Philinte (*Le Misanthrope*), Ariste (*L'Ecole des maris*), and Chrysalde (*L'Ecole des femmes*) give the impression of never having been fools, of never having experienced or even been tempted by the passions and illusions they discourse so wordily about. This accounts for the somewhat abstract character of these armchair "philosophers." They do represent the point of view of good sense and moderation, the point of view of the *honnête homme*, the highest vantage point that can be attained without the experience of oneself as comic. The understanding of the audience, if the comedy has been fully enjoyed, is higher, however, than that of the *raisonneur*, because it is the result of a genuine purgation in the course of which the audience has experienced, as the artist did, *both* terms of the dialogue. This is the position represented by the most modest and least bumptious of all the *raisonneurs*, the endearing Dorante of the *Critique de l'Ecole des Femmes*. "Quant au transport amoureux du cinquième acte," he says, "qu'on accuse d'être trop outré et trop comique, je voudrois bien savoir si ce n'est pas faire la satire des

mants, et si les honnêtes gens mêmes et les plus sérieux, en de
pareilles occasions, ne font pas des choses . . . ? (. . .) Enfin
si nous nous regardions nous-mêmes, quand nous sommes bien
amoureux . . . ?" (sc. 6).

Molière critics are divided among those who argue that the
raisonneurs do express Molière's own opinions (Brunetière, Michaut, etc.) and those who hold that their function is purely artistic
or dramatic, a function of contrast and *éclairage* (Moore, Bray,
etc.). There seems to me to be some truth in both these views, and
yet I find both of them unsatisfactory. Those who see in the
speeches of the *raisonneurs* a set of answers to the questions raised
discount in large measure the *comedy*, transforming it into a kind of
pièce à these. Those who deny any meaning function to the *raisonneurs*, on the other hand, seem to me to be shirking the issue.
It is tempting to hide behind the wall of estheticism but I am not
sure that we do justice to great literature by cutting its links with
the concrete reality in which it has its source and to which it sends
us back. On the whole, however, my own position is closer to that
of the second group of critics than to that of the first group.

The entire wisdom of the *raisonneurs* can be summed up as "do
as the *honnêtes gens* do." The biggest folly is to attempt to be
different from everybody else. Ariste gives a rather extreme expression of this position in *L'Ecole des maris*:

> Mais je tiens qu'il est mal, sur quoi que l'on se fonde,
> De fuir obstinément ce que suit tout le monde,
> Et qu'il vaut mieux souffrir d'être au nombre des fous,
> Que du sage parti se voir seul contre tous.
>
> (I, 1, 51–54)

Not, apparently, a very elevating doctrine, as those who defend
Molière the artist against Molière the "thinker" would be quick to
point out. But there is more wisdom here than meets the eye. This
wisdom is not, however, contained so much in the doctrines and

principles the *raisonneurs* enunciate, as in the dangers that they warn against. However well founded and deeply held your principles, says Ariste, do not loudly flout the ways of the world. For if you do, and this is what the comic heroes teach us, then your principles will be absorbed in your own inauthenticity. They will cease to be ends and will become means, they will become in short the very opposite of what you say they are. If you do hold to objective values, they must be ends in themselves, "terminal values" as the late Professor Lovejoy called them in his *Reflections on Human Nature* (Baltimore, 1961). They must not be merely a means of acquiring the recognition and esteem of others, for this is to make recognition and esteem your only real value. All your preaching thereby becomes a form of self-advertisement, an attempt to impose yourself on the world. The preaching of Alceste and of Orgon is nothing else.

"Adjectival values," however, as Lovejoy describes the ends of recognition and esteem, are vain and empty. Although the desire for recognition and esteem is *prima facie* a desire to invest one's subjective view of oneself with a kind of objectivity, this objectivity is in reality spurious, for it is an objectivity without an object. Noblemen or superior persons have no objective existence in the world as noblemen or superior persons. Objectively they are men, and only in the minds and judgment of others are they noblemen or superior persons. Why, therefore, seek to acquire a recognition that has no objective value? Or at least why deceive oneself into thinking that such recognition has objective value? There is no point, for instance, in changing your title or your rank, for you merely substitute one empty form for another. Chrysalde is amused by Arnolphe's change of name:

> Qui diable vous a fait aussi vous aviser,
> A quarante et deux ans, de vous débaptiser,
> Et d'un vieux tronc pourri de votre métairie
> Vous faire dans le monde un nom de seigneurie?
>   (*Ec. femmes*, I, 1, 169–72)

Molière had none of the stuffy and stupid conservatism which has been attributed to him. He did not laugh at the bourgeois from the smug superiority of the courtier nor did he think that everyone should stay in his place because he espoused the snobberies of the nobles. On the contrary, it was because he saw through the vanity of the nobles and of the King and of all social signs and superiorities that he saw the folly of the ambitions of those below them. As we have already suggested, he was, if anything, more indulgent toward the naïve vanity of the social climber than toward the inverted resentment of the courtier. It was not because he thought there was some inherent value in the existing social conventions that he mocked all attempt to "rise above one's station" or to overthrow the existing conventions, it was because to attempt to do either seemed to him to attribute value and meaning to what in its very nature has none.

Every one of the comedies is in this sense a salutary demystification. The dilemmas of the Alcestes, the Orgons, and the Dandins dissolve in laughter as we see through their deceptions and self-deceptions. Alceste's concern with sincerity is shown to conceal the crassest egoism, his indifference to opinion turns out to be a disguised fascination with those he affects to disregard and his failure is comic because his striving has been revealed as utterly inauthentic. Dom Juan, the supposed libertine and pleasure-seeker, is seen to be incapable of any real pleasure and his apparent autonomy emerges as a base fascination with and dependence on his own servant. Orgon's religious fervor is exposed as mere resentment of and desire to dominate others, to be a little despot in his own home. The seemingly pathetic and persecuted Dandin is his own victim, not the victim of the world, for he is a slave only because he would be a tyrant.

Impostors to the marrow of their bones, these "heroes" find in imposture both the instrument by which they can fulfill their desires and the fulfillment of their desires. Dandin and Jourdain are willing to pay fortunes for a grotesque mimicry of nobility, and it

is their own fault if they are duped, for it is they who invest others
with a prestige they do not possess, it is they who attribute real
value and being to the conventional values and vain appearances
of the world. The Countess d'Escarbagnas, who deems herself so
superior to all the inhabitants of her village and complains that
they do not treat her with sufficient reverence, is appeased by the
grotesquely respectful attentions of a Monsieur Tibaudier, just as
the Sotenvilles, petty monarchs of their provincial parish, seek the
confirmation of their nobility in the submission and respect of a
Dandin. If Philaminte in *Les Femmes savantes* is duped by Trissotin, or Magdelon and Cathos in *Les Précieuses* by Mascarille and
Jodelet, their true qualities are revealed by the deceptions of which
they are the dupes. The baseness of Trissotin reveals the truth
about Philaminte, the degradation of the Sotenvilles reveals the
truth about Dandin, the imposture of Tartuffe reveals the truth
about Orgon. (Significantly enough, Magdelon and Cathos, Jourdain, and Argan are all duped by valets.) One imposture reveals
another; the idol exposes the idolator. The truth is that all these
characters exist exclusively on the level of appearance. Slaves to
illusion, they aspire only to names and forms. The Countess
d'Escarbagnas is vexed because she is not looked up to. Dandin
and Jourdain want to be accepted as noblemen, Philaminte wants
the reputation of a *femme savante*, Orgon desires to be considered
a *dévot* by those around him, Argan wants to be attended by a
doctor of eminent reputation. Philaminte is not primarily interested in learning, Argan is not really concerned about the sickness
that he may in fact be suffering from, Orgon's preoccupation is not
the salvation of his soul. These characters desire only to appear
and they achieve their ends with the help of names and signs. It is
the reputation of Trissotin, of Purgon, of Tartuffe that counts, not
what they really are. Jourdain refuses to learn *la morale*, because, as
he says, "je veux me mettre en colère tout mon saoûl, quand il me
prend envie" (II, 4). He does not aspire to any *real* change, only
to a change in appearances, and only what is necessary to achieve

this change in appearances has usefulness and value in his eyes. He will pay for music lessons and fencing lessons because music and fencing are *signs* of nobility. Likewise he will pay so much for being called "mon gentilhomme," so much more for being called "Monseigneur," and the entire contents of his purse for being called "Votre Grandeur" (II, 5). Jourdain knows of course that in a sense he *is* not any of these things and that no one makes such rapid progress from the one to the other. Since appearances and signs are for him the only reality, however, since no one is anything but what others recognize him for, to carry the sign is to be the thing itself. So long as he is treated as if he were *Votre Grandeur*, he is *Votre Grandeur*. It does not occur to him that he might not really be a *Mamamouchi*, that there might not be any such thing. Provided he is recognized by everyone as a *Mamamouchi* and provided everyone recognizes the existence of *Mamamouchis*, then he really is a *Mamamouchi*.

In so far as it is a *spectacle devant les hommes*, in Goldmann's expression, human life, for Molière, was completely absorbed in the inessential. The comic figure is he who fails to realize this, who takes his acting seriously, who allows himself to be dazzled by the glitter of empty names and signs, who thereby becomes the idolator of others, since the glitter is reflected in the eyes of others. The *raisonneur* also presents himself to some degree, he too seeks the approbation of his fellows. We cannot live in the world and be completely independent of others and of others' judgment of us. To imagine that we can is simply another vanity which the actual facts of our behavior will soon expose. The cardinal principle of the *raisonneur* is that the least inauthentic role is the role we are expected to play, since by playing it we do not ask that it be received otherwise than as a role. We know we are acting a part, but we also know that others know we are acting a part; we are not therefore lying or acting in the way of those who act as if they are not acting. This is the behavior that Philinte tries to make Alceste understand:

Lorsqu'un homme vous vient embrasser avec joie,
Il faut bien le payer de la même monnoie,
Répondre, comme on peut, à ses empressements,
Et rendre offre pour offre, et serments pour serments.
                    (*Misanthrope*, I, 1, 37–40)

Social life is a game that must be played according to the rules,
Molière's *raisonneurs* would say. What we really are is not the concern of the world, and it is foolish to ask the world to be concerned
with it. For this is to attribute to the world a power that, if we are
to be free, it should not be permitted to have, and that in any case
it cannot have, since the world is made up only of men like ourselves. Those who attribute to others a quasi-divine power that they
do not actually have and who try to have themselves judged by
others are the very people who want to usurp this power for themselves and to become the tyrants and judges of everybody else. They
become locked in a senseless struggle for an ever-vanishing prize
which has no reality outside their own minds. Their entire being
becomes absorbed in their being for others, and in their obsessive
preoccupation with their image they lose whatever authenticity
they might have had.

The most authentic characters in Molière are those who are
either so naïvely ignorant of any distinction between appearance
and reality that they never think they might mislead or be misled,
or so completely resigned to the inevitability of the distinction that
they limit their relations with others to the bare minimum required
by life in society. The transparent innocence of Alcmène and the
mask-like enigma of Elmire are the highest examples of these two
modes of being.

❧❧❧

The profundity of Molière's comic vision is testified to not only
by the continued popularity of his works but by their remarkable

prophetic quality. Alceste is the very type of the modern intellectual and in large measure of Western man in general, isolated,
resentful, embittered, affecting to despise society, but in reality
adoring it and suffering because it does not recognize his unique
and immeasurable value. Orgon's dangerous combination of impotence and pride foreshadows the witch-hunters and fanatics of
our own time. Like Molière's comic hero, they too await with open
arms the impostor whose apparently noble ideology will provide
them with the instrument of their revenge on all who have "dis-
dained" (that is, failed to admire) them. And what is the modern
search for "status symbols" if not a new and yet easily recognized
form of Jourdainism? Even to-day the Jourdains are more naïve and
frank in their simple adoration of the world than the Alcestes and
the Orgons with their inverted love-hate of it. The American negro
in his gleaming Cadillac convertible openly avows his mediation by
his "superior" white models, whereas many more highly placed
persons conceal behind a façade of scorn and derision a resentful
fascination with a world that neglects to admire then sufficiently.
What Molière saw three centuries ago and what Tocqueville
pointed to a hundred years ago has become one of the most wide-
spread phenomena of our age. Nearly all of us, from the highest to
the lowest, suffer from the neuroses that afflicted the comic heroes
of Molière.

The great themes of Molière's comedies recur over and over again
in the literature of the eighteenth, nineteenth, and twentieth centuries. (The very titles of his comedies are revealing: *Dom Juan*,
the *Misanthrope*, the *Impostor*, the *Bourgeois Gentleman*, the
Learned Ladies, etc.) To trace their history would be a gigantic
task that would go far beyond the scope of the present study.
Nevertheless some broad lines should be drawn, for, to my knowledge, no one has yet undertaken such a work. There is no question
of "influences," though in many cases it would be possible to detect
a direct impact of Molière on his successors. In the main, however,
the filiations we propose to study very briefly and grossly are not

"influences" and they are not subject to positivist methods of analysis. In pointing them out we do not want to show that the writers who came after Molière were borrowing from him, but that he foresaw in his comedies many of the great themes of modern literature. These themes are handled differently by the various writers who take them up, according to their time and their understanding. The world does not stand still and the problems that Molière could embrace in a three or five-act comedy could no longer be handled with the same simplicity of means two hundred years after him, for the situations themselves had become infinitely more complex, so complex, in fact, that many writers of talent failed to rise to the clarity of vision that distinguishes the seventeenth-century playwright.

The astonishing intellectual power and vision of Molière is not to be looked for or found in the "ideas" of the *raisonneurs*—these form only part of the total picture—but in his deep and prophetic insight into certain crucial problems of modern social life and in his unerring grasp of the true nature of these problems. Among those who followed him and who took up the same themes as he had already exploited, the greatest shared his profound apprehension of the comic. Those who failed to rise to this comic vision became bogged down in myths and false pathos; they became victims of the very inauthenticity he warned against, play-actors themselves, and the first dupes of their own often unconscious duplicity.

The full significance of some of the esthetic problems encountered by Molière also becomes clearer in the light of subsequent developments. The difference between the comedy of *Le Bourgeois Gentilhomme* for instance and that of *Le Misanthrope* has preoccupied many commentators. While agreeing with de Visé's remark that *Le Misanthrope* makes us laugh "dans l'âme," Gustave Rudler wondered what kind of comedy this is that is so muted and inward. We have tried to point out some of the thematic differences between these two works. There is no question, however, that these thematic differences affect the nature of comedy itself.

In the following pages we shall touch on several problems which confront the modern comic author, and we shall see that Molière had already begun to run up against these problems when he wrote *Le Misanthrope*. Signs of the future can be discerned not only in the themes of Molière's plays but in the problems that he met with as a comic artist.

7

AFTER MOLIÈRE

"Gravity is of the very Essence of Imposture. It does not only make us mistake other things, but is apt perpetually almost to mistake it-self. For even in common Behaviour, how hard is it for the grave Character to keep long out of the limits of the formal one?"

Shaftesbury, *Characteristicks.*

"Les prétentions, les fatales prétentions, une des causes principales de la tristesse du XIXème siècle."

Stendhal, *Lamiel.*

IF WE RECALL our earlier distinction between "open" comedy and "closed" comedy in Molière, it would seem at first sight that the "open" comedy such as we find in *Le Bourgeois Gentilhomme* or in *Les Précieuses ridicules* has been practiced with continued success by generations of writers since Molière. The vanities and affectations of those who imitate their superiors would seem to be a favorite subject for comedy. Mrs. Slipslop, Lady Booby's waiting maid in Fielding's *Joseph Andrews*, apes the "distinguished" persons whom she serves with the same clumsiness as Jourdain imitating the nobility. The unfortunate lady's attempts at refined speech are as disastrously unsuccessful as Jourdain's attempts at fencing, music, dancing, and philosophy. The appearance of Mrs. Million at the Marquess of Carabas' house party in Disraeli's *Vivian Grey* reminds one of Jourdain's ornate salutation of Dorimène. Just as Jourdain remains a bourgeois whatever he does, so Mrs. Million remains a wealthy parvenue whatever she does. She arrives at Château Desir with the modest suite she promised— "only three carriages-and-four," "Out of the first descended the mighty lady Herself," writes Disraeli, "with some of her noble friends, who formed the most distinguished part of her suite: out of the second came her physician, Dr. Sly; her toad-eater,[1] Miss Gusset; her secretary, and her page. The third carriage bore her groom of the chambers and three female attendants. There were

---

[1] "Avaleur de crapauds" is Stendhal's translation of this. For a brief explanation of the toad-eater see *Lucien Leuwen*, Chap. 23.

only two men servants to each equipage; nothing could be more moderate, or, as Miss Gusset said, 'in better taste' " (*Vivian Grey*, Bk. 2, Chap. 12). Having arrived sufficiently late to create a modest impression, Mrs. Million decides not to change for dinner. She enters the dining hall leaning on the Marquess' arm "and in a travelling dress, namely, a crimson silk pelisse, hat and feathers, with diamond ear-rings, and a rope of gold around her neck. A train of about twelve persons, consisting of her noble fellow-travellers, toad-eaters, physicians, secretaries, etc., etc., etc., followed" (*ibid.*).

Flaubert's satire of Emma Bovary and of Monsieur Homais likewise resembles closely the structure of an "open" comedy such as *Le Bourgeois Gentilhomme*. Both, like Jourdain, reject the narrowness and ordinariness of the world in which they are born and aspire to distinctions of which they have read or which they imagine, Emma to the exotic world of literary romance, Homais to the important and impressive world of academic and intellectual honors. Emma longs for a great and poetic love, and Homais longs to be celebrated as a scientist and champion of progress. But as everything Jourdain does reveals what he really is and has never ceased to be, everything Emma and Homais do confirms that they are no different from the very provincials to whom they feel so superior. Emma remains a country doctor's wife, petty and narrow-minded. Her great loves are never anything but ordinary acts of adultery, which by the end of her career are scarcely distinguishable from acts of prostitution. Homais remains a provincial pharmacist, stupid and pretentious. His "science" is a characteristic mixture of superstition and crass positivism. Like the old wives he despises, he loves "remedies" and magic cures, though, unlike them, he requires that they have the paraphernalia of Latin names, and he amasses the dreariest facts with the same unimaginative avidity as the inhabitants of Yonville amass money or land. The pompous articles in the *Fanal de Rouen* and the paper which he sends to the *Société agronome de Rouen*, "*Du cidre, de sa fabrication et de ses effets, suivi de quelques réflexions nouvelles à ce sujet"* and which procures him his election to the *section d'agriculture, classe de pomologie* are as clumsy in their imposture as Emma's refinements and false poetic sentimentality. As for his crowning achievement, the Book, to which he gives the learned title *Statistique générale du canton d'Yonville, suivie d'observations climatologiques,* it is as distinguished as Emma's grand passions for Rodolphe and Léon.

The comedy of these texts seems to resemble very closely the comedy of a Jourdain or a Cathos. Some significant changes have, however, occurred, which make the comedy of these later heroes less clear and straightforward than that of a Jourdain.

Between Molière's would-be gentleman and his models the distance was great and virtually unbridgeable, though already narrower than that which separated Don Quixote from his Amadis.[2] Jourdain could openly avow his admiration and his imitation of models whose superiority he never questioned for a minute, while the models, on their part, could laugh freely and generously at the antics of the bourgeois in whom they never for a moment discerned a rival.

In the modern world, however, the imitator is increasingly the rival of his model, from whom he is separated by an ever narrowing margin. Sir Walter and Elizabeth Elliot in Jane Austen's *Persuasion* are shocked at Anne's visiting a Mrs. Smith in Westgate Buildings, while they cannot contain their pleasure at being invited to a concert evening given by Lady Dalrymple. But the manner in which they greet Lady Dalrymple—"all the eagerness compatible with anxious elegance"—indicates the contradictions in their attitude toward her. There is adulation, but there is also proud and resentful unwillingness to admit their adulation, in the Elliots' attitude to Lady Dalrymple. Similarly, their shocked displeasure at Anne's association with *Mrs. Smith* discloses an anxious concern to dissociate themselves from the middle classes, which a gentry

[2] Cf. René Girard, *Mensonge romantique et vérité romanesque* (Paris, 1961).

more sure of its own value would never have had. Even before Jane Austen, however, in the work of Fielding, we can observe how the classes are coming closer together and how everyone is already being swallowed up into a more and more homogeneous "society."

Between Mrs. Slipslop and Lady Booby the difference is no longer very profound. The servant knows the intimate secrets of her mistress, and has no real respect for her. The two are in fact rivals for Joseph's favors and in this rivalry of mistress and servant for the young footman, Fielding shows a real insight into the true nature of their relation, just as a century later Stendhal showed through the rivalry of Mathilde de la Môle and the Maréchale de Fervacques for Julien Sorel, the true nature of their relation. Mathilde may well despise the Maréchale whose nobility is somewhat too recent for her taste: in the end she finds herself competing on a footing of equality with her for the love of the upstart Julien. The very attraction that the lower orders exercise on their "superiors," Joseph on Lady Booby, Marivaux's Jacob on the very aristocratic Mesdames de Ferval and de Fécourt (*Le Paysan parvenu*), Julien on Mathilde de la Môle and on the Maréchale de Fervacques, discloses the inner weakness and degradation of these "superiors." In their attitude to their social inferiors—a strange compound of desire to humiliate and desire to be humiliated—the "superiors" implicitly admit the growing uncertainty of their own position, the breakdown, on a subjective level, of any firm conviction of their own superiority and, on an objective level, the dissolution of the social order on which privilege and distinctions of rank were based.

Disraeli's portrait of Mrs. Million shows a similar awareness of human vanity to that of Fielding, Marivaux, and Stendhal. Mrs. Million has no difficulty in gaining access to Château Desir. On the contrary, she is honored and fêted by her noble host who protests "that her will was his conduct" (*Vivian Grey*, Bk. 2, Chap. 12). For all their contempt, the blue-blooded guests of the Marquess of Carabas are impressed by Mrs. Million and afraid of her.

"The entrée of Her Majesty," writes Disraeli of Mrs. Million's appearance in the castle hall, "could not have created a greater sensation than did that of Mrs. Million. All fell back, gartered peers, and starred ambassadors, and baronets with blood older than the creation, and squires to the antiquity of whose veins chaos was a novelty; all retreated, with eyes that scarcely dared to leave the ground; even Sir Plantaganet Pure, whose family had refused a peerage regularly every century, now, for the first time in his life, seemed cowed, and in an awkward retreat to make way for the approaching presence, got entangled with the Mameluke boots of my Lord Alhambra" (*ibid.*). Mrs. Million, for her part, has none of Jourdain's pure admiration of the nobility. There is dark resentment in her heart, and it is this resentment that Vivian, who studies and exploits the vanities of noblemen, millionaires, and servants alike, plays on with consummate skill. "How beautiful the old Hall looked today!" he exclaims. "It is a scene which can only be met with in ancient families." "Ah! there is nothing like old families!" Mrs. Million answers, "with all the awkward feelings of a parvenue." Vivian seizes his chance. "Do you think so? I once thought so myself, but I confess that my opinion is greatly changed. After all, what is noble blood? My eye is now resting on a crowd of nobles; and yet, being among them, do we treat them in a manner differing in any way from that which we should employ to individuals of a lower caste who were equally uninteresting?" Mrs. Million warms to these unusual and reassuring remarks which give expression to her deepest resentments. Encouraged, Vivian goes on to expound the virtues of the middle class, which permits its children to develop their characters, the true source of their superiority, impartially, without the handicap of "hereditary prejudices" or "hereditary passions." Mrs. Million is gratified but cautious. "I must hear everything before I give an opinion," she says to Vivian who asks her what she thinks of his principles. "When, therefore, my mind was formed," Vivian goes on, "I would wish to become the proprietor of a princely fortune." At last Mrs. Million has heard what she has been waiting to hear, the confirmation of her own superiority to these noblemen whom she courts and hates at the same time, just as they court and hate her. A Million, Vivian has just observed, is worth a thousand Carabasses. Mrs. Million is delighted. She eagerly agrees with the young man and when she leaves him she is determined to invite this brilliant and profound philosopher to visit her in London.

Disraeli's analysis of what he calls the Toadeys—the parasites of wealth and distinction that in Molière's *Dom Juan* go by the name of Sganarelle—emphasizes the same mixture of imitation and resentment. "The great singularity," he writes, "is the struggle between their natural and their acquired feelings: the eager opportunity which they seize of revenging their voluntary bondage, by their secret taunts, on their adopted task-masters, and the servility which they habitually mix up even with their scandal" (Bk. 2, Chap. 15). Miss Gusset, the toadey of Mrs. Million, and Miss Graves, the toadey of the Marchioness of Carabas, vie with each other through their respective mistresses. Miss Gusset complains at having been terrified by the Marchioness' "horrible green parrot flying upon my head." "Horrible green parrot, my dear madam!" retorts Miss Graves. "Why, it was sent to my Lady by Prince Xtmnprqtosklw, and never shall I forget the agitation we were in about that parrot. I thought it would never have got to the Château, for the Prince could only send his carriage with it as far as Toadcaster. Luckily my Lady's youngest brother, who was staying at Desir, happened to get drowned at the time; and so Davenport, very clever of him! sent her on in my Lord Dormer's hearse." Miss Gusset's delicate feelings are outraged by the idea of the parrot's being conveyed in the hearse of My Lady's youngest brother. Miss Graves, however, finds such sentimentality vulgar. "It is all very well for commoners," she declares, and recalls that on the death of another member of the family shortly before, "everything went on as usual. Her Ladyship attended Almacks; my Lord took his seat in the House; and I looked in at Lady Doubtful's where we do not visit, but where the Marchioness wishes to be civil" (that *we* here is masterly!). "We do not visit Lady Doubtful either," replies Mrs. Million's toadey defensively: "she had not a card for our fête champêtre." Before long the two toadeys turn from vying with each other through their respective mistresses to vying with their mistresses themselves. Miss Gusset was clever enough to express a certain admiration for the Marchioness, but Miss Graves suddenly finds that her mistress has serious shortcomings. "Yes," she agrees, "her Ladyship is a dear, amiable creature, but I cannot think how she can bear the eternal screaming of that noisy bird." Mrs. Million, however, "appears to be a most amiable woman." Now it is Miss Gusset's turn to vent her resentment on her mistress. "Quite perfection," she answers; "so charitable, so intellectual, such a soul! It is a pity, though, her manner is so abrupt; she really does not appear to advantage sometimes." Miss Graves agrees that the Marchioness also lacks a certain refinement in considering the feelings of others. The two women now proceed to criticize the dress, the manners, the friends of their mistresses. Disraeli's "toadeys" are torn between resentment of other toadeys, which forces them to extoll the mistresses who are the instruments of their superiority to these others, and resentment of their mistresses, because of their very dependence on them.

It is clear that the type of comedy we are confronted with in these cases is not the comedy of the bourgeois gentleman, but rather that of Dandin and Sotenville, of Sganarelle and Dom Juan or of Orgon and Madame Pernelle. In the relation of Mrs. Million and the blue blood of England, it is the comedy of Dandin and Sotenville, the comedy of vanity and resentment that is being enacted; while in the rivalry of Mathilde and the Maréchale for Julien, whom Stendhal himself likens to Tartuffe, we encounter a modern version of the unavowed rivalry of Orgon and his mother. As the old hierarchies are broken down in the modern world, the differences between classes and persons and the superiority of one group to another become more and more metaphysical, more and more a matter of opinion. The apparent objectivity with which they seemed formerly to be invested disappears. Opinion is no longer determined by established conventions, which seem to be grounded in a fixed and immemorial reality; on the contrary opinion overthrows established and "irrational" conventions and establishes itself as the supreme source of all value. A conflict inevitably arises between "l'opinion que l'on a de soi-même," as Valéry expresses it (*Teste, ed. cit.* p. 82), and "l'opinion que les autres ont de vous," which is the "matière première" of the first. The individual is torn between his own claim to superiority and his need to have this superiority recognized by others, between his opinion of himself and the opinion others have of him, between a boundless "superiority complex" and a slavish "inferiority complex." In such a situation Jourdain's naïve admiration for his superiors is impossible.[3] It is through the nobility that Jourdain seeks to establish his superiority to his bourgeois family and friends and

---

[3] Cf. a telling analysis of the relation of self-esteem to "approbativeness" (the desire to elicit an approving judgment from others) in the third lecture of Lovejoy's *Reflections on Human Nature* (Baltimore, 1961), pp. 100–2:

"Self-approbation is supported by the approbation of others; it is easier to feel satisfied with your qualities or your acts or performances if your fellows appear to think highly of them. On the other hand self-esteem may take the form of an indifference to or contempt for the opinion of other persons, or of some classes or types of other persons. The individual esteems himself the more because he is, or believes himself to be, unconcerned about the esteem of his neighbors. (. . .) And whereas it is obvious that approbativeness tends in the main to compliance with social, that is, external, requirements and standards, the desire for self-esteem—in certain though by no means all forms—may manifest itself outwardly in bumptiousness, aggressiveness, defiance of social conventions and rules. It is, in short, sometimes a revolt of the individual against his own approbativeness, which he feels, puts him into a humiliating position of subjection to other men—that is, to their judgments or feelings about him. It is, in this form, an attainment which the Cynic and Stoic schools in antiquity conceived to be an essential part of moral excellence, exemplified best of all in the traditional pictures of Diogenes as a model of the supreme and godlike virtue of "self-sufficiency"; though as Diogenes was also rather ostentatious about it, Plato and others, according to the familiar stories, intimated that his professed scorn of other men's opinions of him was only a way of 'showing off'. To *proclaim* your freedom from approbativeness is plainly to manifest approbativeness—to make it evident that you wish to be admired by others for your indifference to their admiration."

he freely confesses his admiration for and dependence on the approval of the nobility. It is likewise by identifying themselves with their mistresses that Miss Gusset and Miss Graves seek to establish their superiority each over the other, but at the same time they resent their dependence on their mistresses. Through the sly criticisms they ultimately make of them, they reveal that they are in fact the rivals of their mistresses, that they at once accept and deny the superiority of these "superiors."

In the comedies of Molière this characteristically modern situation is incarnated in several fundamental types of comic structure.

The hero may choose an idol whom he uses as the instrument of his superiority to the world, for whom he loudly proclaims his admiration and for whom he demands the admiration of others, while at the same time trying to maintain a secret control over this idol—secret not only from others but even from himself—so that in the end it may be he, the hero, who is truly superior to the world. In our chapter on *Tartuffe* we emphasized the very real material power on which Orgon's relation to Tartuffe rests. In many respects *Les Femmes savantes* presents a similar structure. The poets and scholars whom Philaminte and her daughters fawn upon are in fact the instruments by which these women would, in a roundabout way, establish their superiority.

In this type of situation the hero is confounded the moment his "instrument" expresses and reveals his independence. And this independence is manifested in two ways, the second of which follows necessarily from the first: by the instrument's *acting or willing* independently of the hero and by his *being* independently of the hero. Orgon is confounded when Tartuffe turns out to have desires of his own and to be other than Orgon took him to be. Similarly Philaminte is confounded when Trissotin turns out to have desires of his own and to be other than she took him to be. Tartuffe desires not to do Orgon's will but to possess his wife, and he is discovered to be no saintly man but a vile intriguer. Trissotin likewise desires not what Philaminte wants him to desire but a substantial dowry,

while he is discovered to be a bad poet and an opportunist. Similarly in Dostoievski's *Possessed*, Mrs. Stavrogin is confounded by
her creation, Stepan Verkhovenski, when the latter develops a will
of his own with respect to Dasha and when he proves unable to
compete for public acclaim with the fashionable and successful
Karamzin. In all these cases the hero's plan is thwarted by the
revelation that his idol is both independent and inferior. The independence of the idol undermines the hero's concealed affirmation of himself through him, while the exposure of the idol's inferiority, of the contempt in which he is actually held by others,
deprives the hero of the approbation he sought to acquire through
him. At the same time, however, the humiliation of the idol is also
the source of a secret joy and triumph for the hero, for this idol is
also a rival.

We saw in previous chapters that a compound of idolatry and
rivalry, of adoration and hatred, characterizes the relations of many
of Molière's couples: Orgon and Tartuffe, Sganarelle and Dom
Juan, Philaminte and Trissotin, Alceste and Célimène, Dandin and
the Sotenvilles. Some of these comic heroes exhibit no elation at
all at the discomfiture of their idol. Orgon and Philaminte, for instance, are not sufficiently threatened with being eclipsed by their
idols for their latent rivalry with them to come to the fore. They
remain throughout the creators and patrons of their idols as well
as their disciples. (This is also, in the main, the case with Mrs.
Stavrogin.)

Among others, however, the rivalry is more overt, and this in
proportion as the idol already commands, in the idolator's eyes
at least, the admiration and respect that the idolator wishes for
himself. Molière incarnates this situation in a slightly different
comic structure from that of *Tartuffe* or *Les Femmes savantes*.
Thus in *Le Misanthrope* Alceste cannot pretend that his choice of
Célimène as a mistress was made independently. It was patently
mediated by others, by the Orontes and the Acastes and the Cli-
tandres, and Alceste is painfully aware of this fact, even though

he will not admit it openly to himself. Not surprisingly, therefore, his fury at Célimène's humiliation at the end of the play is tainted by a scarcely veiled exultation. In *George Dandin* the conflict of love and hate, of idolatry and rivalry is even clearer. Dandin's constant desire is to humiliate his idols, the Sotenvilles, but he can do this only by undermining at the same time his own existence, since it is on his acceptance by them *as superiors* that he has grounded his own value. If Dandin had realized that the Sotenvilles have their superiors by whom they in turn are held in contempt, he would have turned on them in *fury and delight* and screamed that he had been cheated.

This is what happens in Chekhov's *Uncle Vanya*. Vanya's love of Serebrakov's wife Yelena reveals both his dependence on him and his rivalry with him. In Act II Vanya wonders why he never wooed Yelena when it would have been possible to win her—before she became the Professor's wife: "I met her first ten years ago, at her sister's house, when she was seventeen and I was thirty-seven. Why did I not fall in love with her then and propose to her? It would have been so easy! (. . .) Oh, how I have been deceived! For years I have worshipped that miserable gout-ridden professor." Vanya does not answer his own question, but Chekhov expects us to answer it for him. (The sentimental productions of Chekhov that are so common, especially in Anglo-Saxon countries, do not, alas, give us much guidance in finding the answer.) Vanya is incapable of desiring at first hand. He can desire only through Serebrakov, and his entire existence is consumed by his rivalry with a man whom he adores and at the same time resents for the very reason that he adores him. To some degree—the same degree to which Dandin sees through the vanity of titles and ranks—Vanya frees himself from the slavish adoration which his mother still has for Serebrakov, precisely because he cannot bear the superiority with which he himself has invested the professor. Indeed his desire to humiliate the professor is whetted and exacerbated by the very admiration his mother has for him. Vanya's "freedom," however, is merely the outward appearance of an even deeper enslavement than that of his mother. His envy and resentment of his idol constantly urges him to destroy the image that he himself has actively helped to build up. Serebrakov must be invested with enormous prestige so that Vanya can glory in his relation to him, and at the same time the more Serebrakov is illuminated by this prestige, the more unbearable it is to Vanya, who is then tormented by the desire to destroy it. His final cry of rage at his idol is both a triumph of revenge and an agony of self-destruction: "For twenty-five years I have been sitting here with my mother like a mole in a burrow. Our every hope was yours and yours only. By day we talked with pride of you and your work, and spoke your name with veneration; our nights we wasted reading books and papers which my soul now loathes. (. . .) We used to think of you as superhuman, but now the scales have fallen from my eyes and I see you as you are! You write on art without knowing anything about it. These books of yours which I used to admire are not worth one copper kopeck. You are a hoax! (. . .) Wait! I have not done yet! You have wrecked my life! I have never lived. My best years have gone for nothing, have been ruined, thanks to you. You are my most bitter enemy!" The wonderfully farcical shooting scene in Act III sums up the whole of Vanya's relation to Serebrakov. Vanya shoots but misses. His hatred of Serebrakov leads him to shoot, but he must miss or he will deprive himself of the power to affirm himself by belittling his idol. On the other hand his missing also confirms, as he himself realizes dimly, the very inferiority which his contempt denies. His entire existence, as symbolized in the shooting incident, is a set of gestures that never make any contact with reality. He cannot act or will or be in his own right: his whole life is lived, as Dandin's is, in function of another being whom he cannot destroy without also destroying himself.[4] It is characteristic of much mod-

[4] Among many similar situations in Stendhal, one might recall the case of the Comte de Nerwinde in *Lamiel*. Nerwinde, it will be remembered, had formed a liaison with Lamiel, known at that time as Mme de Saint-Serve, but he was incapable of loving or enjoying her. He used her only in order to

ern literature that the idol who mediates between the hero and
all his thoughts and desires is not even aware of or concerned with
those whom he mediates. He may well be obsessed by a mediator-
idol of his own. Serebrakov has his own problems of vanity, and
he genuinely cannot understand Vanya's attitude. This indifference, which is already a notable trait of *Le Misanthrope* and which
becomes more and more marked, as we move by way of Rousseau
and Dostoievski toward the present age, emphasizes the utter
subjectivity of the comic hero. He is the creator of his own anguish.
Andrey's sisters, in the *Three Sisters*, cannot understand why their
brother boasts of his position on the local Zemstvo. They do not
know that, if he is forever impressing them with the dignity and
importance of his place on the Zemstvo, it is because he himself is
perpetually judging himself for not being a professor at the University of Moscow. Andrey cannot bear to be like everybody else.
He insists on being considered and judged as an exceptional being,
even if it means being condemned by his judges. Andrey therefore

---

impress others: "L'essentiel, c'est que, par sa figure et l'esprit que je lui
souffle, elle me fasse honneur dans le monde." But Lamiel charms, not with
any wit that Nerwinde has given or can give her: she charms because she is
supremely natural and unconcerned, utterly ignoring the dreary tone of correct
society and the witticisms that make no one laugh. "Avec son air doux et gai,
elle est l'audace même; elle a le courage plus humain que féminin," says the
old baron de Prévan, "de braver votre mépris, et c'est pourquoi elle est inimit-
able." Nerwinde, on the other hand, cannot bear Lamiel for the very reason
that she is happy and free. Secretly he is jealous of her success and popularity,
so that we are not surprised when one day he tries spitefully to humiliate her in
front of his friends—those very friends whom he was using her to impress! "Eh
bien, messieurs, dit un jour le comte de Nerwinde à ses amis qui admiraient
son bonheur, je ne me laisse point charmer par ce qui vous éblouit; que ce
soit un avantage ou un malheur du caractère que le Ciel m'a donné, je ne
suis point dupe de cette Mme de Saint-Serve, de cette beauté rare que vous
me gâtez comme à plaisir avec tous vos compliments. J'ai les moyens assurés
de rabattre sa fierté; tel que vous me voyez, depuis deux mois, c'est-à-dire
depuis la première semaine qui a suivi mon retour à Paris, nous faisons lit à
part" (Chap. 13). This outburst of vanity has the inevitable effect of degrading
Nerwinde himself. Everyone now wants to teach Lamiel, the astonishing
creature who can be happy even without love, *what Nerwinde had obviously
been inadequate to teach her*. She becomes more popular and more admired
than ever. Nerwinde's attempt to humiliate Lamiel thus results, like Dandin's
attempts to humiliate the Sotenvilles, in his own humiliation.

creates his judges and argues with them. He sets up an imaginary court and acts out his own prosecution and defense. You despise me, he makes his sisters say, because I am not a professor at the University of Moscow, but I think it is a noble thing to be a member of the local Zemstvo. In the loneliness of his study, however, he prepares the case for the prosecution: I am nothing, a failure, etc. Unable to bear his own mediocrity, unwilling to recognize that his lot is no different from that of anyone else, and that he is *quite undistinguished* even in his "failure," Andrey constantly seeks to provoke others into judging him and attributes to others the judgments that they constantly fail to pronounce, the concern with him that they do not have. The silence of the world is the source of his anguish, and it is this "indifference" that he tries to convert into an obsessional preoccupation. This mediocrity would be distinguished on account of his very mediocrity!

Chekhov is one of those modern writers who have not romanticized this situation and who have presented it uncompromisingly as funny. In this respect he joins hands over the centuries with his great predecessor, for Molière's *Misanthrope* is the first profound statement in modern terms of the world's silent indifference to those who no longer have any significant place in it or relation to it.

Alceste, as we saw in our chapter on *Le Misanthrope*, is he who reveals his enslavement to the world in the very act of asserting his independence of it. In reality it is not Alceste who is indifferent to the world; it is the world that is indifferent to Alceste. Alceste's loud protestations of autonomy, his perpetual criticisms, his endless complaints about the insincerity and vanity of others are meant to be *heard*, and to provoke a reaction. *Je veux qu'on me distingue.* It is in fact Alceste who is devoured by vanity, by such enormous vanity that he is unwilling either to be just like everybody else or to recognize that his own value depends in any way on the opinion that others have of him. But Alceste cannot really constitute a world unto himself. He cannot deny the existence of those others whose minds he cannot control and whose very being robs him of the autonomy and absoluteness to which he lays claim. This autonomy and this absoluteness are inevitably his autonomy and absoluteness with respect to others. Alceste must therefore first provoke, then seize hold of and control, the judgments of others. The more he realizes his need to possess in this way the freedom of others, the more loudly he denies it, and at the same time the more insatiable his desire for control becomes. The greater his desire for the approbation of others, the deeper his awareness of their independence; the deeper his awareness of their independence, the more exacting his desire for approbation. No amount of compliments and distinctions can ever satisfy Alceste, for behind them all he sees only the freedom to give them. The silence of the world is intolerable to him, for he must be recognized and distinguished, but in every compliment that is paid him he hears only an underlying silence, the silence of the other who remains independent even as his mouth speaks words of praise.

Through *Le Misanthrope* we are brought to see that proclamations of indifference and misanthropy and the modes of behavior that accompany them, such as living in a barrel or always threatening to go off to a desert place, are theatrical, comic in the purest sense. At the same time however, Molière also shows us that the subjective experience of the misanthrope is one of bitterest anguish. It is a mark of Molière's greatness and of his profound insight into modern life that he understood and portrayed both aspects of Alceste, the anguish and the comedy, the subjective reality of his suffering and the objective insignificance of his being. The objective comic view is the superior one, precisely because it does not exclude but embraces and transcends the subjective one.

Many writers after Molière could no longer sustain the seventeenth century author's clear distinction between objective reality and the comic hero's experience of that reality. This does not imply that those who came after Molière necessarily saw less clearly than he. The protests which Alceste makes against the society of Célimène do not contain, in the form in which they are made, the questions which Molière himself raises about his society. Molière does already question the objective social order of his time, but he distinguishes between his questioning and that of Alceste. Alceste's protest against the court of Célimène is clearly seen as subjective and it does not reach its object, although this object is indeed seen—from the author's perspective—as questionable. The insubstantiality of the "objective" order of society has become so glaring by the eighteenth century, however, that even the author cannot adopt any firm point of view. All he can do is present the hero's protest and society's rejection of it, each of which is understandable only in relation to the other.

In a work such as Prévost's *Manon Lescaut*, for instance, there is no objective key. To try to decipher a fixed meaning in this work is to miss the meaning it really has. This meaning is inseparable from the form of *Manon Lescaut*. The entire story is told from the perspective of the hero himself; we never know more than he, we are as hard put to interpret the signs as he is, and we see the other characters as well as all the events of the story through his eyes. The narrator makes it clear at the beginning that he will report Des Grieux's words as faithfully as he can. Even the author's preface leaves us in doubt as to whether Des Grieux's story is a "terrible example of the force of passion" in the sense that passion itself is a seeking of illusory goals, or in the sense that the passionate individual seeking real goals must be crushed by a society based on and dedicated to empty and illusory forms. At the same time Prévost carefully advises us, and, significantly enough, reminds us by repeating the narrator-audience device of the first part of the book at the beginning of the second part, that what we are reading is a subjective account of events. Des Grieux's own puzzlement when confronted with certain "incomprehensible" and contradictory signs also reminds us of this. Prévost gives us Des Grieux's story of his adventures and only Des Grieux's story, but he does not claim that this story is unequivocally *true*. The significance of the events recounted by Des Grieux is so far from being unambiguous that it is not even clear to him. Can his passion for Manon, for instance, be understood on a single level of meaning?

Structurally the story of Des Grieux's passion resembles that of Alceste for Célimène. Like Alceste, Des Grieux falls in love with the "wrong woman." Like Alceste, he would like his mistress to be simple and faithful and to have few or no relations with the outside world, and yet his love, like that of Alceste, grows and thrives on Manon's "frivolity" and on her very infidelities. After the first infidelity his love becomes a veritable madness and, when she comes to see him at St. Lazare, he finds her "plus aimable et plus brillante que je ne l'avais jamais vue" (*Histoire du Chevalier des Grieux et de Manon Lescaut; texte et ortho- graphe de l'édition de 1753* [Paris, "Les Phares," 1946], p. 37). Far from diminishing the love he has for her, Manon's relations with the world elevate her, as they elevate Célimène, and make her more precious in her lover's eyes. Des Grieux's love takes on the aspect of a kind of cult. She becomes everything for him, while he be- comes practically nothing. In the famous conversation with Ti- berge, Des Grieux himself formulates his adoration of Manon in religious terms (*ed. cit.*, p. 82) and everything he says here is con- firmed subsequently (p. 100). He declares that he does not deserve the grace of being loved by a creature as perfect as Manon (p. 135), that he is nothing compared to her and that it is not for him to question the actions of such a divine being. His final triumph, the possession of Manon, is expressed in terms of a kind of religious asceticism (p. 172).

To the very degree that his passion for Manon grows, however, in the very measure that he elevates her above him, Des Grieux's resentment of her also deepens. The development of his hatred, his frustration, his anguish, and his resentment *accompanies* the intensification of his love after the first infidelity (pp. 29–30, 31) and after each subsequent one or menace of one. Hatred and love feed on each other in this relation as they did in Alceste's love for Célimène; adoring Manon, Des Grieux feels more intensely the need to possess her and thus to humiliate this mistress who is also a rival; at the same time his need to humiliate her confirms her superiority and forces him to adore her.

Des Grieux is afflicted at times with Alcestian misanthropy. On several occasions, in particular after Manon abandons him, he feels an intense desire to flee the world, to renounce forever a society of cruel and heartless people. His misfortunes indeed confirm, as they did for Alceste, the wickedness and valuelessness of the world and his own immeasurable superiority to it. At the same time, however, Des Grieux himself does many wicked things: he lies, he deceives, he steals, he even murders. To maintain the image of his superiority to the world he has therefore to invent another myth, the myth of what we might call his "noumenal" person. According to this myth, his intentions are pure whatever acts he may perform; and even if his intentions at any given moment are not pure, he himself transcends these momentary aberrations by condemning himself for having had them. In the midst of all his evil-doing, Des Grieux can thus maintain the image of his own moral superiority, though, of course, he has to tell his story, to present his noumenal person to the public in order to have it appreciated, approved and confirmed by others—whereby the "noumenal" Des Grieux becomes something of a "phenomenal" one! The Des Grieux who does all the evil acts is the phenomenal Des Grieux, and the phenomenal Des Grieux is regulated by accident. It is thus accident that provokes the world to judge him—he himself, his highest self, is not interested in the world—and by judging him the world reveals its moral inferiority to him, and is confirmed in its pettiness and contingency. As Alceste desires to lose his lawsuit so as to confirm his own superiority to a society that has chosen to base itself on form rather than substance, so Des Grieux appears to seek the condemnation of his society in order to transform this condemnation into a sign of his own superiority to it.

Despite external and structural similarities in the relation in which the two heroes stand to their society and to their mistresses, however, there are significant differences between the two cases. Where Célimène is the center of her society and is accepted, indeed sought after by every member of it, Manon is rejected by hers. In this sense Alceste's desire to win a place in his society is manifested unambiguously in his love for Célimène, whereas Des Grieux's very love for Manon implies at one and the same time his rejection of his society and his love of it. Des Grieux's love for Manon is love for a creature who is rejected by society, and yet his love for her grows as she appears to triumph in society. But in fact Manon's triumphs have the same ambiguity in themselves as Des Grieux's love for her. Those who desire her at the same time degrade her, and she in turn degrades those who desire her.

The role of accident in Prévost's novel is also ambiguous. Alceste, as we saw, presents his love for Célimène as both accident and choice. Accident, however, has no real role in Molière's play. It has only subjective reality in Alceste's mind as a pretext which conceals the objective reasons for his choice of Célimène. In Prévost's novel accident plays an extensive and important role. The entire action of the story is propelled by a series of accidents. On one level these accidents can be, and are, used by the hero to absolve himself of responsibility, much as Alceste uses the "accident" of his love for Célimène. On another level, however, accident has in *Manon* an objective reality. It is both pretext and truth, for Prévost saw the social relations of his time as themselves arbitrary and accidental. In what sense of accident is it accident that brings together persons as diverse socially as Manon and the Italian Prince, or the fugitive lovers and a rich *fermier-général?* The ambiguity of the novel precludes an answer. Prévost does not commit himself to an unequivocal criticism of his society. He is not identical with his hero, nor, however, is his relation to him as clear as Molière's relation to Alceste.

With Rousseau there is complete identification of the author and the literary spokesman. The comedy of Molière becomes the reality of Rousseau. The structure of Alceste's relation to the world in *Le Misanthrope* is repeated once more in Rousseau's relation to his world, but the terms of the relation have again changed. The dissolution of the world of Célimène, Acaste, Oronte and Clitandre, which was already announced, as we saw, in Molière's comedy and which had gone even further in Prévost's novel, has now, by Rousseau's time, been completed. The world of Rousseau's society is a world that wills itself as pure form, a world that seeks to sustain itself by organizing all behavior and all relations in it into set formal patterns. In this world Rousseau inevitably appeared as a comic figure, an intriguer, and a hypocrite. In the champion of sincerity, humility, and the simple life Rousseau's contemporaries found a man devoured by pride and obsessed by the desire to impress others. And all this was in a sense true. Isolated in a world of forms, longing for some real, rather than purely formal, relation to his fellows, terrified by the incomprehensibility of the signs of which formal relations are composed—the polite phrases, the protestations of affection, the honors, the looks of admiration or of interest—not knowing whether they were true or simply conventional, Rousseau, like Alceste, became fascinated with that which constantly escaped him. In the *Confessions* and the *Dialogues* he refers continually to *voiles, impostures, mystères, énigmes effrayants, masques, ténèbres impénétrables, obstacles*, to which he opposes other words like *voir, pénétrer, démasquer*. Confronted with a world which he experiences as masked, veiled, enigmatic, constantly withdrawing from him, Rousseau is seized with a desire to pull aside the veil, to tear off the mask. The only way he can achieve any relation to society, in short, is—paradoxically—by destroying the forms on which it rests. Society is thus at one and the same time the goal of his desire and the obstacle to its fulfillment, in the sense that while the individual, for Rousseau, finds his true fulfillment only through his relations with others in society, the society he knew and lived in stood in the way of such a fulfillment. Rousseau therefore spent his life in vain endeavors to achieve a relation to others that was at once, in the conditions of the salon society of his time, necessary and impossible, desirable and intolerable, longed for and dreaded. Rousseau was not unaware that this paradox made every one of his gestures ambiguous. (Whence his fear of an enormous plot of international proportions to unmask him).

The points of similarity between Rousseau and Alceste are so obvious that they may be rapidly summarized: the adoration of the world and the contempt for the world, the longing for affection and the misanthropy, the constant gestures of departure from the world and the links that are constantly maintained with it. Just as Alceste wants to lose his lawsuit, or Des Grieux to provoke the condemnation of the world in order thereby to prove his own superiority to his judges, so Rousseau provokes the world to the point that he can imagine an enormous plot against him, involving the most eminent persons in Europe, in order both to experience himself as part of society and, by debasing his judges, to dissociate himself from it. With Rousseau as with Alceste, it is not the world that is obsessed by the individual, it is the individual who is obsessed by the world. In a striking passage of his introduction to the *Dialogues*, Rousseau himself refers to his anguish at the silence of a world that seems to be constantly and secretly scheming against him, in a way which leaves no doubt that the world of others has become his God and his transcendence: "Le silence profond, universel, non moins inconcevable que le mistére qu'il couvre, mistére que depuis quinze ans on me cache avec un soin que je m'abstiens de qualifier, et avec un succés qui tient du prodige; ce silence effrayant et terrible ne m'a pas laissé saisir la moindre idée qui pût m'eclaircir sur ces étranges dispositions" (*Oeuvres complètes*, ed. Pleiade, Vol. 1 [Paris, 1959], p. 662). The "silence de ces espaces infinis" which filled Pascal with fear and awe has here become the silence of the world and the awful mystery of the *Deus absconditus* has become the mystery of the Other. Rousseau himself describes this mystery as something "qui tient du prodige." It is in fact on his relation to the world that he both has to and is unable to found his being. His intermittent gestures of revolt themselves make this clear. "N'ai-je donc connu la vanité de l'opinion," he asks himself in a remarkable passage at the end of the *Dialogues*, "que pour me remettre sous son joug aux depends de la paix de mon âme et du repos de mon coeur? Si les hommes veulent me voir autre que je ne suis, que m'importe? L'essence de mon être est-elle dans leurs regards? (. . .) Pourquoi donc est-il nécessaire à mon bonheur éternel qu'ils me connoissent et me rendent justice?" (*ibid.*, pp. 985–86).

The structure of Alceste's relation to the world as Molière drew it in *Le Misanthrope* reappears once again in the literature of the nineteenth century, but once again the terms of this relation have changed. Alceste's protest can be understood as the lament of a disgruntled and displaced *robin* over a social significance that he no longer possesses in the new world of the absolute monarch of the seventeenth century and as his futile and comic attempt to recover this lost significance. But the dissolution of the world of the court itself, which is fairly openly suggested in Molière's play, makes of the comic hero a Janus-figure. To the degree that the comedy is seen from the point of view of a society that is itself losing contact with reality and dissolving into formalism Alceste's protest can foreshadow the later protest of Rousseau against the pure conventionality of human relations in the society of his time. In Molière's case, however, the author could still stand back from his hero to the extent that he still had a relation to society, in this instance to the Court, even though he was beginning to question this relation; in Rousseau's case, the very nature of his relation to society was to question it. The identification of the author with his hero was consequently far greater. Indeed it was complete. In the nineteenth century the relation between the author (and consequently the hero) and society is totally disrupted. Even Rousseau's questioning, which in itself still constituted a kind of relation to his society, now turns inward and ceases to be a genuine questioning. Few of the Romantics had the real concern with social problems or the realistic grasp of them that Rousseau shows in a text such as the *Second Discourse*. The questions asked by the writer are no longer directed at any specific historical form of society but become generalizing and abstract. Paradoxically, however, the more general the nature of the questions, the more subjective is the nature of the questioning. The historical reality of society becomes the subjective concept of "the world," the individual's relation to society becomes "the human condition." [5]

The myth of passion, the loudly advertised uniqueness of the hero, the desire to go off to the desert with the beloved, the rejection of the world, and the adoration of the world are recurrent themes in the literature of Romanticism. The Romantic hero alternately adores and condemns his mistress, just as he alternately adores and condemns the world, passing inevitably in the fury of pride and fear, from the one extreme to the other, experiencing himself now as totally absolute and autonomous, now as totally contingent and dependent, now as a God-like plenitude of being and now as a worm-like absence of being, constantly affirming his independence, constantly discovering his dependence, and con-

[5] In his article "Don Juan and the Baroque" (*Diogenes*, 14, Summer 1956, pp. 1–16), Jean Rousset points to the same rapprochement of author and hero in the case of Romantic versions of the Don Juan legend as compared with versions produced in the seventeenth century. "One constant in the Don Juans of the seventeenth century," he writes (p. 10), "is that their authors are not their accomplices, in spite of their acceptance of inconstancy. They do not confuse themselves with Don Juan, even when they no longer acknowledge the point of view of permanence. Molière maintains a distance between himself and his Don Juan, even though this distance has decreased since Tirso. (. . .) On the other hand, Romanticism—and all of the modern period following it—upset the significance of the Don Juan as conceived by the baroque and, particularly, altered his relationship with his authors. The latter were to conceive of a Don Juan in their own image, their accomplice and their brother. (. . .) We were to see Hoffmann, Byron, Musset and Baudelaire confusing themselves with their Don Juans, and consequently glorifying and absolving him."

stantly denying this dependence in order to reaffirm his independence. The pathos of Vigny's *Chatterton* with its general indictment of an uncomprehending world has its counterpart in the Kafka-like pages of the *Journal* with their bitter and strangely modern-sounding condemnation of *le sale espoir* (the illusions of Romanticism) and their transformation of an ugly and oppressive world into the God before whom we have to bow our heads. The poet would be God and have the world for his slave and admirer; the failure of this dream of dominion transforms the world into Moloch and the poet into its abject slave. All the Romantics want to be distinguished, different from others and superior to them. But to *ask* to be distinguished is to admit a degrading dependence on one's inferiors. A common solution to this dilemma is to cause a scandal (*épater le bourgeois*), without of course intending to—or at least this is how it is to appear—and thus to provoke a judgment, by which one is at once distinguished and at the same time confirmed as superior by the very vindictiveness and stupidity of the judges who pronounce the inevitable condemnation. The infantile nature of this behavior has been beautifully demonstrated by Madame Magny in a chapter on the Surrealists in her book *Histoire du roman français depuis 1918* (Paris, 1950). But its presence is not always perceived. In a paper read to the Johns Hopkins Philological Society in 1962, René Girard pointed out that the murder of the Arab by Meursault in Camus' *L'Etranger* is never satisfactorily explained by the author. It has the appearance of an accident, but if it were only an accident, it would not be enough to give a general and universal significance to the novel and to Meursault's condemnation by the judges at the end. On the other hand, if it is intentional, Meursault must be held to deserve his punishment according to the law of the land, which holds for all, and the judges cannot be considered particularly vindictive or cruel; for Meursault is not in fact condemned for the moral crime or emotional inadequacy of not crying at his mother's funeral—no judge could condemn a man on those grounds—but for the capital crime of murder. The trouble is that, far from everybody's being concerned with Meursault's existence—with knowing, for instance, how he felt at his mother's funeral—no one ever shows the slightest interest in the man. The device used by Camus is in reality one that recurs in countless Romantic works. The murder is *intended* to attract the interest of an intolerably indifferent world, to transform a mediocre and undistinguished character into a distinguished victim, but at the same time it must *not appear intended*, for the little man is to be noticed and singled out by the world without having to ask to be noticed and singled out. Camus-Meursault is in fact the man who is obsessed by an indifferent world and who makes it appear that the world is obsessed by him. Naturally enough he can do this only through the device of the "accidental" murder, for without the murder society would never have noticed Meursault. In the same way the world's persecution of Des Grieux is not provoked by him, but is the result of a series of "accidents." Likewise Alceste sees the situation caused by his refusal to give the customary presents to the judges in his lawsuit as an example of the world's persecution of the virtuous. Whereas Molière points out through Philinte, however, that it is up to Alceste to decide whether he really wants to fight his case, both Prévost and Camus allow the reader to imagine that their heroes are entirely innocent victims.

The modern writer is not entirely *to blame* for failing to reach the clearness of vision that characterizes Molière. One must suppose that other factors, factors to some degree outwith the artist's control, have intervened to make the comic perspective progressively more difficult to achieve in modern times. If we consider even those recent writers who have seemed to us to share Molière's comic perspective, we find that the comedy is darker and more bitter in their works than it is in the plays of Molière. *Madame*

Bovary is not as hilariously funny as *Le Bourgeois Gentilhomme*, although the comic structure is very similar, and there is an element of cruel irony in the novels of Stendhal, and even more so in those of Dostoievski, that is absent from the works of Molière with which we have compared them. Similarly it would seem that something very considerable must have happened to transform Alceste into the utter nonentity that Meursault is.

We noted earlier that the "open" type of comedy, represented in the work of Molière by *Les Précieuses ridicules* or *Le Bourgeois Gentilhomme*, was less common in modern literature than one might at first have expected; and that the "closed" type, in which the hero is actually the rival of his idol, whom he worships and denies at the same time, was far more prevalent. We suggested that the reason for this lay in the dissolution of the earlier hierarchical social order and in a growing perception that differences, which were previously believed to be founded in an objective reality, are formal, conventional, "ideal" (to use Saint-Simon's term), in short, imaginary. "La pantomime des gueux" is seen as "le grand branle de la terre" and everyone is observed to have "sa petite Hus et son Bertin" (Diderot, *Le Neveu de Rameau*). In these conditions, as Diderot's astonishing text implies, the choice must be either to change the existing social order and to construct a new one in accordance with the real equality of men, as the social revolutionary hopes to do, or to accept the unreality of social distinctions and to seek for oneself an imaginary place in an imaginary hierarchy. Every little Rameau will then aspire to be a little Bertin, and the result will then be the progressive denial of the objective, the acceptance of the subjective as primary reality, and the identification of the realm of the imaginable with the realm of the real. Everyone in these circumstances becomes potentially a superior and a rival to every one else, and the anguish and misery of the individual locked in this world of subjectivity becomes at one and the same time more and more imaginary and more and more unbearable. The pain increases, as it were, in proportion as its objective cause disappears.[6] If we compare the world of the Restoration as it is portrayed in the work of Stendhal with the world of the *ancien régime* as it appears in the comedies of Molière, we shall be struck by the interpenetration of the social classes in Stendhal. To the very degree that there

[6] Toqueville, in his *Democracy in America*, gives a profound and prophetic analysis of this situation as it was understood by an acute observer in the 1830's. The following passage is taken from Part II, Book 3, Chap. 16 of the Henry Reeve translation, "Why the national vanity of the Americans is more restless and captious than that of the English" (edition of London, 1862, Vol. 2, pp. 269–70): "In aristocratic countries the great possess immense privileges, upon which their pride rests, without seeking to rely upon the lesser advantages which accrue to them. As these privileges come to them by inheritance, they regard them in some sort as a portion of themselves, or at least as a natural right inherent in their own persons. They therefore entertain a calm sense of their own superiority; they do not dream of vaunting privileges which every one perceives and no one contests, and these things are not sufficiently new to them to be made topics of conversation. They stand unmoved in their solitary greatness, well assured that they are seen of all the world without any effort to show themselves off, and that no one will attempt to drive them from that position (. . .).

"When on the contrary social conditions differ but little, the slightest privileges are of some importance; *as every man sees around himself a million people enjoying precisely similar or analogous advantages, his pride becomes craving and jealous, he clings to mere trifles, and doggedly defends them.* In democracies, as the conditions of life are very fluctuating, men have almost always recently acquired the advantages which they possess; the consequence is that they feel extreme pleasure in exhibiting them, *to show others and convince themselves that they really enjoy them.* As at any instant these same advantages may be lost, their possessors are constantly on the alert, and make a point of showing that they still retain them. (. . .)

"The restless and insatiable vanity of a democratic people originates so entirely in the equality and precariousness of social conditions, that the members of the haughtiest nobility display the very same passion in those lesser portions of their existence in which there is anything fluctuating or contested. An aristocratic class always differs greatly from the other classes of the nation, by the extent and perpetuity of its privileges; but it often happens that the only differences between the members who belong to it consist in small transient advantages, which may any day be lost or acquired.

"The members of a powerful aristocracy, collected in a capital or a court, have been known to contest with virulence those frivolous privileges which depend on the caprice of fashion or the will of their master. These persons then displayed towards each other precisely the same puerile jealousies which animate the men of democracies, the same eagerness to snatch the smallest advantages which their equals contested, and the same desire to parade ostentatiously those of which they were in possession." (Italics added throughout).

is greater movement from one class to another, the signs of distinction are more grossly insisted on, and as the signs of distinction are more grossly insisted on, the substance of these distinctions becomes thinner and thinner. The new aristocracy is more consciously "aristocratic" than the old ever was, precisely because it feels itself constantly judged not only by the old but by its own servants (one thinks of Madame de Fervacques or the Duchess of Miossens), while the old aristocracy adopts many of the so-called bourgeois virtues in order to justify itself before the bourgeoisie (the "patriarchal" nobles of Balzac's novels). The old aristocracy can no longer simply be itself. Even where it is contemptuous of the new ways, it does not escape them. Mathilde de La Môle is also "proving" something to others; her very refusal to follow the new style, her attempt to maintain the old aristocratic style is itself theatrical.

As the area of rivalry, fear, and resentment is gradually extended until it embraces almost the whole of society, it becomes increasingly difficult to get outside it. The follies of Don Quixote take place against a large background of common sense; the comedy of Malvolio's sickly vanity is observed and laughed at by every other character in the play. In the work of Molière, this common sense background is still present. Cathos and Magdelon, Harpagon and Argan are alone in their madness. Against them Molière sets the rather limited but healthy "horse sense" of servants, the real and concrete desires of young lovers, the *honnêteté* of the *raisonneurs* and the—admittedly enigmatic—wisdom of certain of his women characters. Madame Jourdain, stout, solid, and sensible, is a necessary foil for her fantastical and romantic husband. Toinette, buxom and beaming with good health, sets Argan in his proper light. It is true that there is hardly a single honest character in *George Dandin*. Against the vanity and sadistic resentment of Dandin and the Sotenvilles can be set only the scheming hypocrisy of Angélique and her maid and the cold cynicism of Clitandre. But *George Dandin*, like *La Comtesse d'Escarbagnas*, which is in many respects fairly close to it, is set in the provinces and the comedy of provincial life is watched by an urbane Parisian audience of *honnêtes gens*. It is this tacit opposition of Paris and provinces that provides the perspective from which the comedy can be perceived.

If the superiority of the capital be made subject to doubt, however, if the suspicion be aroused that the capital is not really very different from the provinces, *George Dandin* will become a very dark comedy indeed. Petersburg and Moscow are not in fact portrayed in *The Possessed* nor Paris in *Madame Bovary*, any more than the capital is portrayed in *George Dandin*, and to some degree these novels can be considered provincial comedies in the same way that *George Dandin* can. Nonetheless we are vaguely aware, as we read the novels, that the distinction between capital and provinces is finer in the world of the nineteenth century than it was in the world of the seventeenth, and we are more acutely conscious than Molière's audiences probably were that we shall ourselves be dupes if we imagine that not being provincials allows us to escape the ridicules of Homais or Emma Bovary, of Mrs. Stavrogin or of the Governor's wife. Not only are the same comedies, covered by a thin veneer of elegance, enacted in the capital—Proust is one of the great teachers here —the lower inhabitants of the capital ultimately try to humiliate their country cousins, thus joining the two realms of capital and provinces, town and country, in one vast structure of vanity and resentment. Even in *Madame Bovary* this can be observed in Léon's changed attitude to Emma after his—rather wretched— period of study in Paris. Léon feels as superior for having lived in the capital as the Comtesse d'Escarbagnas does for having spent a few days at Court. This interpenetration of capital and provinces, which resembles the interpenetration of the classes during the last century of the *ancien régime* and the even greater fluctuations of the Restoration, had not yet occurred in Molière's time. The comic perspective in Molière's play was thus more firmly established by the social structure itself and was more easily reached by his audiences than is the case with the two nineteenth-century novels. Just as good solid bourgeois and noblemen alike could laugh at the antics of Jourdain, so provincials and courtiers alike could laugh at the antics of Dandin and the Comtesse d'Escarbagnas. Since each group felt sufficiently confident of itself and since neither was dependent on the other for recognition, the spectacle of the social climber was funny to both.

Time has corroded the social hierarchies that constituted the objective, historical condition of the comic perspective in Molière's own age. The privileged perspective of the capital and of the *honnêtes gens* has turned out to be insubstantial and ephemeral, and at the same time the once simple and self-reliant population of the provinces has increasingly sought to vie with its urban counterpart. Very few have not become Dandins or Sotenvilles in one degree or another. In these conditions the vantage point from which *George Dandin* can be laughed at is no longer given by the social structure itself, it has to be acquired. Once it has been acquired, the objective truth of the comedy may be more clearly perceived than it was by Molière's own audiences. In the absence of an historical perspective, the comedy of *George Dandin*, for instance, could well appear more universal to a modern reader than it did to the audience that watched it three hundred years ago and that judged it from its own social perspective, but at the same time the point of view from which such a modern reader might perceive the universality of the comedy would inevitably be more ideal than it was for Molière's audiences. The comedy would then be at once funnier and grimmer than it was for the seventeenth-century audience, and to the degree that the vantage point from which it was being viewed was purely intellectual and mental, it would become very grim indeed, for the reader would have nothing but his own awareness of vanity and stupidity to set against an empirical world that he sees as completely given over to foolish cruelties and empty sufferings. This situation accounts for the rather black and depressing humor of *Madame Bovary* or of *Bouvard et Pécuchet*, for instance. The entire world of *Madame Bovary*, with the single exception of the great doctor who was Charles Bovary's teacher, is engulfed in stupidity, meanness, heartlessness, and vanity. Pretentiousness and folly are no longer the exception, as they still appear to be in Molière, they are now the rule, and it is the man of wisdom and moderation who is isolated in the world, along with dumb and, for this reason alone, authentic creatures, such as Catherine, the old farm servant, who makes a brief but memorable appearance at the scene of the country fair in *Madame Bovary*.

Molière's own work, however, already shows signs of the inroads of modernity. In his most troubling and complex comedies the world of common sense has worn somewhat thin. *Le Misanthrope*, for instance, manifests a considerable narrowing down of the solid background of common sense with respect to simpler comedies such as *Le Malade imaginaire* or *L'Ecole des femmes*. Célimène, Oronte, Arsinoë, and the two marquesses are not quite as deranged in their vanity as Alceste, but their world is not a healthy one either. Even as a world of empty forms and conventions it is not an alternative to the madness of Alceste. The members of this world are themselves unable to sustain the formalism on which their society rests. The vanity of the men ultimately forces them to insist that Célimène declare her hand and pronounce whom she *really* prefers among them, but this is the one demand that is inadmissible in a world of forms. It is as though all the courtiers of Versailles had demanded to know where they *really* stood in the King's favor. The collapse of the united front of Célimène and her society against Alceste reveals clearly enough that the world of Paris and Versailles, which *appears* to provide a foil for the follies and vanities of the comic hero, is itself undermined by folly and vanity. Its cohesion is only apparent; behind the façade of elegant order there is the same seething of destructive pride and anguish as there is behind

Alceste's façade of righteousness and frankness. Philinte and Eliante are the only authentic characters in the comedy, but they are in a sense isolated from society, belonging to no society but their own. Once again, of course, the public of supposedly *honnêtes gens* can be considered as distinct from Célimène and her group, and as closer to Philinte and Eliante. As compared with *George Dandin*, however, the comic perspective is already becoming more and more ideal. In *George Dandin* the world of *honnêteté* which provided the perspective on the comedy could be identified with the world of Paris and Versailles. In *Le Misanthrope* we find that the world of *honnêteté* has shrunk further, since it now excludes part of the society of the town and the Court, a rather considerable part, one would guess. *Le Misanthrope* is, after all, a comedy set in the high society of Paris. We cannot regard as insignificant the fact that the only two authentic characters in this society cut very lonely figures indeed.

The question of perspective is acute, we should insist, only in the most difficult and problematic of Molière's comedies. In them, however, we can discern the shape of the future. We have already referred to the extreme ideality of the perspective in Flaubert's masterpiece and to the effect that this ideality had on the form of his humor. A brief look at Pushkin's *Eugene Onegin* will, I hope, make even clearer the importance of the objective conditions of the comic writer's activity.[7]

Pushkin's verse novel is a beautifully ironical exposure of the

---

[7] Pushkin's *Eugene Onegin* not only bears a striking thematic resemblance to Molière's *Misanthrope*, it occupies a similar position in its author's development to that occupied in Molière's development by *Le Misanthrope*. It was in and through *Eugene Onegin* that Pushkin overcame the Romanticism in his own heart, just as in and through *Le Misanthrope* Molière conquered that part of him which was Alceste. Pushkin's emancipation from certain aspects of Romanticism can be followed in his changing attitude to Byron, his judgment of Hugo and his relation to writers like Shakespeare, Scott, and Goethe. Cf. B. P. Gorodietski, *Dramaturgia Pushkina* (Moscow and Leningrad, 1953); also *Pushkin i Teatr; dramaticheskie proizvedienia, stati, zamietki, dnievniki, pisma*, ed. E. Ivanovna, N. Litvinienko, A. Klinchin (Moscow, 1953).

destructive illusions of Romantic love and of the rhetorical
emptiness of Romantic misanthropy, though Pushkin also shows
that the false attitudes and illusions of his Romantic characters,
their inability to achieve authenticity, cannot be considered apart
from the narrowness and vacuity of the world they live in. His
heroine, like Emma Bovary later, is bewitched by Romantic
novels which she begins reading in imitation of her mother, who
had in turn taken up the habit in imitation of her brilliant
Moscow cousin Princess Aline (II, 30):

> She took to novel reading early,
> And all her days became a glow
> Of rapturous love for the creations
> Of Richardson and of Rousseau.
>   (II, 29)

On Tatyana the reading of novels has a much deeper effect
than it had on her mother or her aunt, both of whom learned
very quickly to accept that radical distinction between poetry
and fact, between literature and life, which Belinsky considered
characteristic of Russian society. Tatyana learns through novels
of a larger world beyond the estates of her father and his neighbors. She learns to desire what neither the boorish friends of her
father nor any mild village idealist can give to her. Unlike her
sister Olga, she is not attracted by Lensky, the enthusiastic young
dreamer who comes home to his village after drinking in deep
draughts of Kantian idealism and literary romanticism in Germany. Lacking any concrete experience of the world or any
acquaintance with people of wider interests and deeper aspirations
than those of the landlords who visit her father's home, she immediately fixes all her longings on Onegin, associating the strange
new neighbor with all the heroes of her favorite novels:

> The lover of Julie Wolmar,
> Malek-Adhel and de Linar,
> Werther, who played the rebel's part,

And that sleep-bringing paragon,
The still unrivaled Grandison.[8]
(III, 9)

Ironically, but compassionately, Pushkin predicts the inevitable
fate of his delightful but dreamy heroine. The hero she is in love
with is a fiction. Onegin himself is, in his own way, a victim of
the sterility and emptiness of Russian life. He too is filled with
ideas and aspirations garnered from books, ideas and aspirations
that are absolutely unrelated to the real conditions of Russian
society and cannot be realized in them. Onegin's whole being has
been poisoned by a spurious education. He is filled with cynical
self-pity, and behind the "interesting" image of the intelligent
young aristocrat there is only a sterile preoccupation with self:

[8] On the influence of novels, the second of Belinsky's articles on *Onegin*,
the ninth in the Pushkin series, should be consulted. I quote at some length a
particularly relevant passage: "The very endeavour of a person to develop
independently, extraneously of society, imparts to him a sort of singularity,
a freakishness which, in its turn, also bears the stamp of society. That is why
with us gifted people richly endowed by nature are often unbearable, and that
is why with us only genius can save a man from vulgarity. By the same token
we have so little genuine and so much *bookish*, *conned* sentiments, passions
and strivings; in short, so little truth and life in sentiments, passions and
strivings, and so much verbal flourish instead of them. The general spread of
reading is bringing us untold benefit; herein lies our salvation and the lot of
our futurity; but it also, on the other hand, breeds much harm (. . .) Our
society (. . .) is the fruit of reform (. . .) It began in the same way as our
literature: by the imitation of foreign forms devoid of all content, either our
own or foreign, for we had rejected our own without being capable of adopt-
ing, leave alone understanding, the foreign. The French had tragedies—so we
must needs begin to write tragedies too; and Mr. Sumarokov combined in his
own single person Corneille and Racine and Voltaire. The French had a
famous fabulist La Fontaine and the selfsame Mr. Sumarokov, according to
the testimony of his contemporaries, threw La Fontaine into the shade with
his Russian parables. Similarly, in the briefest space of time, we begot our own
homebred Pindars, Horaces, Anacreons, Homers, Virgils, etc. Foreign works
were full of amorous emotions and amorous adventures, and we must needs
fill ours with the same. But there the poetry of books mirrored the poetry of
life, the rhyme of love was a reflection of the love that formed the life and
poetry of society: with us love only found its way into books and there it
stayed (. . .) And so, many people with us like to talk about love, to read
and write about it; but as to loving . . . that is an entirely different matter
(. . .) The worst of it is that that other matter necessarily gives birth to a

But oh, Tatyana, dear Tatyana!
The tears are gathering in my eyes;
Already to a modern despot
You've given yourself as sacrifice.
(III, 15)

The prediction is, of course, fulfilled.

Onegin is incapable of love. Like Alceste, he has experienced the deceitful superficiality of human relations—though, unlike Alceste he has also experienced them in himself—and he has turned against the world in dark misanthropy (IV, 1–10). But Pushkin allows his reader to entertain no illusions about the nature of Onegin's boredom and disgust with life:

Lord Byron with his happy wand
Has clothed in dark Romanticism
Incorrigible egotism.
(III, 12)

---

third, rather ugly matter. When life and poetry lack a natural vital bond of unity their disparately-hostile existence gives rise to a spuriously poetical and exceedingly morbid, ugly reality. One part of society, true to its innate apathy, peacefully dozes in the slough of gross materiality; but the other, numerically still the smaller, though already fairly considerable, takes great pains to create for itself a poetical existence, to combine poetry with life. It does so in a very simple and innocuous manner. Seeing no poetry in society it takes it from books and works out its life accordingly. Poetry says that love is the soul of life: therefore, we must love! The syllogism is correct—it is backed up both by the mind and by the heart itself! And so our ideal youth or our ideal maid seeks an object with which to fall in love. (. . .) The ensuing comedy contains everything the heart desires: sighs, and tears, and dreams, and walks in the moonlight, and despair, and jealousy, and rapture, and vows—everything except genuine feeling. No wonder that the last act of this mountebank comedy always ends in disillusionment—and in what?—in your own feeling, in your own capacity for loving! And yet this bookish tendency is quite natural: was it not the book that turned the kind, chivalrous and sensible country gentleman of La Mancha into the knight-errant Don Quixote? (. . .) How many Don Quixotes did we not have between the generation of the twenties and the present time? We had and still have the Don Quixotes of love, science, literature, convictions, Slavophilism and God knows what else! They are too numerous to mention! Above we spoke of the ideal maids; and what a lot of interesting things could be told of the ideal youth!" (V. G. Belinsky, *Selected Philosophical Works* [Moscow, 1956], pp. 274–76.)

Later in the tale Tatyana finds that Onegin's favorite reading, indeed his only reading, for he has renounced everything else, is in fact Lord Byron, his hero, the romantic world-conqueror Napoleon. In his country home she finds well-thumbed and underlined copies of *Don Juan* and *The Gaiour* together with

> Lord Byron's portrait and a stand
> With a small iron figurine
> With hat on, forehead dark, oppressed,
> And arms tight-folded on his breast.
>   (VII, 19)

With innumerable deft touches of this kind Pushkin explores Onegin's romantic misanthropy. The point he wants to make is so important, however, that he drives it home vigorously in an astonishing stanza in Chapter Four:

> Then whom are we to love and trust in
> And count on never to abuse
> Our love, but measure all our actions
> With the same yardstick that we use?
> Who will not slander us, but take
> The greatest pains for our dear sake?
> Who never bores us, but exalts
> Us always, even for our faults?
> You restless seeker of a dream.
> It is yourself you must adore!
> Don't waste your labor any more,
> Reader, for you yourself would seem
> The object to be placed above
> All else, and worthiest of your love.
>   (IV, 22)

The so-called misanthrope is an impostor. Reviling the world for its hypocrisy and deceitfulness, Onegin is shown to be himself utterly inauthentic; he is constantly striking attitudes, acting parts.

The guests at the brilliant reception in the last chapter see him enter and wonder:

> What will he be? Melmoth to-day?
> World-citizen or Quaker, say?
> A patriot, some fanatic soul,
> Childe Harold? What is now his role?

Onegin's vanity and destructiveness are insisted on in several episodes of the novel. He deliberately sets out to turn the head of Olga, the fiancée of his friend Lensky. Not because she attracts him—she does not—but out of pique and self-hatred. He cannot bear the happiness which is the lot of his naïve young friend, and he resents the entire world of the Larins with its simple dreams, simple contentments, simple sorrows, and simple ignorance. Incapable of happiness himself, Onegin seeks to destroy that of those around him, to fulfill in the world outside him the nothingness and despair within him. Lensky challenges Onegin to a duel, but when he finds that Olga still loves him he regrets his challenge. Being young, however, he is ashamed to withdraw. Onegin knows that Lensky cannot withdraw and that he himself ought to apologize in order to close the ridiculous affair. If he really is as superior to the world as he claims to be, he need not care what is said about him. But in fact, this is the one thing Onegin does care about, though, as with Dom Juan, his obsession with the opinion of others also causes him on many occasions to flout it. Zaretsky, an old gossip, having been drawn into the affair, Onegin cannot turn back:

> "(. . .) one of course detests
> And ought to scorn his jeers; but then,
> the mocking words of foolish men. . . ."
> On just such social thinking rests
> That honor which we all revere,
> The very axis of our sphere.
>
> (VI, 11)

So the hero who purports to despise public opinion kills his young friend for the sake of public opinion.

At the end of the novel Onegin meets Tatyana again. She has married a wealthy, high-born, and important general and has become one of the leading ladies of the brilliant society of St. Petersburg. Now at last, having rejected her condescendingly in her country village, Onegin "falls in love" with her. Is his love authentic? Pushkin leaves the question unanswered. The novel expresses, it does not seek to resolve, the ambiguity of the hero's own emotions.[9]

It is strictly impossible to separate love and vanity in Onegin. There is some reason to believe that the death of Lensky and the travels on which he immediately set out have done something to him. To Byron, whom he reads in the French translation of Amédée Pichot, are added now Gibbon, Chamfort, Herder, Manzoni, Rousseau, Fontenelle, and Bayle, "the arrant skeptic." [10] He himself declares that he has seen through his empty independence and his futile attitudinizing, that he longs for a real relation with another human being. This declaration is itself ambiguous, however. It would have been true in a sense at any time in his life. He had always longed for a meaningful relation with others (his affection for Lensky is evidence of this), but his

[9] "Can we unmask him?" Pushkin asks later (VIII, 7). Pushkin never hands us his hero in a nutshell. When Tatyana visits Onegin's home, she learns something of what he is, but Pushkin expresses her insight in the form of a series of questions: "Is he from Heaven or from Hades? / This strange and sorry character, / Angel or fiend, as you prefer, / What is he? A mere imitation, / A Muscovite in Harold's cloak, / A wretched ghost, a foreign joke / But with a new interpretation, / A lexicon of snobbery / And fashion, or a parody?" (VII, 24) As if to ward off too easy acquiescence in these suggestions, Pushkin adds in the following stanza: "Has she the answer to the riddle / And has she found *the word?*" In his comments on Onegin in the Pushkin Speech, Dostoievski singularly flattens Pushkin's profound, yet laconic and ironical, portrait of his hero, his "strange companion," by accepting unilaterally the definition of Onegin as a "parody."

[10] Translators disagree as to who the arrant skeptic is, the Bayle of the *Dictionary* or the Beyle who was Stendhal. While Pushkin is known to have been an admirer of Stendhal, it seems more likely that in the present context the reference is to Bayle.

disgust with a world of ignorance and cant having turned to proud contempt for it, he had become virtually incapable of any relations with others and had in fact come to believe that he desired none. Onegin's cynicism had always masked the bitterness of frustrated hopes and dreams. But in the struggle with the world even those hopes and dreams, which in better conditions might have been simple and direct, had become tainted with the exasperated egotism of the alienated individual. Onegin's desire for Tatyana may well, therefore, be in large measure a desire to re-establish his superiority to her, to conquer her in the eyes of the world and feed his own egotism, as Tatyana says it is. But this motive of vanity in no way excludes its opposite. In the accomplished and experienced Tatyana of St. Petersburg, Onegin rightly sees the woman he can love, for Tatyana, having experienced the world as he has, and having concealed the deepest longings of her heart beneath a mask of social grace and convention, is now in a position to understand and love him not as Saint-Preux or Werther, but as the man he really is. The ambiguity of Onegin's love for Tatyana is entirely rooted in her social being. His vanity is piqued by her social experience and poise, by her self-control and her understanding; but these very qualities of experience and understanding are also what inspires in him a real love and respect, a longing to share his life with her, such as he could not have felt for the simple country girl with her romances, her day-dreams, and her superstitions. Unfortunately this very experience of the world which raises Tatyana to a level of understanding commensurate with Onegin's, also makes her less simple and less trusting than she had been before. Perhaps she was not, as she claims bitterly, "better" in the country, but she was certainly purer and more innocent. She is too much a woman of the world now not to discern the vanity in Onegin's profession of love for her, and she is also too much a woman of the world not to mingle in this discernment her own pique, wounded pride, and vengefulness:

(. . .) I do not doubt,
Onegin, that you still recall
The garden and the avenue
Where fate once brought us, me and you,
And that long sermon you let fall.
I listened to you, still and meek—
Today it is my turn to speak.

(VIII, 42)

.   .   .   .

There in the country far from gossip
And standards based on idle show
I did not please you. For what reason
Must you today pursue me so?
Why have you marked me for your game?
Is it not that I've a name
And riches and because you see
Me move in great society?
Because my husband, wounded in
The wars, is petted by the court
And they would all observe the sport
If such a contest should begin,
So that, if you could drag me down
You'd gain some scandalous renown?

(VIII, 44)

Tatyana's experience of the world, her realism and understanding, the qualities that now draw Eugene to her, to the degree that his love is genuine, are also the qualities that allow her to read the ambiguity of his motivation and to see that there is no place in the world as it is for their love.

Tatyana would gladly give up all the luxury and glitter of her life in Petersburg

For our wild garden and the joys
Of my old books—the modest lands
Around our house, and all the scene

In which I saw you first, Eugene,
And for the churchyard where there stands
A cross, and shady branches wave
Their leaves above my nurse's grave.
                              (VIII, 46)

But there is no going back. The self-conscious, worldly, and dis-cerning woman whom Onegin now loves cannot at the same time be the trusting, naïve, and unselfconscious child of the far-off estate. Tatyana understands Onegin as she did not understand him before. That is why she can say with perfect truthfulness that she still loves him; indeed she loves him more, for she loves him knowing him, but, knowing him, she also knows their love cannot come to anything. There is no escape for Tatyana and Onegin out of the social world which has made them what they are, which has at last brought them together and which at the same time, as Tatyana at least realizes, requires that they part.

At the end of *Onegin* the wheel has turned full cycle: The God of the silent and remote village garden has become the slave of the brilliant Petersburg drawing-rooms. The passionate letter in which Onegin declares his love and places his public reputation at Tatyana's mercy corresponds to the earlier letter in which Tatyana professed her love and placed her reputation at Onegin's mercy. (The parallel is brought out nicely by Tchaikovski when he uses the same theme for the two letter arias.) Onegin's refusal of Tatyana in Chapter Four on the grounds that their marriage would rapidly languish in boredom, unhappiness, and tears—which was quite true at the time—is paralleled by Tatyana's refusal of Onegin in Book Eight on the equally valid grounds that when a woman flouts society and leaves her husband she can bring happiness neither to herself nor to her lover. (It is not hard to see how closely *Anna Karenina* follows up the theme of *Onegin*.) When Tatyana begged for Onegin's love, it was he who understood that their union was impossible, as indeed it was.

Now that Onegin begs for Tatyana's love, it is she who has the deeper insight and who has to teach him that their union is impossible. His respect for her is entirely justified by her very refusal of him. "There are romances," writes Belinsky (*op. cit.*, p. 245), "the very idea of which consists precisely in the fact that they have no ending, because there are events in real life that have no denouement, there is existence without aim, creatures difficult to define, baffling to everybody, even to themselves, in short, what the French call *les êtres manqués, les existences avortées*."

Pushkin's romance is shot through with delicate irony. It is no longer as straightforwardly comic as the plays of Molière. If Pushkin conquered his romanticism in this work as Molière conquered that part of him which was Alceste in *Le Misanthrope*, the victory was even less than in Molière's comedy a clear victory of simple truth and common sense over falsehood and illusion. There are several little cameos of old Russian life in the novel, which the author sets against the romanticism of his hero and heroine, but these are not genuine alternatives. Tatyana's mother gave up her handsome sergeant of the Guards along with her novel reading and settled down to a measured life on the estate of the good and simple man to whom she had been betrothed against her will, making pancakes at Shrovetide and going twice a year to confession. Her husband is described as "a simple squire without caprice" (II, 36) who "loved his wife sincerely / And never gave her cause to frown, / But spent his days serene and trustful, / Attired in a dressing gown" (II, 34). He stands for a way of life that is irretrievably lost, a life of quiet and dull acceptance, lived according to ancestral custom. He has no understanding of the restless desires of the younger generation. For this reason he cannot protect his daughter from the influences that cause her unhappiness:

> Her father, who was good and kind,
> Had long ago been left behind

By modern ways, but in the main,
Although he thought books light and vain,
He did not think them any harm.
And when a man has never read,
The books his daughter takes to bed
With her will cause him no alarm.

(II, 29)

Tatyana's old nurse, like her father, accepts time-hallowed ways. She is appalled and terrified when Tatyana confides that she is in love and crosses herself energetically. Love for her is a madness from which we must be protected. Young people do not marry for love, she tells Tatyana, but according to the plans of their parents.

The character of the father and that of the old nurse are drawn by Pushkin, as similar figures were drawn later by Tolstoy and Chekhov, with great affection and compassion, but not without irony. Pushkin knows, as Molière knew when he created Dom Louis or Dom Carlos or Dorine, that the old order is doomed and that the emancipation of the individual cannot be avoided. Nor does he conceal what is narrow and cruel in the old ways. Perhaps there is some idealization of them. On the whole, however, the picture of Russian country life and of the simple people in particular is beautiful and moving in its plain truthfulness. Tatyana's old nurse is distressed by the child's confession of love, but she does not gild the reality of her own betrothal under the good old system of the marriage-broker:

(. . .) By God's will, my Vanya
Was but a boy, if truth were told,
And I was just thirteen years old.
The marriage-broker kept on pressing
The matter for a fortnight; oh,
What tears I shed you do not know,
The day my father gave his blessing;

They loosed my braids, and singing low
Led me to church. I had to go.

(III, 18)

As for Onegin's contemporaries, those who, like Acaste and
Clitandre, sneer at his constant play-acting, discerning very clearly
the vanity that lies behind his professed contempt for them,
they are no more superior to him than Célimène and her group
are superior to Alceste. If one of the guests at the ball comments
shrewdly on Onegin's theatricality, he is answered by another:

Why do you speak with such disfavor
About him? Is it that we all
So love to meddle and to censure?
Or that unfettered spirits call
Forth either rage or mockery
From every vain nonentity?

.   .   .   .

Or do the mediocre seem
The only subject for esteem?

In *Eugene Onegin* there is only the dying world of the old
nurse and Tatyana's father, the inessential world of Moscow
society, and the illusory world of the hero and heroine. There is
no longer an available position in society itself, such as is
represented in *Le Misanthrope* by Philinte and Eliante, which
allows us to consider the behavior of the principal protagonists
as in some sense exceptional or "abnormal."

This is equally true of Chekhov. In Chekhov, as in Pushkin,
the old family servants represent a world that is moribund. In
the *Three Sisters,* Andrey and his sisters dream of Moscow and
how much better things are there. At one point Andrey asks the
old servant Ferrapont if he has ever been to Moscow or wanted
to go there. The old man replies simply that it was not God's
will that he should go to Moscow. Similarly in *The Cherry*

Orchard, it is old Feers who provides the contrast with the
restless seeking, wandering, and suffering of his educated masters.
But when they close the house up and go away, they forget all
about the old man and leave him abandoned there in the ancestral
home on which they have turned their backs for ever.

Immediately the empirically real social perspective from which
Molière presented the follies and vanities of Jourdain or Philaminte or Argan narrowed to the already somewhat ideal perspective offered by an Eliante and a Philinte, his comedy lost something of the gross heartiness that characterizes *Le Bourgeois
Gentilhomme*, *Les Femmes savantes*, *La Malade imaginaire*, and
even *Tartuffe*. The virtual absence of any such perspective in
Eugene Onegin obliged Pushkin to renounce this hearty type of
comedy altogether. *Eugene Onegin* remains a comedy, but it is
a comedy of irony, not a full blooded satire.[11] Pushkin's vantage
point already has a greater quality of ideality than Molière's
had, even in *Le Misanthrope*, and Chekhov's has more ideality
still (whence the excessively romantic interpretations that bedevil
many modern productions of Chekhov). The perspective from
which Pushkin portrays the illusions of his beloved Tatyana—his
vierni ideal, his true ideal—and of his strange companion—*moi
sputnik strannij*—Onegin, is an ideal one in which the freedom

---

[11] It is not altogether surprising that Bert Brecht, with his astonishing satirical talent, was a socialist, and that he worked at a time when the socialist
movement seemed to offer a concrete ground for confidence in the future.
Brecht was able to rediscover all the heartiness of Molière's heartiest satire and
all the verve of his farce in part, at least, because his association with a
broad and empirically real workers' movement provided him with a firm
platform from which he could look upon the follies, affectations, and impostures of the decadent "ruling classes." Brecht, of course, is more combative
than Molière was, for the victory of socialism in which he believed so intensely had not yet been won. It would be an error to discount his political
faith in any discussion of his comic genius, or even of his dramatic tech-
niques. How justified this faith was, is another question. What seems certain
is that genuine satirical comedy becomes less and less possible as the writer
loses faith in humanity and human life, as his public becomes more and more
infected with inauthenticity and hypocrisy. Irony seems to occupy an inter-
mediate position between satire and the bitter, self-mocking parody that
flourishes in times of despair.

and uniqueness of the individual will have been truly achieved
and will no longer be a blind for sterile imitation and resentment
of others.[12] The perspective from which Chekhov views the
vanity, boredom, restlessness, and inauthenticity of his characters
is likewise a kind of ideal future, which he himself is the first
to poke fun at. "It may be that posterity, which will despise us
for our blind and stupid lives, will find some road to happiness,"
says Astrov, the doctor in *Uncle Vanya*. Astrov himself, however,
is not only profoundly pessimistic about the future, he resembles
all the other characters in the play in his pursuit of vain illusions.
As Alceste prefers Célimène to Eliante, Astrov prefers the elusive

---

[12] The interpretation of *Eugene Onegin* given here is somewhat schematic.
I am painfully aware that, for the purpose of my argument, I have simplified
a work in which a complex and deeply experienced reality is expressed with
marvelous poetic economy. I myself prefer Belinsky's interpretation of *Onegin*
to Dostoievski's, although it is perhaps to the latter that the interpretation
sketched here might seem to bear the stronger resemblance. (Belinsky's study
of *Onegin* can be found in V. G. Belinsky, *Estetika i Literaturnaia Kritika v
dvukh tomakh* [Moscow, 1959], Vol. 2, pp. 434–501. This work contains all
his other articles on Pushkin. The two articles on *Onegin* have been translated
and published in V. G. Belinsky, *Selected Philosophical Works* [Moscow,
1956], pp. 211–98. Dostoievski's interpretation of *Onegin* is found in his
Pushkin speech, published in his *Diary of a Writer*, for August 1880. There
are, besides, many allusions both to Pushkin and to *Onegin* elsewhere in the
works of both writers.) To correct this impression, I should like to quote a
passage from a letter Belinsky wrote to his friend Botkin on September 8,
1841, published in translation in Belinsky, *Selected Philosophical Works*, ed.
cit., pp. 169–79. This letter, which goes some way toward explaining Belinsky's
intimate understanding of Pushkin's text, expresses something of what I myself
tried to say about *Onegin* on p. 291 of the present text. "We made friends,
quarrelled, made up, quarrelled again and made up again, were at loggerheads,
loved one another madly, lived and fell in love by theory, by the book, spontaneously and consciously. That, I believe, is the false aspect of our lives and
our relations. But must we blame ourselves for this? We did blame ourselves,
we swore and took vows, but it was no better, nor will it ever be. Our constant cherished (and rational) dream was to sublimate our whole lives to
realities, and, consequently, our mutual relations as well; and well! the dream
was but a dream and such it will remain; we were phantoms and will die
phantoms, but it is not our fault and we have nothing to blame ourselves for.
Reality springs from a soil, and the soil of all reality is society. (. . .) Society
regards us as peccant tumors on its body; and we regard society as a heap of
fetid dung. Society is right, but we are still more so. (. . .) We are men
without a country—nay worse—we are men whose country is a phantom and

and "interesting" Yelena to Sonia with her simplicity and devotion. But the concrete situation in *Uncle Vanya* is already very different from that in *Le Misanthrope*. Eliante is a real alternative for Alceste. She is his equal in every way and a perfectly suitable match. Sonia, however, stands to Astrov rather as Tatyana stands to Onegin when they first meet. She does not understand him. Her life, good, simple, and pure as it is, is remote from his. Of the frustrations that eat at Astrov's heart she has no glimmering. Similarly, Chekhov both affirms and mocks Trofimov's belief in progress in *The Cherry Orchard*. Trofimov is right when he cries out in Act II: "The whole of Russia is our orchard. The earth is great and beautiful and there are many, many wonderful places on it. Just think, Anya: your grandfather, your great grandfather and all your forefathers were serf-owners—they owned living souls (. . .) and it has perverted you all, those who came before you and you who are living now. (. . .) We are at least two hundred years behind the times." But Trofimov too is enslaved to dreams and illusions. Happiness for him is always somewhere in the future and he never sees it before his very eyes. "I can see happiness, Anya," he says, "I can see it coming. (. . .) Yes, the moon is rising. (*A pause*) There it is—happiness—it's coming nearer and nearer. I seem to hear its footsteps. And if we don't see it, if we don't know when it comes, what does it matter?

---

no wonder that we are phantoms ourselves, that our friendship, our love, our aspirations, our activity is a phantom. (. . .) You see what it is, my dear: we realized directly that there was no life for us in life, and since, by our natures, we could not live without life, we plunged headlong into books and began to live and love by the book. (. . .) However, our natures have always been higher than our intelligence, and therefore it became tedious and trivial to be constantly hearing the same thing from each other and we got bored to death with one another. Boredom passed into annoyance, annoyance into animosity, animosity into discord. Discord was always rain for the dry ground of our relations and brought forth a new and stronger love. (. . .) But the stock was soon drained and we relapsed back again to the old, to our personal interests, hungering for *objective interests* as manna from the skies; but these interests did not exist, and we went on being phantoms and our life was a beautiful content without a rationale."

Other people will see it!" With his blind faith in the *future*, Trofimov has forgotten about the world around him. He is incapable of experiencing ordinary desires that have real objects and that can be satisfied. His idealism is grotesquely comical. "Vanya's afraid," he says to Anya, "afraid we might suddenly fall in love with each other. (. . .) She's so narrow-minded, she can't grasp that we are above falling in love. To rid ourselves of all that's petty and unreal, all that prevents us from being happy and free, that's the whole aim and meaning of our life. Forward! Let's march on irresistibly toward that bright star over there, shining in the distance! Forward!" Perhaps only Anya really escapes from the inauthenticity that inhabits all those whose destinies and desires have been shaped by the Cherry Orchard. But even the luminous faith and love of her words to her mother at the end of Act III are shot through with a vein of irony. "The cherry orchard's sold, it's quite true, there isn't any cherry orchard any more," she exclaims, "it's true . . . but don't cry, Mamma, you still have your life ahead of you, you still have your dear, innocent heart. You must come away with me, darling, we must get away from here! We'll plant a new orchard, even more splendid than this one—and when you see it, you'll understand everything, your heart will be filled with happiness, like the sun in the evening; and then you'll smile again, Mamma!" There is a chance that Anya will be able to create a more real existence for herself than those who surrounded her youth were able to do, but her mother's life has already been wasted in perpetually fleeing from reality. She does not have her life ahead of her and her "dear, innocent heart" is already somewhat worn with use.

The writer is not alone to blame for the weakening of his faith. The objective conditions of his experience, the world itself, in short, gives him less and less cause to have faith in it as it becomes progressively more corrupt and inauthentic, as the contradictions in its pursuit of "freedom and happiness" become more and more patent. From Molière's time to our own the process by which wider and wider sections of humanity have been engulfed in inauthenticity has continued unabated. Compared with Molière, Stendhal had to look hard to find any vantage point from which he could satirize the society of his time, and he found it where it was least expected, not in Paris, but in the provinces, not usually among men but among women. Stendhal's vantage point is already so *different* from that of the majority of his readers, that he could only hope he would be understood by future generations. It is already far more personal, far less social than Molière's. With Flaubert even the oases of authenticity, out of which Stendhal constructed his perspective on society, have dried up. There is virtually nothing left in the society of Flaubert that is authentic or genuine. In these circumstances the superior position from which the writer obtains his comic view of the world isolates him even further from it, instead of reuniting him to it; it aggravates his misanthropy and his disgust instead of curing them.[13] His transcendence of the world becomes the very source of his anguish and his loneliness, for he is the first to experience the futility of a superiority that allows him only to see the utter vanity of every-

[13] Astrov's conversation with Sonia in Act II of *Uncle Vanya* illustrates this point very clearly. Astrov sees the absurdity and vanity of his society but he is himself sick, unable to reach the world and frustrated because he cannot impose on it his own ideal patterns. "I like life as life", he says, "but I hate and despise it in a little Russian country village, and as far as my own personal life goes, by heaven! there is absolutely no redeeming feature about it. Haven't you noticed if you are riding through a dark wood at night and see a little light shining ahead, how you forget your fatigue and the darkness and the sharp twigs that whip your face? I work, that you know—as no one else in the country works. Fate beats me on, without rest; at times I suffer unendurably and I see no light ahead. I have no hope; I do not like people. It is long since I have loved anyone." To Sonia's desperate question: "You love no one?" he replies with a cruel egoism reminiscent of Onegin's first encounters with Tatyana: "Not a soul. I only feel a sort of tenderness for your old nurse for old time's sake. The peasants are all alike; they are stupid and live in dirt, and the educated people are hard to get along with. One gets tired of them. All our good friends are petty and shallow. (. . .) Those that have brains are hysterical, devoured with a mania for self-analysis. They whine, they hate, they pick faults everywhere with unhealthy sharpness. (. . .) Simple, natural relations between man and man or man and nature do not exist."

thing around him, including himself. The sly superiority of a Marivaux ends in the agony and madness of a Céline. Brilliant flashes of comedy are still possible for writers like Flaubert and Céline, but it is a bitter and angry humor that soon reveals the loathing and self-loathing behind it. Emma Bovary is cured of her illusions only to be filled at the moment of her frightful death by a terrible vision of universal futility, irony, and nothingness. "Emma Bovary, c'est moi," Flaubert declared in a celebrated epigram. Flaubert's relentless pursuit of his heroine is in fact the mirror of his own despair.

Earlier writers found a basis for that faith in human life and in human beings, without which there can be no comic liberation, in the world around them. Molière grounded his in the *honnêtes gens* of his time, whatever their shortcomings, in his robust family servants, in his solid and sensible bourgeois characters, in his young lovers. Even the craftiness of valets has a healthy and positive side to it in Molière. Stendhal found his, with greater difficulty, in the provinces of France and in the small cities of Italy, and he coupled it with a certain confidence in the future, with an idealistic radicalism that comes out not only in his satire of the "ruling classes" or in his political views, but in the biting social criticism of texts like *Rome, Florence et Naples* or certain chapters of *Lucien Leuwen*, and in a character like Palla in *La Charteuse de Parme*. But Stendhal is already very skeptical of the future. "Prenez un petit marchand de Rouen ou de Lyon, avare et sans imagination, et vous aurez un Américain," Lucien says to his radical friend Gauthier. The world of the future often appears to Lucien a world of petty meanness, vanity, and vulgarity. "Je ne suis pas fait pour vivre sous une république," he declares; "ce serait pour moi le triomphe de toutes les médiocrités, et je ne puis supporter de sang-froid même les plus estimables. Il me faut un premier ministre coquin et amusant comme Walpole ou M. de Talleyrand." In the end Stendhal himself comes close to a kind of romantic quixotism when he finds that only rank idealists and madmen are admirable and authentic beings. "Excepté mes pauvres républicains attaqués de folie, je ne vois rien d'estimable dans le monde," Lucien tells Gauthier; "il entre du charlatanisme dans tous les mérites de ma connaissance. Ceux-ci sont peut-être fous: mais du moins ils ne sont pas bas." It is true that Stendhal quickly corrects his hero and warns him to wait until he has a little more experience of the world before he presumes to decide on such momentous issues. Lucien's love for Madame de Chasteller will in fact deepen his understanding of what the authentic values in human life are, but the attitude he expresses at this point remained a constant element in Stendhal's own view of the world.

Nevertheless, neither Stendhal with his mocking realism nor Chekhov with his irony ever attempted to satirize the whole of humanity; they did not turn their wit against the human condition itself. They had no naïve optimism, but they continued to look for something substantial and real against which to set the follies of those whom they ridiculed. In recent times, however, human existence itself has become more and more frequently the cause of disillusionment and disgruntlement and the object of the writer's angry witticisms. Such total condemnation and mockery of humanity transforms the author into the very character that Molière made the butt of his satire in *Le Misanthrope*. The author's own activity, literature itself, becomes, like Alceste's attacks on the world, a form of parasitism, a connivance with and participation in the very inauthenticity and absurdity it exposes. How the writer is to recover that rudimentary confidence in the goodness of human life that seems to be the necessary condition for the creation of great comedy, is, of course, another question, one which each man must answer for himself if he wishes to be something more than a successful peddler of despair.

The objective historical conditions in which Molière worked were extremely favorable to his comic genius. He stood, historically speaking, at the crossroads of the old and the new, and he saw the old with the eyes of the new and the new with the eyes of the old. He could laugh with the society of the Court and the *honnêtes gens* at the outmoded pretensions of Cathos and Magdelon, the resentful rivalries of Dandin and the Sotenvilles, the grotesque impostures of Orgon and Tartuffe, or the "Jansenist" revolt of Alceste. At the same time, however, his satire of the old order embraces the new order as well, for the absolutism of the seventeenth century was in the end a compromise solution of the conflicts at the heart of French society. It brought a temporary and provisional equilibrium, but the conflicts it was designed to control were not disposed of; they assumed new and more complex forms and the absolutist compromise itself soon appeared as a formal, and therefore inadequate, answer to the problems of the time, just as the ideology of *honnêteté*, which accompanied the absolute monarchy, was rapidly recognized as an abstract theory which did not really correspond to social reality. For this reason Molière's satire reaches more than its immediate objects. Indeed, the greatness and richness of works like *Le Misanthrope, Dom Juan,* or *Amphitryon* rest on a vision that is capable of embracing both the outworn order of the author's immediate past and a present order that was itself already showing signs of being bypassed by events and reduced to an empty formalism. Are the proud and tyrannical heroes of these comedies representatives of the new or of the old? Is Dom Juan an old style *grand seigneur* or a new-style individualist? Is Jupiter a superb anarchist or is he the monarch himself, the upholder of law and order? Is Alceste a disgruntled *robin* or is he the very image of the Acastes and the Orontes as it is reflected in the prophetic mirror of the author? These comic heroes are in fact both. Their impostures and contradictions are discerned from the point of view of an ordered and structured society, and yet at the same time they are revealed as the inner image of that society. As Molière came closer to this marvelous dialectic of order and revolt, of individual and society, he found it harder to portray within the plays themselves the position from which they were to be viewed. The audience is required to look on the protagonist from the point of view of the antagonist, on the antagonist from the point of view of the protagonist, and then again on both from a point of view which is not really given in the play and which includes and transcends that of protagonist and antagonist alike. In the achievement of this final perspective, the comedy achieves the liberation that is its deepest purpose.

For Molière this liberation was positive. It did not simply raise the audience to a new and futile superiority, for it implied a transcendence of all illusory superiorities. The possession of truth does not feed our vanity; on the contrary, it raises us out of our vanity and restores us to reality. In the very act of laughing at illusion we recognize the difference between reality and appearance, truth and illusion, and we side, whether we want to or not, with reality against appearance, with truth against illusion. So it is that the better we understand the comedy, the more realistic our own vision will be. Molière himself always tried to see things honestly and truthfully. He did not romanticize his Sotenvilles and his Dandins, his Dom Juans and his Jourdains, but he did not spare himself either, and he did not romanticize Alceste and Arnolphe. His own position was often that of *la Cour et la Ville*, which, as he realized, expressed far more accurately than that of a Sotenville and a Dandin, of a Dom Louis or of a Dom Carlos, the objective reality of the world in which he lived, but in *Le Misanthrope*, for instance, he showed that he was able to go beyond the position of *la Cour et la Ville* to a still more realistic and comprehensive one—one in which *la Cour et la Ville* are themselves seen in their contingency. *Le Misanthrope* uncovers the discrepancy between the forms of the new social life of the so-called *honnêtes gens* and its reality, between the ideal of *honnêteté* that was professed by society and the actual behavior of men and women in society. As we pointed out in our chapter on this play, there are few *honnêtes gens* at the court of Célimène.

In our own day we still have much to learn from Molière's unflinching honesty. Every time we laugh at one of his comedies we are "instructed," as he would have said, for our laughter to-day commits us, as it committed the audiences of three hundred years ago, to siding with truth and to rejecting lies and imposture. Molière is a great comic writer in large measure because he always tried to see both the world and himself as they really were, to lay bare every illusion, every form that had no real substance, every trick that men play on others and on themselves.

Index

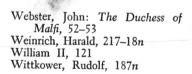

MEN AND MASKS
A Study of Molière

Lionel Gossman

designer: Edward D. King
typesetter: Vail-Ballou Press, Binghamton, N.Y.
typefaces: Electra text, French Old Style display
printer: Vail-Ballou Press
paper: Warren's 1854 Medium Finish
binder: Vail-Ballou Press
cover material: Columbia Riverside Linen